Social History of Africa

THE MOON IS DEAD!
GIVE US OUR MONEY!

D1113178

Social History of Africa
Series Editors:
Allen Isaacman and Jean Hay

THE MOON IS DEAD! GIVE US OUR MONEY!

The Cultural Origins of an African Work Ethic, Natal, South Africa, 1843–1900

Keletso E. Atkins

University of Michigan
Ann Arbor

HEINEMANN   JAMES CURREY
Portsmouth, NH   London

Heinemann
A division of Reed Publishing (USA) Inc.
361 Hanover Street
Portsmouth, NH 03801

James Currey Ltd.
54b Thornhill Square,
Islington
London N1 1BE

ISBN 0–435–08076–8 (Heinemann cloth)
ISBN 0–435–08078–4 (Heinemann paper)
ISBN 0–85255–658–6 (James Currey cloth)
ISBN 0–85255–608–x (James Currey paper)

First published 1993.

Library of Congress Cataloging-in-Publication Data
Atkins, Keletso E.
  The moon is dead! Give us our money! : the cultural origins of an
African work ethic, Natal, South Africa, 1843–1900 / Keletso E.
Atkins.
    p.   cm.
  Originally presented as the author's thesis (Ph.D.)—University of
Wisconsin.
  Includes bibliographical references and index.
  ISBN 0-435-08076-8. — ISBN 0-435-08078-4 (pbk.)
    1. Working class—South Africa—Natal—History—19th century.
2. Work ethic—South Africa—Natal—History—19th century.   3. Natal
(South Africa)—Social conditions.   4. Natal (South Africa)—
History—1843-1893.   5. Natal (South Africa)—History—1893-1910.
I. Title.
  HD8801.Z8N3722   1993
  305.5′62′09684—dc20   92-41611
                                                                CIP
British Library Cataloguing in Publication Data
Atkins, Keletso E.
  The Moon is Dead! Give Us Our Money!:
  Cultural Origins of an African Work
  Ethic in Natal c. 1843–1900. – (Social
  History of Africa Series)
    I. Title II. Series
306.3609684

ISBN 0-85255-608-x (Paper)
      0-85255-658-6 (Cloth)

HD
8801
.Z8
N3722
1993

Cover design by Jenny Jensen Greenleaf.
Cover photograph ("Natives Eating") from the Killie Campbell Africana Library.
Text design by G&H Soho Ltd.
Cartography by Helena Margeot and Raymond Poonsamy.
Printed in the United States of America.
98 97 96 95 94 93   EB   1 2 3 4 5 6 7 8 9

To the newest members of my family,
Tsedai Keletso and Jelani Claude

The Zulu always expected his wages at the end of *every month*. Many English got a bad name because they insisted on paying the wages at the end of every *calendar* month. I got a good name for honesty because I paid regularly at the end of every *lunar* month. As soon as the new moon first shows the small thin crescent, the Zulu month commences.

H. J. Barrett, *Fifteen Years Among the Zulus and the Boers*

CONTENTS

ACKNOWLEDGMENTS

This book is based on a 1986 Ph.D. thesis for the University of Wisconsin. In the course of my graduate studies and during the preparation of the original thesis, I received financial help from many sources: first, from the University of Wisconsin-Madison, to whom I am enormously indebted for the continuous support provided under the Affirmative Action Advanced Opportunity Fellowship program; from the Social Science Research Council and Fulbright-Hays for the main period of research in London and the Republic of South Africa; and from the American Association of University Women for a final year of study and writing. I am deeply grateful to all these institutions. I also wish to express my appreciation to the staffs of the libraries and archives where the bulk of my research has been done: the Houghton Library of Harvard University, the library of the School of Oriental and African Studies, the archives of the United Society for the Propagation of the Gospel; and the Pietermaritzburg Depot of the South African Archives (with particular thanks to Karansing Chutterpaul, Mary Mclean, Joan Pretorius, and Judith Richards). I also received generous help from John Wright and John Benyon at the University of Natal, Pietermaritzburg. Thanks are also due to the University of California-Santa Barbara and the University of Michigan-Ann Arbor, whose support allowed me to revise the manuscript for publication.

There were a number of individuals who showed genuine hospitality, kindness and concern (*ubuntu*) for my welfare, and their warmth and friendship helped to lessen the trauma of my first prolonged encounter with the sad realities of South Africa. My love especially to Ellen and Alois Hlengwa and family; and many, many thanks to Dr. C.L.S. Nyembezi and family, Khaba and Kwenzi Mhkize, Percy Khumalo, Jabulani Dhlamini, Nelson Ntshangase, Kate Zondi and family, Sebongile Myandu and family, Oregan Hoskins, Geraldine de Lange, Daphne and Edward Grantham and family, Myrtle Matthias and family, Usha David and family, Ahmed and Rookaya Bawa, Aideen Gonlag and family, and Glen Flanagan.

There are two individuals who have contributed much to my thinking. Steven Feierman, who supervised my thesis, has proven to be not only a great scholar, but a wonderful teacher, wise counselor, and good friend. Jan Vansina, whom I had the great fortune to have as a mentor as well, was extraordinarily generous with his time, and his brilliant scholarship has been a constant source of inspiration.

My indebtedness to Fred Cooper, Jean Hay, David Henige, Allan Isaacman, and Shula Marks, who read various drafts of the manuscript and offered useful comments and suggestions.

I have to thank Geraldine Brewer, Tammy Davis, and Joanne Hall who shared in the experience of this project.

In regards to orthography I am indebted to Harold Scheub who took great pains reading through the whole manuscript in order to check the spelling of Zulu words. Where I have employed Zulu words with English suffixes, those usages were adopted from spellings used by Colin Webb and John Wright in their editing of *The James Stuart Archive of Recorded Oral Evidence Relating to the History of the Zulu and Neighbouring Peoples*. I take full responsibility for the interpretations and final method of presentation of the materials contained in this book.

My greatest debt of gratitude, a very special thank you from the heart goes out to my family and friends, whose patient understanding and continued belief in my efforts through the long years of preparation were all the support and encouragement I required to accomplish the goal. I thank everyone who has taken an interest in my work.

ABBREVIATIONS

ABC	American Board of Commissioners for Foreign Missions
CNC	Chief Native Commissioner
CO	Colonial Office Series
CSO	Colonial Secretary Office Series
DCL	Durban Corporation Letters
DCSPRB	Durban Corporation Superintendent of Police Report Book
DTC	Durban Town Council
MMS	The Methodist Missionary Society
NA	*Natal Advertiser*
NC	*Natal Colonist*
NGG	*Natal Government Gazette*
NH	*Natal Herald*
NMA	*Natal Mercantile Advertiser*
NS	*Natal Star*
NW	*Natal Witness*
SDN	*Standard and Digger's News*
SNA	Secretary of Native Affairs Series
TN	*Times of Natal*
USPG	United Society for the Propagation of the Gospel

GLOSSARY OF ZULU TERMS

Note: Complete forms are used here, with the noun class capped to indicate how the word would be found alphabetically in a Zulu–English dictionary. In many cases, both noun and verb prefixes are dropped when the terms are used in the text.

ukuBhala: to write, record, register
isiBhalo: system of forced labor introduced in Natal
imBongi (izimBongi): bard, poet, praise singer
isiBongo (iziBongo): clan name; (plural) praises, praise names
ukuButha (pass. *ukuButhwa*): to form young men or women into age grades; to enrol into new military units
iButho (amaButho): regiment; warrior, soldier
uDibi (izinDibi): boy (girl) who carries a warrior's or traveler's belongings; mat bearer
inDuna (izinDuna): civil or military official; headman; person appointed by the king or chief to a position of authority
umFana (abaFana): boy; young person
isiGodlo (iziGodlo): women of the king's establishment; girls presented to the king as "tribute" or selected from the households of his subjects
ukuHlobonga: to practice premarital(external) sexual intercourse
ikhafula (amakhafula)\[Arab. infidel]: kafir; used disparagingly, a term of contempt
iKhanda (amaKhanda): royal homestead where soldiers are quartered; major military center
iKhehla (amaKhehla): man who has put on the headring; elderly or married man
ukuKhonza: to pay respects to; to wait upon; to serve under a chief or white man
isiKhonzi (iziKhonzi): servant; messenger or envoy
isiKhulu (iziKhulu): man of high standing in the Zulu kingdom
inKosi (amaKhosi): king; paramount; chief
inKosikazi (amaKhosikazi): principal wife of a king, chief or *umNumzana* (head of a kraal)
ukuLobola: to give cattle for a bride
iLobolo: cattle or goods given for a bride; bridewealth or bride price
umLungu (abeLungu): white person; European
iMfecane: a period of intensive warfare; social, political and demographic upheavals in southeast Africa of the 1820s and 1830s
iMpi (iziMpi): military unit; regiment; army
ukuNgena: to marry the widow of a deceased brother

xiv

umNguni (abeNguni): people who are linguistically and culturally related and who occupy the coastal area of southeast Africa from Zululand and Natal to the borders of the Cape colony

iNsizwa (iziNsizwa): youth approaching manhood

iNtombi (iziNtombi): grown up girl; virgin; sweetheart

ubuNtu: good moral disposition; humaneness; hospitality

umuNtu (abaNtu): human being; African; one with human feelings

umNumzana (abaNumzana): head of a homestead; head of a family

iNyanga (iziNyanga): moon; expert; a professional person or one skilled in some craft

ukuQoma: to select a lover; choose

ukuQomisa: to court

ukuSoma: to practice premarital (external) sexual intercourse

umThakathi (abaThakathi): one who uses supernatural forces for evil purposes

iToho (or Togt): piece work; service for the day; one who takes it

umuZi (imiZi): kraal or family homestead; village; collection of huts under one headman

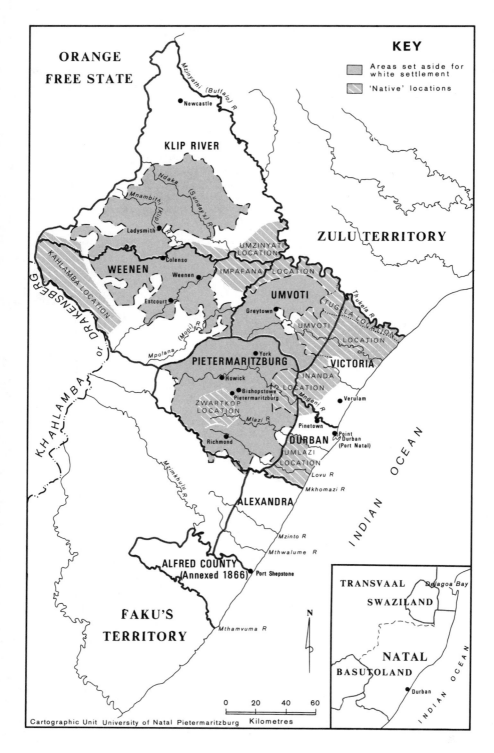

KEY

Areas set aside for white settlement

'Native' locations

ORANGE FREE STATE

Newcastle

KLIP RIVER

Mzinyathi (Buffalo) R

Ndaka

Mnambithi

(Sunday's) R

Ladysmith

(Klip) R

ZULU TERRITORY

UMZINYATI LOCATION

Colenso

IMPAFANA LOCATION

WEENEN

Weenen

Estcourt

(Mooi) R

Mpofana

UMVOTI

Greytown

TUGELA LOCATION

Thukela R

UMVOTI LOCATION

KAHLAMBA LOCATION

DRAKENSBERG

York

PIETERMARITZBURG

Howick

Bishopstowe

Pietermaritzburg

ZWARTKOP LOCATION

INANDA LOCATION

VICTORIA

Verulam

Mngeni R

Mlazi R

Richmond

Pinetown

Point Durban (Port Natal)

DURBAN

KHAHLAMBA

Mzimkhulu R

UMLAZI LOCATION

Lovu R

Mkhomazi R

ALEXANDRA

INDIAN OCEAN

Mzinto R

Mthwalume R

ALFRED COUNTY (Annexed 1866)

Port Shepstone

FAKU'S TERRITORY

Mthamvuma R

N

TRANSVAAL

Delagoa Bay

SWAZILAND

NATAL

BASUTOLAND

Durban

INDIAN OCEAN

0   20   40   60

Kilometres

Cartographic Unit University of Natal Pietermaritzburg

NATAL'S GEOGRAPHIC HISTORY

Introduction

The "Kafir labor question" was in the mouths of most colonists in nineteenth-century Natal. It was an issue that bristled with controversy, a topic from which few stood aloof. Labor shortages affected up-country farmers as well as coastal planters; the dearth was experienced on government works, at Durban's dockside by landing and shipping agents, and by merchants and shopkeepers in both the leading boroughs. This was also generally true for artisans and craftsmen. Likewise, ordinary house-holders shared the same problem in the management of their domestic establish-ments, but got no sympathy whatsoever since nearly everyone else was competing for the same commodity. Another way of stating the matter is to say that all classes and groups were simultaneously exposed to recurrent shortfalls in labor; all focused obsessively on the problem; and all complained incessantly of their hardships. So preoccupied were Natalians with the manpower crisis that they gained for them-selves a reputation for being a colony of inveterate grumblers.

Not only did the settlers lament the quality of life in their community, in the early years in particular they felt that the very survival of the colonial venture was at stake. These concerns were the subject of essays, orations, and debates that were given considerable coverage in the press. Indeed, local news journals provided more specific details regarding all levels of this discourse, which came to dominate nineteenth-century politics, than can be found anywhere else in the contemporary records, giving us an incisive view into the public's mind. The foremost concern of the settler community was what to do about the "Kafirs," who were looked upon as the basic radical source of their problems.

British Natal had a population of five thousand Europeans by the 1850s; the indigenous inhabitants numbered between one hundred thousand and one hun-dred fifty thousand. The latter figure had more than doubled by 1881. Initially, the European colonists expected to profit from these statistics. That is, from the start the African population was viewed as an immensely valuable asset, its members repre-senting potential labor units, a massive reservoir of cheap, complaisant workers. So white settlers suffered not only economic inconvenience, but great mental distress at the realization that, despite their overwhelming numbers, Africans appeared to be making no noticeable contributions to the colonial labor market. Etched in the white imagination was a picture of black men idling on the sidelines or "away in the native locations with not a care in the world except to kill time"; and nothing, either by way of cajolery or threats, it seems, was sufficient to induce these "shiftless layabouts" to undertake long work engagements.

Yet Natal Africans were themselves experiencing an unprecedented socioeconomic crisis; and both private and governmental agencies had already invested time and energy designed to mold blacks into a European ideal of what workers ought to be like. From the very beginning, however, the results of their efforts were discouraging. Finally, the European recognized that only by a complete immersion in Western culture—that is, only after a prolonged process of acculturation—would the preindustrial African worker be transformed into a model based on the Protestant capitalist work ethic, itself a contested area in nineteenth-century Europe.

Inevitably, a campaign of public vilification was launched against these nineteenth-century Africans who had failed to measure up to the capitalist construction of the worker. They became objects of ridicule, constantly derided for what they were supposedly not doing, unsparingly criticized as lazy and unreliable, and scathingly put down for a host of other deficiencies and shortcomings. In due course, whites began to purvey the fantasy, accepted almost universally as infallible truth, that "Kafirs" were "a fickle race," as "fitful and capricious as children who worked while the humor was on them, but [who] reserved to themselves the right to start off to their kraals whenever the humor changed." What is more, it became important in the settler's mind to view this negative construct, or some cruder version of it, as *the* explanation for virtually every failed colonial enterprise. As with so many crude labels, the widespread popularity of the "lazy Kafir" epithet is exemplified in the fact that whites still use it today to describe Natal Africans.

Thus the latter half of the nineteenth century was taken up in innumerable projects of economic experimentation and social engineering, the sole purpose of which was to secure and make more valuable the services of the black population of Natal. At the same time, though, immediate action was required to keep local industries afloat. The recruitment of laborers from abroad was initially conceived as a short-term strategy to relieve commercial agriculture, an industry especially hard pressed. During periodic peaks in the economy, private recruiters and colonial authorities encouraged foreign workers to migrate from the region around Delagoa Bay; Zulu migrants also arrived from Zululand, Basotho from Moshweshwe's country, creoles from the island of St. Helena and a contingent of liberated slaves from Zanzibar. Interestingly enough, freed slaves and their descendants from North America were under consideration as a potential source of supply. The most significant overseas consignments, though, were indentured workers from India, the first drafts arriving in 1860. None of these sources, it should be noted, produced a level of in-migration sufficient to meet colonial demands, which remained high.

Throughout these developments, then, commercial farmers and other interest groups continued to harangue government, demanding the implementation of poverty-increasing programs to stimulate "native" productivity. The idea was to institute a "gate of misery" and squeeze Africans through it. With precisely that end in view, a number of regulations were passed abridging land in the African locations, elevating the hut tax, and introducing marriage fees. Furthermore, the wholehearted support for a system of low wage payments and long service contracts must be seen as additional ways of swindling black people and driving their labor onto the market.

The dominant white attitude was that short contracts and high wages were detrimental to systematic industry and retarded colonial growth.

A further charge—namely, that Africans would not work with any degree of certainty for stated periods—brought whites to the conclusion that the sanctity of master-servant agreements was beyond the comprehension of "untutored savages"; that being the case, the situation urgently called for official remedies. Broadly speaking, these took the form of a registration system that mandated both statutes regarding vagrancy and the use of pass laws. Such mechanisms were meant to assist authorities in locating and punishing runaway servants, while, at the same time, operating as deterrents against future breaches of labor agreements.

Another controversial component of "native policy" involved the dismantling of core social and ritual institutions (like polygamy and *lobolo*, or bride price) that governed basic interactions in African life, but which were perceived as interfering with the labor market. Missionaries were in the vanguard of these aggressive campaigns to reshape traditional structures and transform the Africans' vision of the world.

Needless to say, attempts to implement these drastic measures undermined any feelings of racial harmony that might have resulted from a more discreet handling of the labor crisis; instead a rupture was produced between the indigenous communities and the colonial population. For the present, it is enough to point out that Africans did not passively give in to these attempts to destroy their core institutions, and hence their social existence. Years of struggle rendered much of the above legislation ineffectual.

A central contention of this study is that the settlers themselves were the leading impediment to the colony's acquiring the labor it sorely needed—in rural areas for plantation and farm work, and in the towns for domestic service, keeping the streets and roads in good repair, working the docks, and so forth. The settlers were, for one thing, woefully ignorant of the African cultures that their elaborate plans sought to destroy. Public perceptions of the indigenous population were based on a set of misguided assumptions and foregone conclusions derived in the main from a "kitchen knowledge of the Kafir." Ironically, those whites who undertook "to civilize the heathens through the gospel of labor" were often totally oblivious to aspects of the traditional work culture that might have been accommodated to colonial needs. European employers were often so warped by prejudice, so quick to act upon their wrong impressions and so self-righteous in their approaches to the labor question that there was scarcely room to negotiate for a practicable application of indigenous customs and norms. On the contrary, the settlers' habit was to brush aside traditional practices as irrelevant and meaningless; whites routinely tossed off any suggestions that Africans might have had their own agendas, with their own clear-cut goals and strategies for achieving them.

Such deep-seated contempt was fed by racialist notions of African inferiority. Absolutely nothing tended to incense whites more and to rigidify their thinking along these lines than the unwillingness of the "Kafir" to accept the indignities attached to his newly assigned status, defined in terms of his "proper relations to the white man." Because Africans were not eager to serve and obey whites, they were often confronted with open, oppressive violence. This tendency to violence created an atmosphere in which employer-servant relations badly deteriorated into arrangements characterized, on the one side, by profound suspicion and mistrust, and on the other, by a raw bitterness of feeling that often results from frustrated desire, a special kind of animus chilling in the intensity of its loathing for the black man.

"I was once interrogating a young intelligent superintendent of machinery in the Colony as to the labour he employed," recorded Anthony Trollope, a visitor to the settlement, "and asked him at last whether he had any Kafirs about the place. He almost flew at me in his wrath,—not against me but against the Kafirs."[1] The missionary Greenstock was similarly moved to write, "settlers can not speak of the present state of things calmly. It was enough to drive them wild to see thousands of idle people around them.... "[2] That these feelings existed is corroborated by Frances Colenso, who tells us that "the hatred which the typical colonial bears to the native *is quite a phenomenon in the history of mankind*" [emphasis added]. This was because, she explained, "They have never been allowed to make slaves of them which they want to do, and they have hitherto looked upon Mr. S[hepstone] and his policy as the great hindrance to their doing so."[3]

Presumably because so much evidence exists reflecting the popular prejudices regarding the Natal African's disinclination to enter wage employment, researchers have dismissed the idea of a nineteenth-century labor history of Africans in the region. The most telling commentary in this regard is that despite the spate of labor histories produced by the self-styled "radical" or revisionist school of South Africanist scholars, not one of their students found Natal's "Kafir labor question" a sufficiently worthwhile topic to direct their attention to it.[4]

I came to the subject intrigued by a historical puzzle of the best kind. On the one hand, as mentioned before, great prominence is given in the contemporary record to stereotypical Natal Africans whose one ruling propensity was "unconquerable laziness." It was commonly held that Africans were so comfortably provided for by a bountiful nature, there was no necessary inducement to labor. Yet such a simplistic assessment hardly accorded with social realities. My research has shown that these same communities were threatened with an internal crisis of such magnitude that it should have compelled their members to hire themselves out in the colonial labor market for long stretches of time. But that is precisely what did not happen! Our task, therefore, is to coax the sources into revealing why this might have been so. What I hope to present in the following pages is a nuanced analysis of the available data. Using various approaches, I looked for loose ends that might allow me to unravel some of the complex factors underlying both the African responses to the wage economy and those elements within white settler society that contributed to British Natal's prolonged experience with labor shortages.

The greatest challenge of the book came in finding new ways to explore the reality behind the images and words associated in the public's mind with the "lazy Kafir." In this sense my study tackles head-on certain enduring social attitudes about race. But more fundamentally still, it was the desire to arrive at a more exact understanding of the so-called "Kafir labor problem" that led me to ask a series of questions about the preindustrial African worker—unsophisticated yet sensible questions that have not previously been probed to any significant depth.

In taking these matters under investigation, preconceptions had to be rigorously set aside. I had constantly to remind myself, for instance, that it is only against an alien standard that African actions appear "baffling" and seem to defy economic good sense. In order to enter intimately into the life of these early African laborers and to experience what they were about, we must actually put an end to a certain way of thinking. For try as we might, we shall never come to understand what their behavior signified by isolating these workers from their cultural context. Indeed, the very answers that we seek are to be found in the traditional values that permeated these workers' lives.

My approach, therefore, is African-centered. By this I simply mean that I brought to the primary sources a list of inquiries, the answers to which I hoped to elicit directly or indirectly from the workers themselves. Basically this entailed following up clues that hinted in the slightest way at the existence of an African work culture. From the beginning there were pieces of evidence from the ethnographic records to serve as a guide. Such data provided decisive keys to grasping how northern Nguni-speaking people thought about and responded to the natural and social environment in which they traditionally operated. Supplementing these sources were materials from the James Stuart oral history collection, as well as documents from government and municipal archives. Missionary accounts, travelers' diaries, settler memoirs, colonial newspapers, and other popular literature of the day, such as Zulu–English phrasebooks, were minutely and rigorously examined. Phrasebooks, which were deemed such useful tools in master/servant relations that every nineteenth-century household would have been lost without one, and which have largely been overlooked by historians, proved to be documents of crucial social importance. This particular genre of print vernacular offers insights into such things as how job tasks were structured, how workmen kept track of their time, and so on. These sources also provide clues elucidating the system in vogue for apportioning punishment and rewards. In addition, by comparing various editions one can derive some idea about changing pay scales over short periods.

Other exciting approaches to interpreting the content of these small volumes were found: contrived though they may be, these texts can still be viewed as snippets of "dialogue" frozen in time between masters and their servants. And because industry was seen as a vital part of religion, missionaries, who were primarily responsible for controlling the written vernacular, focused mainly in these publications on subjects dealing with work discipline, such as duty and obligation and conformity to accepted standards of conduct. So in countless settler households it would not have been unusual to hear mistresses and masters not only uttering homilies on ethical matters; but also, their patience being quickly exhausted, they frequently resorted to issuing threats and admonitions (scripted in the Zulu–English phrasebooks) to their domestic servant, drumming into the head of their "dim-witted boy" the instructions required to fulfill various job functions. The thing is, in the process of analyzing the full body of data at my disposal, I began to notice that masters and servants repeatedly seemed to clash over very particular details in these work scripts. Much of this study has been dedicated to identifying those flashpoints and explaining their root causes. The reader will come to appreciate the enormous value of the information conveyed in these texts as some of the scenes are played back in the pages of this book.

As stated, all the sources of data mentioned above, including these less orthodox ones, were minutely examined, rigorously interrogated and compared, until, bit by bit, I was able to expose some of the everyday concerns and struggles of black working men in colonial Natal. This account is told from their point of view and wherever possible in the workers' own words.

I am not unaware of the difficulties associated with this approach. The major problem, of course, is that the bulk of these sources were written by Europeans whose testimonies were hostile, for the most part, and therefore must be suspect. The most delicate point of all, then, was how to derive the African point of view from narratives constructed by whites and from which the latter drew negative representations of the black man. While this is quite a serious and tricky question, I did not consider the problem insurmountable.

The strategy ultimately adopted here is one I imagine a criminal attorney would be compelled to fall back on in preparing the defense of a client whose case seems hopeless, but yet in whose innocence she persists in believing despite the array of eyewitnesses lined up to testify against him. That is, I proceeded under the assumption that if the hostile witnesses talked long enough, they would incriminate themselves, and, most important, that in their unconscious acts of self-betrayal they would also involuntarily disclose crucial information that could vindicate the defendant.

Although they did not know it at the time, European employers, who were exceedingly garrulous when it came to the "much vexed labor question," left a veritable gold mine of details about the nature of the preindustrial African response to the colonial labor market. The big task was to winnow out the interpretative biases. This was accomplished with the aid of ethnographic records, Zulu–English dictionaries, and other corroborative accounts. With the rich material that remained, the study will endeavor to convey the African wage earner's conceptualization of his workaday world.

One broad example will have to suffice as representative of the direction in which this approach is headed. It would scarcely have occurred to most white folk in colonial Natal to discover on what basis the black worker had agreed to sell his labor time; or to learn the African's views and notions of a fair day's work. Nor, it seems, did the vast majority of colonists ever imagine—or care, for that matter—that black workers might have understood the concept of the dignity of labor and attached status, prestige, and self-respect to jobs and tasks assigned and performed. As will be shown from evidence that, by and large, was intended as a sweeping indictment of African labor, this latter group had very definite views and a body of customs pertaining to all these issues; in addition, they drew strength from a moral code that bound them to their fellow workers and was expressed in institutions (an alternative to Western trade unions) that proliferated throughout the rural and urban areas during this period.

Another broad concern here centers on the experience of race and cultural contact. By that I mean that in a crucial way the book must be seen as an investigation of the intersection of two very distinct cultures in order to appreciate their fundamentally different notions about work, time, and status values, as well as a number of related matters. The book attempts to analyze what those encounters meant in terms of the behavioral consequences, especially for those Africans who participated in the nineteenth-century labor market.

A degree of satisfaction comes with knowing that the effort expended in pursuing the lines of inquiry set down in the pages of this book has been generously repaid. For now we have an image of the nineteenth-century African as wage earner that differs profoundly from any previous assumptions. In the chapters to follow, and in details not previously thought possible, the book will show that the African working community was actively involved in the colonial labor market and made their combined presence felt around issues affecting their objective day-to-day existence. Quite possibly, though, the most radical finding is that these men exhibited a set of patterned responses, guided by a body of corporate values and shaped by structural practices, that unmistakably constituted an African work ethic.

One thing more remains to be stated. It has to do with the audience to whom this book is primarily addressed. From the outset, my overriding concern was to reach beyond the academy to a much broader population, especially black people. As I commenced this work I was mindful that young black South African sisters and brothers and African American youths are desperately in need of access to histories about themselves—written in a clear, unspecialized, demystifying language—that confirm their humanity and show in concrete terms that even in the competitive labor market, far from being "shiftless niggers," backward, and disorganized, African people, almost from their first encounter with the white-dominated economy, reached within themselves and often bested the white man at his own economic game. So I began writing this study with a relatively limited end in view: to tell the story plainly, to move beyond the arid, often theoretical interpretations that have merely served to frustrate a broad awareness of a truly remarkable era in the socio-economic history of the continent.

It is my hope that young scholars of African descent, in particular, will come away from this study not just with a more balanced picture of black working men in nineteenth-century South Africa, but also convinced about the possibilities of conducting historical research from an African-centered perspective. The author looks forward to the publication of such studies by their hands that will amend, enlarge, and go beyond such findings as this work has been able to make.

The book is organized as follows. The problem is placed in perspective in Chapter 1, where we deal with the disastrous impact of the *mfecane* (period of intensive warfare) and post-*mfecane* turmoil on Zulu refugees returning to Natal. This initial chapter also examines attempts by successive white communities to control the labor of the returnees, and the latter's response. Chapter 2 focuses more closely on the socioeconomic ramifications of the crisis confronting the wounded households returning to Natal; it not only examines the efforts employed by African women and men to recover from the trauma of the crisis, but also explores their motives for doing so. The purpose of both Chapters 1 and 2 is primarily to show that African peoples in Natal were the absolute antithesis of the "lazy Kafir" stereotype that was incorporated into white popular consciousness. I do this by effectively demonstrating that it was not only a series of misplaced circumstances, but a range of positive incentives as well, that served as inducements for black males to enter the colonial labor market in great numbers.

Chapter 3 discusses the northern Nguni work ethic, the social prescriptions that intertwined status and occupations. This chapter sets the stage for much that follows, since it illuminates the theme that the African laboring population behaved in accordance with rules, beliefs, and norms of northern Nguni culture. Chapter 4 deals with two prolific causes of breaches of master-servant agreements—time disputes[5] and the withholding of wage payments, and as a consequence, the developing preference among African workers for minute forms of labor contracts.

Chapter 5 examines the rural and urban dimensions of *togt* or day labor. There the worker's ability to shape the conditions of labor is explored within the broader context of what was happening in the political economy of the colony. Chapter 6 continues to develop the idea, introduced in Chapter 3, that the persistence of northern Nguni cultural traditions in the colonial workplace not only assisted laborers in adjusting to their new surroundings, but those traditions and structures provided a ready program of action by which Africans achieved worker power. This chapter also describes in concrete detail the strategies and activities in which these African workmen engaged, and it recounts the long record of municipal and private failures to control the organized efforts of the African guildsmen and other forms of labor associations and clubs. The conclusion attempts to draw out the implications of some of the ideas discussed in the foregoing chapters.

1

"Forbidden Journey": Natal's Refugee Problem

This story begins in the early nineteenth century against a backcloth of upheavals known popularly today as the *mfecane*. The destruction spawned by these events caused massive dispersals of peoples, dislocated mixed farming economies, and ultimately reshaped the political landscape of southern Africa. Reports filtering out of the area starkly amplified the impact of the *mfecane* with details about how, as a result of the devastation, Natal (the territory lying directly south of Zulu country) was virtually emptied of its inhabitants.[1] In reviewing the contemporary accounts, however, one needs to be mindful that these reports were written as much to impress the reading public with the "remorseless violence" wrought by Shaka, as to make known the existence of depopulated areas suitable for European settlement and enterprise. On the whole, therefore, not much direct information can be found either in the early record or, for that matter, in recent historical treatments regarding the ways in which the survivors of these wars sought to piece together the shards of their lives once normalcy returned to the region. This chapter will discuss the plight of Natal's returning refugee population, the initial attempts by white traders and settlers to regulate their movements and exploit their labor, and the various responses of the refugees to those efforts at control.

The years 1817 to 1828 mark off that turbulent episode in the history of those northern Nguni-speaking people who had occupied Natal in ancient times.[2] Military operations allegedly mounted by Shaka against pocket chiefdoms drove throngs of refugees southwards, "impelled by the assegai and by fire," where they rebounded against settled homesteads and then erupted, plundering here and there, before pushing on. The cold moons of winter ushered in the season of hostility. It was then that the *amabutho* (Zulu warriors) were dispatched to scour the countryside, lifting cattle and pillaging granaries, while the *izibiba* (younger reserve forces) retreated before them with booty taken from the razed settlements.

During these attacks and surprise ambuscades, many of Natal's people were captured or carried off, or independently reached Zululand where they were incorporated into Shaka's kingdom. Just as many others, determined to resist Zulu over-lordship, poured headlong across the southern borders into Pondoland or beyond, where they joined still-intact communities. Even chieftains who had sent envoys to the Zulu king to offer the submission of their people were compelled to evacuate their *imizi* (villages); otherwise they might become frequent targets of forays depriving them of their domestic herds and winter stores. In the frantic rush to withdraw, those unable to keep up were left behind; and while the bad times persisted, the stragglers remained well hidden, urgent necessity alone forcing them to venture from their camouflaged dwellings and barren nooks to hunt, fish, and "bushrange," (i.e., grub and forage for food). Thus we are told that by the time the turmoil subsided, the open country of Natal had disgorged most of its population, and had become an immense buffer zone defined by the Thukela River in the north and the Mzimkhulu River in the south.[3]

Shortly after 1824, when the English established a trading post at Port Natal (later Durban), motley-looking bands began to emerge, one after another, from their places of concealment, seeking protection at the port. By Shaka's favor these men, women, and children were permitted to gather without fear of molestation in the vicinity of the bay. This was because the king viewed the trading settlement as part of his dominion and the white traders as his "relations."[4]

Then in 1827 or 1828, around the time of Shaka's murder, the first party of refugees from Zululand appeared in Natal. Again, after the customary consultation, they, too, were granted permission to reside near the port.[5] Now up until this time, Shaka, supremely self-assured, probably cast only a half-contemptuous glance at the miserable refuse begging relief at the commercial outpost. And as no great significance was attached to these occurrences, he was inclined to be mercifully disposed. Indeed, royal forbearance seems to have been the norm in past cases dealing with fugitives. But in light of the historical assessments of Shaka's career contending that the Zulu monarch had broken radically with tradition, his recognition of this archaic practice becomes all the more noteworthy. In retrospect, we know his continued tolerance of refugees was a strategic mistake of monumental proportion: a profound miscalculation that, in effect, sanctioned the port as a place of political asylum for Zulu defectors, a springboard from which future attacks could be launched against his kingdom.

From one point of view, a sanctuary in the neighborhood of the "despotic" Zulu government acted like a magnet upon political dissidents and other malcontents seeking alternatives to submission to Zulu leadership.[6] From the vantage point of the English traders, two hardheaded imperatives encouraged them to dispense food and protection to the numerous individuals desiring independence—namely, the number of wards (i.e., potential laborers, hunters, and fighters) seeking attachments would measurably enhance the port's economic possibilities, and they would also bolster its capacity for self-defense.[7]

Directly in the wake of Shaka's assassination, the Zulu kingdom fell into disarray. Without his genius and charismatic leadership, the union Shaka had welded immediately began to crumble. Further, a series of military defeats caused a loss of morale in the army and a decline in prestige abroad. During this period of disintegration, several subject chiefdoms not fully absorbed into the Zulu polity saw an opportunity to secede. The most notable movement was led by Nqetho. On the reassertion of his authority, the Qwabe chief gathered his people and hastily withdrew beyond the Mzimkhulu River, taking with him a portion of the royal herd. Following Nqetho's lead, other groups renounced their nominal allegiance and quit Zululand as well. A sense of urgency therefore confronted Dingane, Shaka's brother and assassin, upon his accession to the throne. The clear and obvious dangers inherent in this dynamic forced the new king and his principal men seriously to rethink their southern strategy, to enable them to act quickly and put the matter right.

To Shaka, Port Natal represented a vital commercial outpost. And as there were critical benefits to be derived from this link, the Zulu monarch had been careful to eschew aggressive action in the neighborhood of the bay.[8] Dingane took a less lenient view, however, particularly as the kingdom continued to sustain population losses. One sure sign of gathering problems was the incident reported in 1834 by an English trader J. Collis. In that year the Injanduna, one of Dingane's military regiments, ran off to Natal. As soon as the fact was discovered, an alarm was raised and three royal regiments were dispatched to head off the escape, strict orders at the time being issued to refrain from crossing the Thukela River.[9]

Ordinarily, even in pre-Shakan times desertion to another chief was regarded as a form of sedition because it weakened the strength of the abandoned chiefdom and increased that of a possible enemy. It was customary, therefore, for pursuers, if they could, to apprehend the fugitives before they crossed the boundary and to take their cattle. However, it was universally recognized that once the border had been crossed, runaways were under the protection of the chief whose territory they had entered.[10] With the rise of the powerful Zulu, these punitive campaigns became more violent. Persons running away who were subsequently caught on the road were put to death. Furthermore, total vengeance was exacted on chiefs found harboring fugitives, especially if the latter's infractions entailed theft of the king's cattle. In that case, the king's *izimpi* (regiments) relentlessly followed up the royal herds, destroyed the defectors, and summarily chastised the chieftain who had had the unpardonable impertinence to receive the fugitives. In one instance involving the Cele people, there is a tradition to the effect that their chief, Magaye, was executed merely for allowing Nqetho to pass through his district with cattle stolen from the king.[11] The message, therefore, was stark and unambiguous, a warning not to be lost on future deserters or their would-be protectors.

Presumably the renegade Injanduna had not been sufficiently foolhardy to abscond with a portion of the national treasure, which may, of course, explain why Dingane ordered his detachments not to cross into Natal—a decision which, as already noted, had been upheld by his predecessor in 1828. Nonetheless, it seems quite appropriate to speculate here that had Shaka lived, no doubt he would have taken great pains to reassess the situation in light of new developments unfolding in the region, and very probably would have rescinded the rule allowing defectors to settle in uncomfortable proximity to the kingdom. As indeed, the wisdom of that outmoded principle was now strenuously being challenged in the aftermath of his death.

For some time Dingane had been under pressure from his principal *izinduna* (civil and military officials) to adopt a course of action that would ensure Zulu hegemony beyond the Thukela. The king was urgently advised to deliver a swift, retributive attack aimed at sweeping away all the black people at Port Natal, thus resolving the matter at a blow.[12] Arguments for a major application of force came in the wake of a string of increasingly disturbing events that had roused the suspicions of the king's advisers. For one thing, the body of Zulu deserters could no longer be ignored as insignificant flotsam—their numbers were growing (as was the number of whites); and, by 1832, several thousand displaced persons and other fugitive elements had collected at the bay. For another, a substantial number of these refugees were ostensibly being trained as hunters in the use of firearms. Sensibly, any one of these developments would have proven ominous, but when, in the following year, blacks and whites residing at the port banded together and tested their "sticks of fire" against a weakened Zulu *impi* (regiment) returning from an unsuccessful campaign against the rebel, Nqetho, the mounting concern of the Zulu chiefs turned to genuine alarm.[13]

Threats of reprisals in consequence of the number of Zulu who had taken refuge at the bay provoked so much anxiety that a meeting of whites was held in 1835 to devise a plan for their mutual security, and to consider methods to prevent future desertions of Dingane's people. Allen Gardiner, the port's resident missionary, entered into negotiations with the king, and by treaty it was agreed that the lives and property of every individual, black and white, would be guaranteed, provided that the whites would agree not only to discourage "and never more to receive any deserters from his dominion," but also to return future runaways. Subsequent events soon canceled out the treaty and, as a result, all whites were debarred from entering Zululand, except Gardiner and his interpreter.[14]

Another crisis was building at just about the same time, but from a new direction. The Zulu nation was to experience its most formidable test with the appearance of four thousand *voortrekker* or Boer (Dutch) emigrants, accompanied by four thousand colored servants, who had left the British Cape with the intention of setting up a republic in the interior. Towards the end of 1837 an advance party of these emigrants arrived in northern Natal. By prearrangement, their leader, Piet Retief, preceded them in order to treat with the Zulu monarch for a grant of land. The incident is well known. Dingane, who correctly understood that the continuous white encroachment upon his dominions would ultimately lead to the subjugation of the Zulu people, killed Retief and massacred most of his followers, who had gathered near the Thukela riverbank. Several months later, the remaining *voortrekker* (emigrant farmers) groups met Zulu forces in a decisive campaign in which the king and his war councillors badly underestimated the Boers' superior weaponry, expert marksmanship, and discipline. On 16 December 1838, at a place that later came to be known as "Blood River," the Zulu army suffered a staggering defeat.

Thereafter Zulu internal affairs plunged to their lowest ebb. The nation literally began to unravel as thousands of people in tumbled disorder crossed the Thukela into Natal, their ancestral homeland, while others began to reenter the district from the south. Before the kingdom could recover from these losses, it experienced yet another major blow to its integrity—"the breaking of the rope" (*ukugqabuk' igoda*), an expression used among Zulu to describe the major rent that took place in the kingdom when Mpande, Dingane's half-brother, crossed into the district with a vast concourse of people (the greater part of the nation) and tendered allegiance to the Boer Republic of Natalia in exchange for protection.[15] In January 1840, Mpande returned to Zululand with Boer backing. After Dingane was put to rout and shortly thereafter reported executed by the Swazi, Mpande was proclaimed king.

Immediately the new sovereign, whose position was fast eroding, set about garnering support. Two major challenges had to be met: the preservation of the empire from disintegration, and the assertion of his authority.[16] Within scarcely four years, from 1839 to 1843, tremendous numbers of deserters had swelled the refugee population in Natal to between eighty thousand and one hundred thousand souls.[17] Petty chieftains who had crossed over at the time of "the breaking of the rope" were unwilling to follow the newly proclaimed king back to Zululand. Failing to reconquer the apostates, Mpande retaliated by confiscating their cattle and grain supplies.[18]

Removing his enemies, both the political supporters of his predecessor and members of the royal family suspected of conspiring against him, was crucial to securing the throne. The execution of Gqugqu, the king's half-brother, was meant to foil just such a plot. But as it happened, instead of surmounting the crisis, restoring calm, and thereby preventing further desertions, the attack on Gqugqu and other principal persons precipitated another massive flood of deserters, led by Mawa kaJama, Mpande's aged aunt, in 1843. Although many of the would-be emigrants were killed, the old woman and a sizeable following survived the crossing. It is important to note that at the time of her flight, Mawa daringly managed to seize an immense amount of state wealth (i.e., royal cattle) and take it out of Zululand.[19]

Colonial Adoption of the Cattle Confiscation Rule

While matters were in this unsettled state, Britain declared Natal a colony in 1843. For the next twenty years or more, the central focus of foreign and domestic relations in the region consisted of attempts by both the English and Mpande to staunch the outward surge of people and cattle from Zulu country, in order to prevent roused hostilities from escalating into war.

No Zulu was oblivious to the perils. The "forbidden journey" was a treasonable act, and by their actions defectors sacrificed the whole of their possessions. Or to put the matter another way, the life, cattle, and all other property of runaways were forfeited to the king.[20] From the start, Mpande pushed aggressively for the full recognition of this law in the newly established British territory. In June 1843 he sent a royal delegation to Major T. C. Smith, commander of British forces in the colony, to request on the king's behalf that "Mawa and the other fugitives, with the whole of their cattle, be compelled to return."[21] But in Major Smith they "found a rock," for this officer was adamantly opposed to the "barbarous law" and convinced that such a measure would send fugitives "to certain destruction"; Smith felt that to admit "the Kafir principle alluded to, and strip them of their cattle, would be to leave them to starve or to become marauders for their subsistence."[22] When, in October of the same year, Colonel Henry Cloete, Her Majesty's special commissioner, arrived in Zululand to settle by treaty the question of boundaries, Mpande reiterated his grievances and renewed his request that the British "drive all his runaways back to his country, and restore his cattle." Assurances were given that attempts would be made to discourage such robberies, and that every effort would be taken to restore those cattle that could be clearly traced. Mpande was further told that the influx of his people had created a state of consternation and alarm in the white inhabitants; nonetheless, the commissioner was firm in stating that "no authority would venture to force the refugees back to Zululand against their will."[23]

Cloete's approach established the course of future procedure. The policy set down in 1846 on the formation of the new government repudiated the idea of extra-diting fugitives from bordering countries.[24] At the same time, however, strenuous steps were taken to remedy the influx by forbidding defectors to bring property out of Zulu country. Arrangements were therefore made for the seizure of cattle the moment they entered the district, and for their restoration upon peaceable applica-tion. Chiefs along the Natal side of the border were issued strict orders to retain such cattle, and to report to the lieutenant governor that they had done so; moreover, they were instructed to give the cattle up to Mpande should his messengers demand them in the meantime.[25]

Every attempt to implement the above instructions met with obstacles. As soon as cattle crossed the colonial boundaries, a large number were stolen by white farm-ers and Africans living in the border divisions; others were scattered and secreted among friends and relatives of the refugees. Many of the overdriven beasts died from the hard pace set during the crossing, from accidents and attacks by wild animals, and from diseases induced by sudden changes in pastures. To keep the women and children alive, cattle from these herds were bartered for mealies; and when grain could not be obtained, beasts were slaughtered for food. In addition, the said live-stock were seized on the government's behalf and used to cover administrative costs involved in implementing the regulations: food was supplied to the *izikhonzi* (mes-sengers) sent by Mpande to request the return of pilfered stock. These envoys from the king were provisioned while in Natal, as well as given slaughter cattle and blan-kets for the return journey to Zululand. Another expenditure was incurred in deploying African policemen on these assignments. The general practice was to reward the men with a few head of cattle once the whereabouts of the latter had been discovered. In short, upon entering the colony contraband herds underwent a steady depletion.[26]

Understandably, this situation provoked Mpande's ire. Time and again, he expressed the strongest displeasure with the working of the confiscation act, a futile, toothless law, which held not the smallest chance for recovering his property unless decisive steps were taken to circumvent the ineffectual British handling of the prob-lem. Reinforcing these sentiments, of course, was the latter's inept handling of the case of Mawa, the king's renegade aunt. The royal herd the old woman had absconded with reputedly "would cover the site of Pietermaritzburg, and their track was like a wagon road," yet only a few head had been restored and those only after repeated representations to the colonial authorities.[27] To Mpande's way of thinking, "the shortest and best plan" was to intercept the cattle before they could be dispersed.[28] But the execution of the king's plan, a series of "hot pursuit" actions, led to inevitable boundary violations. On one occasion, Zatshuke, a colonial messenger, was sent to inform Mpande of two border infractions committed by the forces sent out to thwart escapees. But when called to account for these breaches of agreement, according to which, as already stated, the colony had undertaken to restore his prop-erty, the Zulu monarch exclaimed in a burst of anger:

> Whose cattle were they then? Were they not mine? No one in Zulu country owns cattle but me. They are all mine, and I shall follow them wherever they go. My people did right by following them, and they shall do so again. . . . What business has anyone to insist upon a lot of talk about the return of my property![29]

As if to punctuate his remarks, Mpande repeated the above declaration, which carried the warning that "he would give his people orders not to stab or use the assegai until they were resisted; and then," added he, "you will see a blaze."[30]

The white fear of Zulu reprisals intensified. Up to this point colonial efforts had accomplished little towards diffusing the crisis. No matter how assiduously they may have tried and despite the "hot pursuits" initiated by Mpande, defections by the king's people had only been slightly checked. "From information I have lately received," wrote Theophilus Shepstone, diplomatic agent in 1848, "I find that the Zulu willingly sacrifice their property to purchase a better form of government, and avail themselves of every opportunity that promises personal safety to abandon their cattle and enter this district."[31] And on a journey along the Thukela in 1852, Reverend Dohne was told that while he was there, several parties had gone into the Zulu country in order to get out their friends, who had been preparing for this purpose. Dohne was also informed that in all probability, after five years, all the "oppressed subjects" of Mpande who lived in the *emaphahleni* (outer fringes of the kingdom) would have quit Zululand for the same reason.[32]

Tough border interdictions were attempted to halt the momentum of the exodus, including, for example, the appointment of Chiefs Soqweba and Umvula, with a considerable number of Mpande's soldiers acting as surveillance teams under their command, to patrol the Zulu border along the Thukela riverbank.[33] To achieve the objective on the British side, twenty African constables were appointed and stationed at the four principal passes through the Thukela, which were represented by Mpande's messengers as almost exclusively used by refugees entering the lower part of the district.[34] These maneuvers, however, were soon revealed to be inadequate. Tension between the two governments continued to mount.

Two great issues of vital moment claimed public attention and virtually monopolized the political agendas of the successive white communities from the late 1820s through nearly the whole of the 1860s. The first was foreign policy. Securing the borders against incursions by Zulu military forces was inextricably bound to the topic of regulating the influx of refugees. The second question of great magnitude had reference to harnessing the labor of the resettled population for commercial endeavors recently undertaken in agriculture. Both these matters featured prominently in the proceedings of the 1852–1853 "Kafir Labor Commission."

The Apprenticeship Ordinance

It was probably with feelings approaching panic that the short-lived Boer Republic of Natalia (1839–1843) faced the steady traffic flowing through the escapeways along the Thukela. The Afrikaners (or Boers) regarded Natal as theirs by right of conquest and treaty agreement, deeply resented the intrusion of this fugitive population, and tried to suppress the migration with a law that forbade any African to cross the northern boundary into the district. However, the sheer volume of the traffic and the Boers' need to obtain labor prevented enforcement of a policy of exclusion. Accordingly, a more workable scheme was sought—one that would protect Boer interests, keep Africans under strict control, and simultaneously ensure a constant labor supply.[35]

With the eastern Cape behind them, the Boers continued to practice a system of apprenticeship (the origins of which can be found in the period of Dutch East India Company rule) in the frontier districts. As early as 1840, the Republic of Natalia made legal provision for state control of African labor when it decided that all orphan children had to be registered as apprentices (inboekselings), the boys until the age of twenty-five, girls till that of twenty-one. The law was intended to encompass not only orphans but also children of parents and guardians who had "voluntarily" agreed to place them under European masters.[36] Three years later the legislative body, the Volksraad or People's Council, determined to eliminate the "excessive" black population resettled on land throughout the district, proposed a plan for the strict sharing-out of labor at the rate of five African family units, with their families, to each occupied farm, and the compulsory registration of their children as apprentices.[37] Employers would be required to guarantee that the children would be well treated, and every apprenticeship was to be registered with the landdrost (district magistrate). All "surplus" blacks were to be forcibly removed from white areas into one large location.[38]

Just as had been the case in the Cape Colony, the system of child labor in Natal was accompanied by serious abuses, which brought harsh criticism from the English, who viewed the apprenticeship program as a practice akin to slavery. Accusations of slavery stemmed especially from the Boer custom of taking African children as captives. Zulu youngsters, for instance, were seized by parties of voortrekkers (emigrant farmers) after the defeat of Dingane. Recent research indicates that commandos were formally constituted in Natal and particularly in the eastern Transvaal primarily for the purpose of raiding African villages for this form of labor. As a result of these coercive methods, a class of African children was incorporated into Boer society, where they fulfilled household requirements for domestic labor and acquired a number of other skills that allowed them to work in a variety of capacities.[39] On the other hand, little evidence exists to suggest that the emigrant farmers attempted to take adult captives on a large scale. While some men and women were seized during commando raids, few were successfully retained within trekker society. This was because Boers lacked the means of control to integrate full-grown Africans into their system of domestic slavery. Children could be easily managed, and their young minds could be shaped to conform to European institutions and customs.[40]

Among other considerations, then, charges of slavery and slave dealing prompted the British to occupy Natal. When the area was taken in 1843, the English circulated a proclamation declaring the essential conditions under which the new administration would govern. The statement of conditions maintained that no distinction or disqualification on the basis of color, origin, language, or creed would be tolerated; that aggression against Africans beyond the limits of the colony by any private person or by any body of men would not be sanctioned, unless undertaken with the immediate authority and orders of the government; and that "slavery in any shape or under any modification" was absolutely unlawful.[41] To most Boers, the above terms were totally unacceptable. And to crown it all, when the English failed to provide an adequate solution to the land disputes contested by the returning African population and the emigrant whites, the majority of the trekkers packed their belongings, inspanned their oxen to their wagons, and withdrew to the north, where charges of slavery followed them, especially in the Transvaal Republic.[42]

The salient point is that British Natal was thoroughly familiar with this history of labor abuses, and with the outrages committed by Boers in the interior. Thus when some English colonists began to broach the subject, suggesting the introduction in Natal of a modified, more judicious indentureship program, some felt the need to tread warily. Indeed, the issue evoked contradictory feelings in Theophilus Shepstone, who advocated a cautious approach to the refugee question. For instance, he advanced the view that "it would be a great advantage to the black and white population, if the youth of the former could be induced to enter the service of the white employer and thus early acquire habits of industry," which he felt was "one of the first steps towards moral and social improvement." On the other hand, he was disinclined to openly endorse "any measure which had for its object the direct compulsion of one individual to work for another."[43]

There were wide differences of opinion. In some quarters, a few moderate spokesmen echoed Shepstone's position, arguing for a well-guarded system of apprenticeship with voluntary engagements of up to and not to exceed three years in the service of Europeans.[44] At the other extreme, some invoked the impassioned judgment that compulsion was the only effective answer to the labor problem. Whatever the particular viewpoint, it is clear that most settlers envisioned the apprentice system serving essentially a threefold function. In the first place, such a program would act as a deterrent and prevent many of Mpande's people from availing themselves of the open frontier; second, it would enforce labor from the new arrivals and assist in distributing workers among the colonists; and finally, it would be useful as an instrument for civilization.[45]

These matters go a long way in explaining why British Natal, not yet a decade in existence, jettisoned its principled stance—the one which in 1843 denounced "slavery in any shape or under any modification." Faced with a classic dilemma—that of finding a balance between a potentially disruptive situation involving deserters from Mpande's country on the one side, and pressures from indigenous commercial interests on the other—the response was to sacrifice British "liberal ethics" for the sake of expediency. In no time, more stringent regulations followed, which laid down new conditions of entry to the district. As it turned out, the new regulations were more punitive than deterrent. Though they did not halt the flow of traffic, they sanctioned the forced return to their "home" country of all who refused to submit to the labor demands of the new order.

The key feature of the 1854 Refugee Regulations was the compulsory apprenticeship rule, which required the registration and assignment of every able-bodied male refugee to the service of a colonist for three years, at a wage rate fixed by the authorities, the payment of which would be ensured through the magistrates. As stated, incoming fugitives refusing to work would be turned back to the Zulu country. Any chief or head of a kraal found harboring deserters or cattle would incur a fine of ten beasts for every such refugee, and five head of cattle for every beast harbored or concealed; upon repetition of the offense, he faced expulsion from the district.[46] Detailed guidelines were gazetted two years later with respect to procedures for registering fugitives for service.[47]

Priority was given over all other applications for apprentices to sugar cultivators,[48] and the available information indicates that preferential treatment was shown to town merchants as well. From the outset, both planters and merchants sought to strengthen the regulations. The thrust of their concerns was embodied in an 1857 petition to extend the term of service. It was proposed that individuals under eighteen years of age should serve for five instead of three years, and that masters should be legally vested with power to inflict corporal punishment. Neither suggestion was adopted. Yet it is worth mentioning that under the Masters and Servants Ordinance of 1850, resident magistrates were empowered to flog servants in their jurisdiction for breaches of the law (not to exceed twenty-five lashes according to instructions circularized in 1851). Whipping, as an instrument of control, was liberally made use of.[49]

A special challenge to law enforcement was that of devising ways to distinguish refugees from other categories of African servants, in order to monitor the former's movements and apprehend those who had decamped from service. One solution offered in 1854 by Durban's magistrate required apprentices to "exhibit some particular badge, or wear his [sic] hair in a particular way" that would "at a glance proclaim their identity" until their period of servitude expired.[50] While this idea was immediately rejected as impracticable, a bounty or reward system (offering 2s. 6d. for apprehending registered refugees who had deserted) was urged by the same individual and instituted three years later.[51]

Despite recurrent efforts to aid in the "more effectual accomplishment of the objects," the apprenticeship law failed in its design. That failure was due in part to the fact that the fledgling British colony, like the Boer republics, lacked the repressive machinery to prosecute such an ambitious plan. It was also due to a lack of official foresight in anticipating the needs of the resettled communities. Thus, insofar as its main goals were concerned—to register and settle the refugee population, to discourage emigration from Zululand, and to assist the agricultural industry by providing it with a steady supply of labor—the law was rendered essentially a dead letter. In the upcoming years, however, the ordinance (extant till 1891) remained useful as an instrument for entrapping unwary travelers, intimidating the general black populace, and preying upon the youngest and most vulnerable members in the African community.

Implementation of the Refugee Law

Fugitives arriving in the several northern frontier divisions were rounded up by border agents and forwarded in batches to magistrates applying for them. At the seat of each magistracy, it was left to the discretion of the resident official to dispose of refugees either in lots or singly to "respectable" European colonists. The absence of precisely worded instructions gave magistrates considerable latitude in the interpretation of the law. As a result, the conditions and practices for executing the regulations varied greatly from one division of the country to another. The inevitable outcome of such a procedure—that is, of placing these officials in enormously powerful positions with minimal restraints at a time when the demand for labor was growing increasingly competitive—laid the system wide open to large-scale abuse and corruption.

To get a sense of those abuses, it is only necessary to state that nowhere did the 1856 refugee guidelines consider the needs of the basic Nguni socioeconomic unit (which in peacetime ideally consisted of a kraalhead, his one or two wives, and their children); nor, it should be noted, was the apprenticeship of females contemplated.[52] Such glaring omissions created enormous problems in terms of the law's effective execution. Almost immediately, the authorities had to contend with resistance arising from attempts to apply the instructions, especially to women and girls of marriageable age. The Tugela magistrate reported a "system of passive disobedience" among the refugees, and was obliged "from inability to apply the instructions to women to allow several of them to go to their relatives"—an objectionable alternative, as it was felt that the practice held out "direct encouragement to our own Kaffirs to pursue a course fraught with danger and inconvenience to the government."[53] In another case, a party, consisting mostly of women and children, repeatedly demonstrated their stubborn defiance of the law by acts of passive resistance.

> On the 8th instant I dispatched to Pietermaritzburg under escort ... 109 of these refugees. I have this morning been informed that nearly the whole of that body decamped on the night of the 9th inst. and are now once more scattered over the country. I have already sent to recollect them. . . . I am more at a loss to conceive their reasons for this unwillingness to be sent to Pietermaritzburg [a distribution center] as I have striven to persuade them that it is to their own advantage.[54]

Whatever interpretation one cares to attach to this near-universal response, one explanation that can be promptly dismissed as erroneous is the refugees' utter aversion to working for white people. J. T. Kelly's investigation at Ladysmith revealed cases in which absconding parties had contracted themselves to Boer farmers. These farmers, he alleged, were primarily responsible for "exciting groundless fears in the refugees as to the consequences should they go to Pietermaritzburg."[55]

A case can be made to support the charge that early resistance to the ordinance stemmed from the instigations of Afrikaner farmers. For northern farmers would have benefited immensely by inciting the refugees in this sense: so long as the fugitives harbored feelings of dread about the fate awaiting them in the lower divisions, so long could the upland farmers—by exploiting those fears and thereby obstructing government's policy of favoritism towards the planters—be reasonably assured of labor being available for their own use. But as pertinent as this argument may be to the subject at hand, the origins of African resistance to the ordinance have to be sought elsewhere. For a more systematic investigation of this development, we turn to the journal of John William Colenso, bishop of Natal.

Colenso's diary is one of the best chronicles that we have for gaining insight into the practical workings of the refugee law and its ramifications on the apprenticed population. What is known at present, which his journal resoundingly confirms, is that the refugees' "groundless fears as to the consequences should they go to Pietermaritzburg" were in far too many cases implacably real.[56]

The bishop happened to be present at the border in 1856 when four fugitives— a man, a widow, and her two children (a little boy and girl)—arrived in the district, whereupon he immediately took charge of the party, in accordance with the terms of the 1854 Ordinance. Tied to the actions of the Anglican divine was his desire to establish a frontier mission station, a place to which every refugee child sufficiently young would be sent and subjected to the Christianizing influences of education.[57] It was a humanitarian service he never accomplished. Such corrupt practices were linked to the apprenticeship program that had the facts become generally known, they were sure to have outraged the public conscience. Colenso realized this. He further understood that being a willing partner in such a scheme meant not only risking damage to his reputation, but possibly calling down opprobrium upon the church.

At very least, the politic thing would have been for the framers of the regulations to include a conditional clause, one stating that every consideration should be taken to prevent further trauma being inflicted on the broken social units seeking shelter in the colony. From the start, however, the ordinance was arbitrarily and callously applied. No regard whatsoever was shown for surviving kinship ties, as the following excerpt demonstrates. Thus about the widow and her two small children, Colenso wrote:

> It was an affecting sight to see her, with her little ones nestling to her, one on each side . . . and to see the sorrow which overspread her face when told that she could not take them with her to settle among her friends. But this, the magistrate, acting under the Ordinance, refused to allow, for the boy at all events; and at last she consented to go with them into my service, rather than be returned, as otherwise might have been, in the Zulu land.[58]

Even though the mother was given assurances that her children would be cared for, and that she might go and live near them if she liked, or go herself and live at the kraal of her friends, and return from time to time to visit them, the family remained totally inconsolable. And on several occasions when the bishop inquired after the woman, he was told "she was crying bitterly, and the little maiden too." Finally, he was enjoined by conscience from acting upon his plan.

> It is hopeless, I find, to think of taking the mother and her two children to Maritzburg, at least without some painful scene or other, which I should be sorry to be the cause of. . . . I have decided, with Mr. W's [Mr. Walmsley, resident magistrate] approval, to let them go at present to the kraal of a neighboring chief, the friend with whom the woman wished to reside; and to send shortly for the man and boy, and leave the mother and daughter to continue there, on the understanding that the little girl is to be surrendered for three years to the occupants of the new mission station, so soon as it shall be established.[59]

Not only was it impossible to ignore these flagrantly objectionable aspects of the apprenticeship program, the time came when the bishop could no longer morally permit such proceedings to go unchallenged. Essentially what happened was this. Alarmed by the allotment practices operating at Durban, he was compelled to bring charges in 1857 to the effect that the distribution of refugees in the port town took on the appearance of a slave mart or "Kafir fair"; that instead of being privately assigned by the magistrate, at his discretion, the unfortunate victims were publicly exhibited to the gaze of white people, who, in the manner of a slave auction, "made their remarks freely, then and there, upon their personal qualifications," and were allowed to pick and choose from among them at their own liking; and that children were being separated from their mothers against their will.[60]

Though these scandalous revelations resulted in explicit orders being issued from time to time from the office of the secretary for native affairs, prohibiting the separation of refugee families and the indenturing of females,[61] such practices were still prevalent in following years. In Umsinga and Stanger, where apparently a popular unwritten practice superseded the legal code, the custom of apprenticing small children, boys and girls, continued unabated and on a large scale. The appropriation of numbers of these children seemed to have been such a common phenomenon that it very likely accounts for the statement made by John Knight, the border agent and administrator of native law, who freely admitted that more refugees were indentured at Umsinga than at any other place in the colony.[62]

The Umsinga case is noteworthy not merely because violations there were so blatant and shocking, but rather because the administrative center of the colony was tied into the scandal. The majority of children apprenticed from Umsinga were taken from protesting parents by African policemen, escorted cross country, and disposed of to white householders at Pietermaritzburg.[63] The extent to which this trafficking in child labor perverted the spirit of the regulations came to light in an incident involving two female children. Not by the largest stretch of the imagination could the family of the little girls be construed as refugees.[64]

This latter case points to one very prolific cause of abuses—namely, the broad meaning attached to the word "refugee."[65] Any black person entering the colony stood the risk of being impressed into three years of servitude. Without being given a chance to remonstrate, unwary migrant workers or visitors—including traditional doctors and other professional men on their seasonal circuits—from Pondoland, Basotho, and Tsonga country were waylaid into indentureship.

> I heard some strange things at Estcourt. A man of a Basotho tribe had been detained for three years in the service of the Government Border Agent. He had entered Natal with the intention of seeking instruction for his children, but had been seized as a refugee. When he pleaded that his wife and family would be destitute in his absence, it was of no avail: he was told that he must work for the agent. The three years were up, but still he was not liberated, being detained six months longer on some trifling pretext.[66]

The injustices of another well-publicized affair in 1873 prompted R. E. Ridley, editor of the *Natal Witness*, to assert angrily that "it would be called slavery by Englishmen if practiced in the Transvaal by the Boers."[67] To allay the fears engendered by this system of impressment, which threatened to interfere with Natal's foreign labor supply, the matter was brought before government where in an 1885 ruling it was secured that a "refugee" was and could only be someone who left Zululand to settle in Natal. The court further decreed that refugees would become the sole monopoly of the government for three years of enforced labor (*isibhalo*) on the public roads. Private parties henceforth were legally denied the right to claim them.[68]

Great effort was taken to outline this episode in the colonial history of Natal in order to establish the context and to set the tone of future developments. Before proceeding, the reader should be made fully aware that the early determined resistance to the apprenticeship law emanated from the needs of the refugees to salvage the traditional kinship unit. Close attention must be given, therefore, to the reasons such as those offered by the planter Ralph Clarence in 1847 for preferring the residence of African families on his farm. It was not just that he found children and women more useful in performing light work; he also observed that "boys" did not leave their employers so frequently when their relatives were near at hand as when they lived at a distance.[69]

Presumably this was the rationale in 1843 when, it will be recalled, the Volksraad or legislative body of the Republic of Natalia proposed a plan for the strict sharing-out of labor at five African family units *with their families* to each occupied farm.[70] Former experience had taught that this precondition was so singularly critical to the smooth functioning of rural labor arrangements that it is astounding so few colonial administrators made official note of it. One was Walter Macfarlane, the resident magistrate for Weenen. Macfarlane fully recognized that *"On the question of distribution, it was the families one ha[d] to consider* [emphasis added], because it [was] vain to expect that the young men [would] remain contented for any lengthened period if entirely separated from their kraals."[71] Similar observations were made by Theophilus Shepstone with respect to a party of refugees that fled into the colony in 1865.

> I believe these refugees are as yet without their families and I do not think there will be any advantage in removing them to the Klip river until they have been either joined by or know the fate of their women and children. It is useless to try to distribute them under the refugee regulations until they are satisfied on that point. I suggest whether it would not in the meanwhile be better to leave them where they are and then distribute them as families to farmers requiring their service.[72]

As things turned out, no serious attempt was made to draw closer scrutiny to the matter. The advice of Weenen's magistrate and that of the secretary for native affairs went largely unheeded. This fact would explain why, despite "the most diligent search and watchfulness" and the stiff penalties and fines awarded chiefs and heads of kraals found harboring refugees and contraband cattle,[73] it was well-nigh impossible to implement the apprenticeship measures effectively. Meanwhile, public dissatisfaction continued to be raised owing to the lax way in which "fugitives, unapprenticed and at large," were "allowed to overrun the country."

> It is found that very few of these who have recently sought, in such numbers, asylum in Natal from the oppression and cruelty of their king, Panda, are willing to fulfil the conditions of servitude to the colonists, under which they are allowed to remain. . . . Thus the whole system is useless, both as a check to further immigration and as a means of supplying labour. It is, therefore, doubly plain that our government should resolutely co-operate with Panda for putting a stop to the further influx of his subjects. If they will not conform to reasonable conditions of service imposed, as a price for our protection, and as a slight compensation for the perils we incur in harbouring them, there is no longer any reason, social or political, why we should continue to risk a collision with a powerful barbarian neighbor, otherwise disposed to friendly relations with us.[74]

Profile of the Refugee Population

The refugee population fell roughly into two classes: those who sought asylum in Natal from political or other causes of persecution, and those who were members of communities that had begun to reestablish themselves in the district before it was declared a British colony. The great majority of ordinary refugees were of this latter class. During the Great Zulu Revolution of 1839–1840, individuals had become separated from their families when large numbers of their menfolk who crossed with Mpande placed themselves under the Boers and resettled on land formerly occupied by their forefathers.[75] Ever since that time, a steady stream of Zulu hazarded the flight in order to reunite with relations or to establish fresh social ties. Many of these individuals, weary and disoriented, managed to clear the river before dropping from sheer exhaustion and hunger. Rounded up in that condition, they were supplied with rations, but, in spite of such efforts by the authorities, large numbers in this weakened state died on their way down.[76] Survivors were registered and parceled out to white masters.

An intense longing to join clan members already settled in the district was the great motive inducing those who had been impressed into service to make good their escape. At first opportunity, fugitives negotiated their way to the nearest homestead, where they enlisted assistance and protection, and where they hoped to receive intelligence on the whereabouts of kinspeople and friends. This stopping place or "safe house" was but one in a series of forwarding stations along which they were passed until, at last, they were safely secreted in some out-of-the-way terminus to elude detachments of "native constables" who had been specially deployed to apprehend fugitives and registered runaways.

The first year no new huts were built; the refugees would bide their time in concealment until they could establish themselves openly without fear. Even along the Thukela border, "kraals of refuge" were reported where Zulu deserters were received and housed in old huts, vacated for their use, while new ones were erected for the old residents; and since the latter were long-time inhabitants well known by whites living in the division, no notice was immediately taken of the subterfuge. In due course, the fugitives were marched further into the district. The process took place "so quietly," reported Lewis Grout, "as scarcely to attract notice. Numerous and populous villages have sprung up, as if by magic, in almost every direction around us. . . ."[77]

During the period of sequestration, refugees destitute of cattle and other property were entirely supported by the charity of the people in whose kraals they found refuge.[78] Attempts by the authorities to penetrate this network of "intertribal" solidarity, and to undermine the spirit of *ubuntu* (hospitality), were frustrated time and again, as these remarks by the Kahlamba magistrate show.

> If any duty approaches in character and influence that of a sacred obligation in the Kafir's mind it is hospitality and so strongly is this felt among the natives generally, that, I believe, there is a mutual compact among all tribes to defeat in every way not openly hostile any attempt to apprehend the refugee, after he has once demanded and obtained the protection of a chief. Any informer would be abhorred among them and at once cast out of the tribe.[79]

Preindustrial people long understood that survival came from acts of charity. But apart from this spirit of altruism, other principles were actively operating here.

There can be little doubt that minor chiefs looked to derive power from such accretions to their communities; that individual heads of kraals, in a like manner, sought personally to improve their lot.[80] Men of undistinguished lineages, who possessed no rights to chiefly claims, hoped nonetheless to build a following and augment their cattle wealth. Not surprisingly, among those entertaining lofty aspirations were persons of dubious character, unprincipled men known to extort allegiance from fresh arrivals by holding over them the threat of exposure. Since no statute of limitation existed beyond which a fugitive became exempt from the apprenticeship law, an individual who had managed to elude the compulsory regulation for several years was, on being discovered, still liable to three years of servitude. That information, put to use by venal and corrupt men, was a powerful weapon for manipulating and controlling male youths who had entered the district illegally.

These matters are explored at great length in Chapter 2. For the moment, it is necessary to concentrate on the scope of the refugees' predicament. Brought down to its essentials, it was this: in all the chaos and confusion of the wars, they had become separated from loved ones, were presently suffering the extremities of privation, and had no idea what lay ahead for them. We must also keep in mind that when the refugees fled to Natal, it was in anticipation of finding some relief from their troubles. They came fully expecting to be "wrapped in a mantle of British protection." As one latter-day informant observed, it was customary that when men in Zululand fled from one chief to another, the family system in its new environment was not in any way tampered with; "if protection was shown in Zululand, it was only to a complete unit of the state, not to mere solitary individuals."[81]

Imagine what these people must have felt when, on entering the district, they encountered this assault upon their future—a policy aimed to scatter their children broadcast, and to indiscriminately separate women, girls, and young men from the influence and protection of their guardians. If their feelings could be summed up and spoken, they would have been that the government was out to finish them; the desperate thought must surely have been that the refugee policy would utterly shatter what remained of their fragile surviving connections. These considerations are what made the apprentice system repugnant; this is what rendered the laws unworkable.

From the colonial standpoint, there were powerful external and indigenous pressures urging an immediate solution to the fugitive problem, a plan that would mollify Mpande and simultaneously benefit commercial farmers and other employers. Political and economic necessity was thus the justification for taking advantage of the misery and distress of these people by imposing a sentence of indentureship upon them. Furthermore, as already shown, in their efforts to achieve a double objective—to stem the floodtide of Zulu deserters and to create a cheap, malleable work force—government officials failed to act aggressively in halting the excesses committed under the labor ordinance. The result was that British Natal's earliest system of African servitude bore striking resemblance to the institution of bondage for which they had so severely criticized the Transvaal Boers.[82]

In 1864 Theophilus Shepstone was asked to assess the overall effectiveness of the registration system in diminishing the annual number of ordinary refugees seeking asylum in the colony. While the secretary for native affairs felt the existing regulations had been sufficient to check ordinary emigration from the Zulu country, he was disposed to add that given the "despotic" nature of the Zulu government, there would always exist causes for flight which no regulations could overcome.[83] He reckoned the average number of emigrants settling in Natal from Zululand at about six hundred persons annually.[84] This figure is, of course, a gross understatement.

In a report furnished fifteen years later to the 1881–82 Natal Native Commission, John C. Walton admitted that,

> We are not in a much better position to-day to give any precise information
> as to the number of Natives in the Colony, inasmuch as no census of these
> people has ever been taken, nor any registration made of the births and

deaths amongst them. (Marriages alone being registered.) The number of Refugees and other Natives who have flocked into the country since it has been under British rule has never been ascertained. Some information, however, is obtained from a Return during the years from 1856 to 1881, inclusive, 10,978 came here to settle permanently. But this Return is manifestly incomplete, since the County of Weenen is altogether omitted therefrom, and no mention is made therein of the arrival of large numbers of Zulus about the year 1856, who fled into this country through the Lower Tugela, after the death of Umbulazi; nor of those who came through the Buffalo River in 1859 under Chiefs Umtongo, Digidi, and others, who settled chiefly in the County of Weenen; nor of the large tribe of Amaswazi, which migrated hither with their cattle, under Mavovo, about the year 1860, and settled in the District of Klip River. On the other hand, nothing is said of those tribes under Dushani, Sidoi, Matyana, Langalibalele and others, who fled the Colony during that period. . . . [85]

After almost forty years of British rule, careful and accurate population estimates for the African communities were still unobtainable. Statistics compiled for the year 1881 (based on occupied huts counted during the annual tax season) suggest the enumerated population of Africans within the district totaled about 367,152 souls[86]— a figure that represents more than a 250 percent increase over estimates given in 1843 when the district was declared a British colony. If these numbers have any relevance whatsoever, it is that they show the Refugee Regulations were an abysmal failure.

2

Crisis of Reconstruction and the Mobilization of Labor

An explicit theme running throughout the nineteenth-century literature is that Natal's indigenous households were flush in cattle, land, and women, an idea that came to be firmly implanted in the popular colonial consciousness. Of course, we know now this picture of wealthy African communities, luxuriating in "savage freedom and heathen idleness," is an invented fallacy. All the same, it is a curious experience reading the literature for what it does *not* say. It is as if the havoc wrought by the wars and the turmoil produced in their wake had had no telling impact on the African population; it is as though the subsequent social ferment within Natal's black communities had failed to intrude upon the notice of white men. Our sources move beyond the early misleading accounts to reveal a radically different picture, one that accords more with the shared experiences of the vast number of black people who had recently returned to Natal.

The argument is uncomplicated. The reimmigrant communities faced an internal crisis of staggering proportion. The weight of evidence to support this is commanding. Here we will explore the dimensions of that crisis, the state of affairs that slowed down the program of recovery, and some of the strategies employed by Africans, women and men, to restore the subsistence base. Finally, we will examine the motivations that propelled them in their efforts to resurrect and infuse these communities with a new vitality. Before we begin, however, let us briefly turn to Henry Slater's lucid discussion of the northern Nguni "homestead production complex,"[1] for it was institutions similar to this ideal model, but ones that had been sucked into the turbulence set in motion by Shaka and other forces of change, that were at root of the crisis.

All of the resources in the production complex—the socioeconomic triad consisting of women, cattle, and land—together with the maintenance of certain social practices, were necessary to the operation of the homestead. That is, loss or deficiency in any one of these variables created a precarious imbalance in the subsistence level of the domestic unit. For instance, deficits in cattle precluded the transfer of *lobolo* (bridewealth) for wives, which, in turn, reduced the size and strength of the polygamous family, the self-sufficient unit of production and consumption. Similarly, without land cattle could not graze, crops could not be grown, and a surplus could not be produced for trade. The usefulness of this model lies in the fact that it allows us to make a damage assessment of those groups that resettled in Natal.

The crisis lay in the cumulative losses—both human and material—sustained during the *mfecane* (period of intensive warfare) and in its aftermath. There is no question but that these people were cattle-poor; that, as will be argued, they were experiencing great stress due to an undersupply of women; and, as is generally well known, that they suffered from a critical shortage of arable land in the locations that had been set aside for their use in 1847. By any criteria, then, their resources fell disastrously short of what was needed to maintain subsistence levels. Furthermore, it seems certain that this state of things would have led to very grave consequences indeed had it not been for the willingness of black and white residents in the district to provide immediate relief aid.

Given their straitened circumstances, one can see why the new arrivals would be favorably disposed to external market forces. The fact that they very readily adapted to their altered condition and surroundings, and were able to absorb a new system of values, is what made their survival and rapid recovery possible.

To deal adequately with the crisis of reconstruction, special attention must first be given to the period from about 1840 through the 1860s. These twenty or more years saw an intensive movement of repopulation. It was a time in which Natal reluctantly received the bulk of its repatriate refugees. More importantly, though, from an African perspective, this period coincided with the beginning of colonial rule, portentous of a much greater eventual loss. Still, for a brief spell at least, and this despite the refugee law, the new order seemed to hold out unprecedented opportunities of trying new things and new ideas. Not only were members of these fragmented social units receptive to the advantages, they were wide-awake to the fact that pursuing them would contribute to the reformation and formation of cohesive households. The essential point is that this was a time of significant recovery and change, a time when Africans were confronted with tremendously difficult choices and displayed great shrewdness and ability in using traditional and nontraditional stratagems in order to achieve their goals. For all these reasons, it is important that we be clear about what those goals were.

While Natal's Africans were motivated by a combination of many needs and desires, it seems fairly clear that three areas in particular engrossed them. Their immediate aim was to secure protection and stabilize the subsistence base; second, was the need to either comply with or avoid obligations in the form of colonial hut and labor taxes; and finally, of paramount concern were issues of authority and prestige. With respect to this last matter, it should be noted that the emphasis placed on the value of "being first," and the competition stemming from it, underlay much of their actions. One could be "first" and "senior," as Kopytoff shows in his splendid essay, [2] in a variety of contexts—such as age, kin group, the settlement as firstcomer in a locality, and so on. The operation of this pan-African cultural principle is clearly discernible on all these many levels in the present analysis. For example, one critical factor at this time was related to the power vacuums created during the *mfecane* and post-*mfecane* years; in consequence of the great void in leadership, a scramble occurred among members of the various age groups who, in pushing themselves forward, hoped to be reinstated or to make a name for themselves and emerge publicly for the first time as "big men."

Women operated from very similar motivations, being guided as they were by the same rule of precedence. Their diligent efforts to attain primacy of place in the homestead is one reflection of this. Deliberative thought and conscious maneuvering often went into winning the position of either senior wife or favorite wife in plural households. Great care and attention, moreover, were directed toward becoming a successful merchant of farm produce or an *inyanga* (a professional person or one skilled in some craft), for such strategies enabled women to acquire not only property in their own right, but an undeniable measure of prestige and power.

Reaccumulation of Cattle Funds

Apart from providing *lobolo* (bridewealth), cattle and cattle keeping in northern Nguni society were associated with several key institutions. Livestock were a primary source of food (milk and meat), clothing, and fuel (as *amalongwe*, or cattle dung). Wealthy individuals who possessed more stock than needed for their own consumption could lend (*sisa*) the unencumbered portion of their herd to less fortunate men over whom they then exercised some authority. Cattle were, moreover, a source of entertainment and "poetry and great care was lavished on them." Indeed, one can show that in their emphasis on cattle the Zulu possessed a deep aesthetic appreciation for the qualities of their herds.

Domestic animals also played a central role in the ritual life of the people. Cattle furnished the means of propitiating the spirits with sacrifices made to avert evil, or to procure a blessing, or to make a thanks-offering.[3] It is a matter of record, for example, that Zulu refugees demonstrated their gratitude for their safe flight by sacrificing the first cow earned in Natal.[4] Furthermore, beasts were slaughtered and commonly offered after the building of a new kraal, by parents when sons were absent on long-distance and dangerous missions, and by prophets to procure inspiration. Cattle were required to pay for the services of the *inyanga* (such as a medical person), or to ransom relatives seized by the enemy during times of strife.[5] In the one episode of which we have knowledge, though such cases must have abounded, refugee parents paid a cow for the redemption of their daughter captured and held in Zululand after an abortive attempt to escape.[6]

All this demonstrates rather vividly their need to revive the "cattle complex." It further explains why some fugitive parties took tremendous risks to bring herds out of the Zulu country; and why, once in the district, they adopted numerous ploys to conceal them in noncompliance with the confiscation order. Such evasions were supported not only by Africans living in the border divisions, but also by Boer farmers desiring a steady supply of laborers. For example, groups of frightened refugees were approached by white farmers with attractive work offers and warned that proceeding further into the district would lead to certain government seizure of their stock. Runaways were persuaded to remain on white-owned land where, they were told, their herds would be safe and allowed to graze with the farmer's cattle.[7] Various ruses were employed to outwit magistrates and "native detectives." Fugitives surrendered a portion of the smuggled herd and then gave sworn testimony that the cattle relinquished represented all that were brought out of Zululand, while the greater portion of the herd was concealed among the farmer's stock in exchange for labor. These arrangements were fraught with problems, however, and refugees quickly discovered it was not always possible to redeem herds distributed under such conditions.[8]

To calm apprehensions and gain trust, other forms of rural agreements were held out as enticements to the fugitives. As pointed out above, the measures taken to disperse refugees among the colonists failed largely because these practices were viewed, often rightly so, with trepidation and therefore resisted. But where registered contracts appear to have been smoothly executed and made acceptable to all parties concerned, it is likely that those arrangements were workable because they offered a safe haven for every surviving household member. From the farmers' standpoint, such a strategy offered only temporary relief from their labor problems. This was because after amassing sufficient resources and on completing the terms of their indentureship, refugee groups usually abandoned their white benefactors in order to establish homesteads of their own.

In 1849 a party of deserters was rescued from imminent starvation by the Coetzee family. The refugees were allowed to squat and cultivate "a good deal of ground"—the produce of which was continually exchanged for cattle—on condition that some of their numbers worked for the farmers whenever called upon. In addition, the Coetzees were in "the habit of paying them in cattle, blankets, or picks for any work beyond that ordinarily required."[9] Some of their "blanket wages" were sent with trading parties to the Zulu country for bartering cattle,[10] and in this way a few became very well off. Goliath, for example, earned twenty-six head of cattle in four years. And as he and his party had accumulated enough to live upon, they now "wished to leave and go away where they need not work [for the white man]."[11] Such "base displays of ingratitude" were a great source of vexation to the colonists. By some twisted logic, the settler community had apparently arrived at the conclusion that Africans owed them a life-term debt, payable in labor, for having provided an asylum from Mpande.

The overworked stereotype that Africans entered labor service for two reasons only—namely, to pay hut taxes and to increase the number of their cattle so as to increase the number of their wives—tells us more about the limitations of those contemporaries who asserted this view than the individuals they purported to describe. Yet this statement nonetheless contains a significant grain of truth, for Africans *were* in very many cases converting their earnings into livestock. A measure of this is seen in the brisk cattle trade that had developed in Natal by the early 1850s. Commenting in 1852, the hunter/trader William Baldwin asserted that he had "sold forty or more [cattle] in one day and had upwards of six hundred on the place at one time, averaging in those days before the lungsickness, from 10s. to £2 a head, *for which the kaffirs in Natal always paid cash*" [emphasis added].[12] From this piece of information we may conclude that efforts were well underway to restore African homesteads to levels of self-sufficiency.

As late as 1872, individuals, families, and small groups of coconspirators residing in Zulu country could still be found plotting strategies and making preflight plans, aimed ostensibly at recouping previous and/or anticipated property losses. Numerous getaway schemes unfolded whereby parents plotted to send ahead, first, their daughters and other female wards, to provide for their needs in the new locale.[13] The idea seemed to have been that if the young women could be gotten out safely, their parents or guardians would be assured of claims to cattle (*lobolo*) in case they were presented with the necessity of fleeing at some future date.[14] Grave danger attended these activities, but given their extremely limited options, and considering the heightened risks involved in the crime of pilfering the king's herds, perhaps no other course suggested itself as sensible.

Rebellious young maidens made the perilous flight, in defiance of the king and often against their parents' wishes, sometimes eloping with a young man but frequently absconding on their own. Numbers of these young female runaways made their appearance in the Newcastle division, where they were promptly apprehended. The arrangement originally was to send the girls back, or at least attempt to do so, but, according to Shepstone, "this produced disgusting scenes and the girls as is usual the world over got their way." The more practical course afterward adopted was that of allowing the girls to marry long-time residents in the colony, with the magistrate's consent. The cattle resulting from such unions were demanded by Cetshwayo (Mpande's son and successor) and delivered up to him as Zulu property.[15]

As will be shown in greater detail in the next section, illegalities of all sorts arose in connection with this traffic. Deliberate fraud was perpetrated so boldly by the refugees themselves that the colonial authorities were forced to take notice. One government source, for instance, disclosed that among the Zulu who entered the colony as refugees were some in the company of their married sisters, whose husbands were also fugitives. Their lawful marriages, which had been previously contracted in Zulu country where *lobolo* was considerably below that existing in the district, were not acknowledged by the women's relations in Natal. The upshot was that legal spouses were illegitimately being deprived of their wives, who were remarried to men willing to pay the higher rates.[16] The young men allegedly instigating these transactions were then in a position as their sisters' guardians to receive the bridewealth, which they, in turn, "borrowed" in order to acquire wives for themselves.

Equal zeal was applied to the lucrative practice of cattle rustling. Ordinance No. 1 of 1855, the object of which was to prevent cattle stealing, apparently accomplished little in that regard.[17] In all events, at the very point at which these households seemed to be making a phenomenal recovery, after years of unremitting effort and collective commitment to restocking their cattle byres, the disastrous lungsickness struck. Large Natal herds owned by white farmers and Africans were decimated by the disease which spread with fearsome results throughout Zululand as well. In 1856 Umsiyane, an *induna* (army officer) at the Indabakawombe military kraal reported an *indlala* (famine) there, and further stated that the cattle were all dead and that the great body of soldiers had been sent to their homes in the country so as not to be a burden to the king.[18] The scourge still prevalent in Natal in 1857 prompted Bishop Colenso to remark that "a native now, who used to be so eager for it, will rather decline a cow, as a present, or reward for a piece of labour."[19] And the Inanda magistrate reported that "money is rapidly becoming the substitute medium in the purchase of wives; ten pounds sterling being the standard value of a damsel of average attraction."[20] Another more common response was to "bank" (or hoard) wage-earnings and other money received from trade in hawking farm produce, home crafts, and European manufactures, till the day the lungsickness passed, whereupon the "deposits would be withdrawn" and then invested in restocking their cattle pens.[21]

The *"Intombi* Trade" (Trade in Young Women)

Authors have argued that land shortages and the buildup of demographic pressures in and around Zululand in the late eighteenth century may have been the key contributors to the violence and chaos of the *mfecane*. It was apparently to halt the degradation of the environment and contain the population explosion that Shaka instituted drastic measures to control relations between the sexes.[22] Strict rules of celibacy were put in force; and the timing of marriages, which had come to be associated with the regimental system, was now determined solely by the king, whereas that prerogative had previously rested with individual heads of households. Though statistical proof is lacking, Bryant's observations suggest that in addition to the constant warfare, such radical reforms had a decisive effect on curbing population growth within the Zulu kingdom.[23]

Aside from the question of achieving a reduction in fertility, it is the nature of the social historian to wonder about the public's reaction to any changes of such magnitude, especially within the most intimate areas of people's lives. The immediate response of many, no doubt, was to capitulate to their fears of Shaka's "awesome powers"—to comply obsequiously with the marriage law and the restrictions placed on sexual expression. Others, probably festering with resentment and rumbling discontent, submitted, for the time being, to the offensive codes. In later years, after his excesses had gotten out of control, Shaka was assassinated. But what is most instructive in this context is a passing statement made by Henry Fynn regarding Shaka's murder. Fynn tells us that among the national songs composed by Dingane at this time, which reflected on the conduct of the deceased king, "was one exposing the folly of depriving people of the right or liberty of marrying."[24] From this and other remarks made by the same observer, it is clear that dissident voices were being raised around the question of late marriages, as well as other critical issues, before the regicide occurred. Grievances were taken up in high-placed quarters, where the decision ultimately reached was to do away with Shaka. Yet if Dingane's coconfederates anticipated the inauguration of a regime whose hallmark would be the institution of more compassionate measures, their hopes were quickly dashed when steps were taken by the new king to entrench the national marriage law. The episode that precipitated Nqetho's flight from Zululand during the early years of Dingane's reign will illustrate the point.

The Qwabe chief, Fynn recounts, had just married two wives. Since one of these was the widow of his deceased brother, who by custom automatically became Nqetho's wife, he reported only one marriage to the king. Hearing of the former *ukungena* (the levirate) marriage, Dingane arrested Nqetho's messengers, who were tried for attempting to deceive the king. Dingane, in ruling against the findings of his council of chiefs, argued that no marriage of any kind was to be entered into without his permission. On the basis of these proceedings, Nqetho wisely concluded his life was in jeopardy. As Chapter 1 recounts, he hastily collected his people and fled Zulu country with a substantial portion of the royal herd.[25]

Ndukwana, who drew on the recollections of his grandmother, stated that in the days of Senzangakhona[26] and before, it was the custom for girls to choose (*qoma*) their sweethearts and for such couples to engage in the premarital privilege of *hlobonga* or *soma*,[27] a form of unconsummated intercourse. The custom was generally viewed as a preliminary step to matrimony. Yet no choosing of lovers could be done in Shaka or Dingane's days—the custom was prohibited for young males. Girls could *soma* only with grown men. To emphasize the state policy on celibacy, Zulu regiments of younger females and males were given the distinctive name "Imvokwe," by which they were known for the duration of time that their class was placed under restriction not to have intercourse of any kind with members of the opposite sex. It is noteworthy that these prohibitions were relaxed in Mpande's time.[28]

During the latter's reign the policy was to allow young male *amabutho* (regiments) to court (*qomisa*) and *soma* with girls of their age. The king's ruling had two unintended consequences. In the first place, it accentuated social contrasts; and second, it fed the tendency toward rebellion. When full-grown, girls were ordered to put on the "top knot" (*isicholo*, a distinguishing hairstyle that proclaimed their marriageable status), and then, under compulsion, they were given to older men. These men, some of whom were of the "white" regiments, had long ago finished *thungwa*-ing (i.e., they had sewn on the headring, a badge symbolizing they had entered the nuptial state), and already had wives and children.

> A girl who was putting on the top knot would cry, for she knew that she could no longer go to her lover; she was bound to take a husband among those men who were putting on the headring. Their mothers too would cry; they would cry at the river. They would cry for their daughters, whose lovers had not received the order to put on the headring. There would be great lamentation. Some people would take their daughters and cross the river to the white people's country. *This is what caused people to cross over. This is what destroyed the country* [emphasis added].[29]

Mpande's people were thus well acquainted with the fact that residence in the colony held out prospects for a lightening of constraints endured under the system of age regiments. Indeed, the very proximity of Natal produced restless aspirations, especially among the youths, for an improvement in their condition. As indicated above, full-grown girls (*amaqhikiza*) were discontented because they could not marry men close to their own age. And I am inclined to believe that another source of dissatisfaction may have been the fact that many of these conjugal arrangements precluded their chance of becoming the first or senior wife. Girls of the king's household (*izigodlo*) frequently found themselves being "married off by degrees to men with cattle when they had got old and flabby in the cheeks."[30] To avoid an unwelcome marriage, young maidens were known to deceive their lovers (i.e., their *hlobonga* mates) by declaring themselves to be pregnant, as a way of pressuring the youth into crossing the river. Such a ploy was almost surely guaranteed to work. "Illicit amours" were punishable by death, especially involving girls of the royal establishment, whether the act resulted in a prenuptial pregnancy or not. Consequently, the only recourse available to the ill-starred couple was voluntary expatriation or banishment—flight to Natal.[31]

Even more extraordinary were the disabilities placed on young men. Marriage and careers were delayed by the king under the Zulu military system until soldiers had completed about twenty years of army service. The central fact to remember is that this prolonged state of bachelorhood forestalled advancement to senior rank.

Men without headrings, even if "youths of mature age" approaching their forties, were nonetheless considered socially immature, and occupied a marginal state: that is, they were juridically adults with the potential capacity to act socially, but in reality, they were sexually restricted and prohibited by the norms of the community from assuming critical roles and social functions.[32] By withdrawing from Mpande's reach, a young man moved closer to the possibility of acquiring a wife, producing on his own account, and becoming a recognized member of the community. Thus it was, as Bryant relates, that Sikonyana started his public life by falling in love, against the law—for neither his own regiment nor that of the girl had been *jutshwe* by King Mpande (i.e., permitted by proclamation to marry). Rather than face the consequences, the pair fled to the white man's land.[33]

This emphasis on early betrothal as the means to enhance status set in motion a train of other events. From the time these "youths" made it through the escapeways, it seems their plans were fraught with disappointments and reverses. By the worst of luck, both Sikonyana and his sweetheart were promptly captured by the government border agent and indentured to European employers for a term of three years.[34] But it was not the refugee ordinance so much as it was mainly on account of women being in short supply that young men were only gradually able to marry over the span of many years. And as mentioned above, only after marrying could a young man hope to realize his ambitions fully.

Let us consider more closely the proposition that there were more marriageable men in the colony than there were young attainable females. To do this, we need to return to the immediately preceding years.

The Zulu say the way to Natal was opened by Mpande. This was so in a double sense, for the king made two decisions of consequence. The first was represented by the "breaking of the rope," after which many of the soldiers who had crossed over with the prince decided against returning to Zululand, where most of their kin continued to reside. Meanwhile, there followed years of quiescence, which ironically ushered in a whole set of unique problems for the aging monarch.

Few military campaigns were waged by the Zulu against their African neighbors during the period of Mpande's reign, primarily because his field of operations had been limited by the presence of British Natal and the Transvaal Republic. One obvious and tangible effect of these comparatively placid years was that an entire generation of Zulu youths were spared the ravages of war. Precisely on this point there is evidence from contemporaries, who chanced to note an indisputable fact—namely, there was a growing percentage of junior males within the kingdom, a demographic increase that would not have been possible under the bellicose regimes of Shaka and Dingane.[35]

We have seen in Chapter 1 how Mpande was confronted by two enormously difficult challenges on his accession to the throne—those of consolidating a rapidly disintegrating kingdom and asserting his authority over it. Compounding his problems was an inactive army. The lessening of opportunities for warfare among this restive population of unemployed warriors had created a potentially dangerous situation. A matter of persistent concern, therefore, was how to prevent pockets of rebellion from erupting within the armed forces. In the past, field maneuvers and drill exercises, plus the prospect of frequent sorties against neighboring chiefdoms and long military campaigns, had offered distractions and minimized opportunities for political intrigue. Furthermore, a side benefit of these "manful diversions" was that they served as outlets for the soldiers' libido.[36] With the cessation of much of these martial activities and war games, rules intended to inhibit contact with the opposite sex quite possibly were proving unenforceable.

Until recently historians have gone along with the view that the social edicts pertaining to marriage and sexual conduct issued under Shaka were upheld in their entirety by the rulers who followed him.[37] Yet we know that the second decision of consequence made by Mpande was that of allowing young people greater sexual freedom. It was a decision driven by necessity—a palliative gesture meant to moderate the intensity of youthful aspirations. But instead of muting popular discontent, revival of the age-old custom respecting *hlobonga* seems to have aggravated existing problems and eventually brought matters to a crisis. That is, the reform helped to ignite a widespread movement that resulted in an outflow of young dissidents from the kingdom. Junior subjects belonging to the Zulu polity bitterly resented that while they were now unrestrained to openly love whomever they chose, they still were not free in the choice of whom to marry. Control of marriage remained firmly in the hands of the king.

By all accounts, it was the young cadets and soldiers, either in companies or singly, and mature Zulu men from senior regiments who most frequently fell afoul of traditional authorities and who jumped at the earliest opportunity to desert the country, because more avenues of escape were open to them. Very often their precipitous departures entailed abandoning deep personal attachments, including wives, children, sisters, and sweethearts. This situation suggests there was a marked disparity in the sex ratio in Natal; that such an imbalance was bound to be aggravated by the continuation of polygamous practices;[38] and that as women became even greater objects of competition, acute rivalry sprang up between junior men and the community patriarchs. These matters deserve our careful attention.

Elderly Zulu informants testify to the fact that during these years the conventions governing sexual conduct and marriage were vigorously contested by young women and men, many of whom eventually left Zululand in protest.[39] And unless I am much mistaken, it can be further argued that the young people's continued open defiance of the marriage rules led to a restructuring of that institution in the colony. What does all this mean? That steps were taken by the elders in Natal to make the laws regulating matrimony more relevant and effective in the new surroundings. How do we come to know this? As much as any single fact, the proliferation of comments that bridewealth or "bride price" had soared, from an average of between two and six head of cattle to an exorbitant twenty, fifty, sometimes sixty head for the daughter of a commoner,[40] alert us to the conflict. Indeed these steep increases in bride price serve as a sort of barometer, an indicator that something akin to a revolution was taking place within the institution of marriage.

Of course, one can suggest a coherent alternative to this argument—that, for instance, these outrageously inflated rates signified attempts to rebuild herds lost during the epidemic or on the flight to Natal. Likewise, one can point to the dominant sentiment expressed among missionaries that a mercenary interest played a large part in the matter. This latter view reflected the general belief of whites in the cupidity and greed of Zulu elders. And one can find in both currents of thinking more than a sediment of truth. But, in point of fact, things were not so simple, and if the problem is left to stand there, we would miss much.

For a long while after returning to the district, the refugees were in a state of flux—caught up, as it were, in a dynamic of fresh realities struggling to assume visible form. In such an atmosphere, new desires conflicted, sometimes violently, with codes of the past. Every community witnessed movement toward reestablishing affective ties and building up new associations, thereby enabling a few lucky individuals to acquire effective social and political power. We must constantly keep in mind that, more than anything else, this was a period of fierce competitiveness and change, where serious generational cleavages surfaced again and again in struggles over leadership and the exercise of authority. During these tumultuous years, elders were impelled to erect safeguards to protect their privileged station. Such, in my judgment, was the meaning behind the excessive *lobolo*, a signal event of the first order. It revealed the social tension at its heart; it communicated the seniors' disapproval of those individuals who had attempted to overstep conventional bounds; and it proclaimed to all that fundamental steps had now been implemented to curb these radical trends.

To grasp more fully the nature of this increasing rivalry, imagine, after they had recovered from the initial trauma of the flight, what the young people's response must have been now that the right to marry was no longer dependent upon the king's will. This loosening of institutional authority brought the suspension of many of the rules ordinarily regulating their lives. What is more, this shedding of constraints implied a potential gain in independence, particularly for the young men. From this can be inferred an accentuation of antagonistic interests between age-groups and among kin. And the truth was that deeply rooted customs were degenerating; the authority structure, already suffering wounds sustained during the disorders, was presently undergoing great internal stress as it sought to ward off mission values and assaults from the colonial state.[41] The idea that traditional norms were undergoing a modern test is affirmed in these comments by Lewis Grout:

> As a general thing in Natal, the young man thinks himself at liberty to marry as soon as he can find cattle enough to pay for a wife. *The idea of looking to his chief for permission to be "of age," and meddle with matrimony* [emphasis added], if it comes at all to his mind, comes more from respect to old national usages than from any sense of dependence upon the will of his father. . . . [42]

Elsewhere he remarked that

> [u]nder British rule many a rigid native custom is growing lax. Most of the sable sons of the colony are beginning to find out that it is better to earn their own cattle, as they can, in these days, by working for the white men, than to depend upon father or guardian for them.[43]

Further corroboration that permissive *abelungu* laws (white men's laws) were undermining traditions is seen in Mrs. Shooter's observations of her nearest neighbor, Bambula, "a dignified old gentleman" of considerable means and importance, who had a horror of white innovations and their influence, particularly on his junior son, Habe. Habe, who by Shooter's estimate was only twenty years old, had two wives and wanted very much to take a third, which his father objected to.

> In his day, he [Bambula] said, a man was content with one wife until he was thirty years old, but in these degenerate days mere boys had their second and third wives; no son of his should do so, he was determined. He supposed, as Habe had already made overtures to the father of the girl, he must

allow *this* marriage to take place; but if he were not then content, but wanted a fourth wife, he must understand that the first step towards the accomplishment of his wish must be his removal from his father's kraal. . . . [44]

Habe's case, of course, is atypical in the sense that here was a young man in a wealthy household with apparently easy access to bridewealth payments. Yet this simple narrative illustrates better than anything the attitude of elders who feared the baleful influences and degeneracy of the present age on African youths. As near as we can discern, the general response of the old men to these disquieting developments was to drive up the required number of marriage cattle. And until the Marriage Act of 1869, which fixed bridewealth at ten cows for the daughter of a commoner, the old men must have calculated that this stratagem would lock junior competition out of the matrimonial market. Such a step also theoretically guaranteed the elders' control over the available supply of young women, thereby securing their role and continued prestige in the community.[45]

Several practices came to the fore at this time to circumvent the colonial Marriage Act. For example, in Alfred County, fathers of girls now began to insist that ten large oxen or ten cows in calf must be given, which of course cost the would-be husbands more than the twenty head of small stock they would have given before.[46] Interestingly, too, the custom known as *imvulamlomo* ("the thing by which to open the mouth") came into wide use. *Imvulamlomo*, a fee (in cattle, blankets, horses, saddles, and cash) added to the *lobolo*, was charged by the bride's father for his consent to the marriage, a custom which, though widely practiced in Natal, was utterly foreign to original Zulu marriage practices.[47]

Ways were found by resourceful young men to overcome some of the difficulties placed in the path of acquiring and multiplying wives. Outlawry was one recourse; and plundering and looting herds were activities endemic to the times. Mr. Bergtheil, a member of the Legislative Council, was definite in his assertion that the increasing incidents of cattle stealing in the colony were linked to inflated *lobolo* prices.[48] Cattle rustling aside, a clear indication of their motives comes from numerous accounts of females being smuggled into the district. Reports received as early as 1835 tell of Europeans misbehaving themselves while trading in Zululand by persuading the people, particularly young women, to desert, after which they were conveyed by stealth into Port Natal.[49] Eight years later Henry Cloete, Her Majesty's commissioner in Natal, reported:

> There are two vices, I fear, too deeply rooted in the disposition of the Zulu to be easily eradicated—the first is the plunder of cattle, and the next abduction of women. During my rapid progress through the Zulu country, I witnessed numerous instances of the latter, and a fearful exhibition of the former propensity. . . . it is self-evident that the aggressions will ever originate with the Zulu refugees now in this country; for, having left their numerous connections behind, smarting under injuries inflicted upon them, they are but too prone to give vent to feelings of revenge and hostility. . . . [50]

No sooner had they arrived in the district, and gathered their wits sufficiently, than immigrants set about establishing communication networks linking refugees to their families and sweethearts stranded abroad. Intelligence passed along in this manner was most useful in aiding defectors in accomplishing their object. Mention of these clandestine operations appears again in a news item in 1854:

> The Kafir servant of an English Zulu trader having been discovered in the act of bringing Zulu women across the Tugela into this district, was severely flogged for the offence by order of Mr Walmsley [border agent].[51]

From a similar incident involving the death of a Natal African in Zululand, we learn of other disreputable English traders encouraging their servants to induce young girls to leave Zulu country, "under protection of their wagons." These young women were then offered as payment (in lieu of cattle) to the young men in the white traders' employ.[52]

White authorities were fully aware of the fact that such activities could erupt at any time into a situation likely to engulf the colony. Following in the wake of Jambu-ya's death (the servant slain by the Zulu), the public was put on notice regarding the "numerous irregularities" practiced by Africans and whites from the district.[53] Magistrates were instructed to discourage Africans from entering Zulu country; traders were warned that any of them found doing so without permission would not be "shielded by the government from any punishment which their proceedings in that country may bring upon them." A proclamation issued the same year reiterated these admonitions. The traffic nevertheless persisted, with women being brought in from other bordering communities as well.[54]

At the height of these illegal doings, by December 1855, Mpande, who had previously been inflexible on this issue, astonishingly began to give thought to an entirely different approach to the fugitive question. Throughout the 1840s he attempted to cope with the refugee problem by creating a buffer zone between his people and the borders of the colony. All of his efforts in this regard failed, so that in the early 1850s the Zulu people were again permitted to inhabit the territory contiguous to the district. Now he generously suggested that "a closer union should exist between his people and those of Natal." Mpande wished them to intermarry and visit each other freely. Moreover, he hoped the laws of one country would be recognized and enforced by the other. The motivations behind this remarkable proposal may have been far more complex than a simple desire to prevent further desertions.[55] But whatever it was the king desired to accomplish, this relaxation in policy gave encouragement to former subjects to appeal directly to Mpande for permission to bring their wives and children out of Zulu country. Requests of this nature were sometimes granted, but not without establishing obligations.

An instance of this occurred in 1859 when Sikota, formerly Mpande's *induna* (army officer), applied through the intercession of Bishop Colenso for the release of his family. A decade earlier Sikota had abandoned status, family, and possessions, and had ever since lived alone in the colony. By traveling to Zululand under the bishop's protection and having Colenso speak on his behalf, Sikota hoped he would be allowed to gather what remained of his thirty wives, eight sons, and forty daughters, leaving, of course, all cattle and other property in the hands of the king. Those among his wives and daughters who had married since his departure were likewise lost to him. Another supplicant, Madala, sought to bring out one wife, three daughters, and two sons. Both appeals were granted, it being conditionally agreed that if at a future date their services were called upon, the two men would respond with cheerful readiness to the royal summons.[56]

Still, the stretch of years from 1855 to 1872 seems hardly to have brought an adequate solution to the pattern of desertions and certainly not the illegal withdrawal of women from the kingdom. Mrs. Wilkinson, a missionary in Zululand during Cetshwayo's reign, wrote:

> It is a fact, which you will hardly credit, that in Natal they have quite as misty and fearful ideas of Zululand as anyone in England. The fact is, the Natal Kafirs have been so often trading and stealing Zulu cattle, and at the same time helping boys and girls to run away across the Tugela to the colony to such an extent, that Cetewayo has given orders that all Natal Kafirs travelling without a white man are to be seized and beaten, and their cattle taken from them; but that all Kafirs travelling with the missionaries' letters are to be respected. This on the other side of the Tugela, has been construed into, "every Natal Kafir is to be killed."[57]

In an attempt to regain stability and to enforce discipline, Cetshwayo (who acceded to the throne on the death of his father in 1873) overturned Mpande's momentous reform and proclaimed anew that "girls were not to be *hlobonga'*d with." This law was—indeed, had apparently always been, even under Shaka and Dingane—extremely unpopular. Since Shaka's days, however, significant changes had unfolded in regional power relations, which served to vitiate the king's authority in this area. Clearly, so long as flight to a powerful neighbor was an option, willful youths would continue to flaunt the law contemptuously. As it turned out, the present effort to execute the injunction had an effect for only one year. After that, we are told, "girls of the king's place went to the youths." Reports state that the girls brazenly said, "Cetshwayo would finish them off, for they would not leave off, as they wanted to and liked to *hlobonga*, and asked if, when a prince, he also did not like to *hlobonga*."[58]

Such eager disregard for consequences left the king few alternatives; an example had to be made of these women, by persuasion or by force. In 1876 a regiment of girls were ordered to marry the men of one of the king's regiments; they complained there were too few men. Cetshwayo gave in to them, and named another regiment; but again the young women stalled, making further objections. Some of them just outright refused to marry, courting fate for the last time. A male regiment was sent out to punish the refractory women. According to several accounts, this was done, and their bodies were strewn on the highways to serve as an example to other disobedient subjects. Cetshwayo allegedly said he "was determined to show his people who was the master."[59] After this wholesale massacre, things within the Zulu kingdom would never be the same.

The open insurrection of Zulu girls of the Ingcugce regiment, who refused to obey authority and marry old men at the king's orders, may be seen as the culmination of a long history of popular protests against repressive controls over the most intimate and private areas of their lives.[60] Led by young people, the movement—which was essentially about the freedom to express their sexuality (within the context of ancient customs) and the right to choose their marriage partners—reached alarming proportions under Mpande. Cetshwayo's stubborn resolve to expunge these demonstrations had profound repercussions. Caught by historical forces beyond his control and comprehension, the tragic confrontation with a number of females of the Ingcugce precipitated a deadly clash with colonial forces as well. For the massacre of these women was used as a partial pretext by the British for the 1879 invasion and destruction of Zululand and the exile of the king.

Adjustments in the Marriage Code: Marriages Between Juniors and Widows

Until now our general focus has been on how the young men and a few young women (for we have no way of gauging the actual volume of the traffic) contrived to circumvent the age rule governing marriage. One must not assume that the elders residing within the colony, who by virtue of their position were conservative in outlook, were necessarily incapable of responding either pragmatically or innovatively to the imperatives affecting the lives of their people. No doubt this popular resistance sparked off an excited debate in the Council of Chiefs, and after profound consideration, they must have quite sensibly arrived at the view that the marriage reforms introduced by Shaka were unsustainable in Natal. This, one can deduce, brought about a legalized return to pre-Shakan practices; other moderate measures seem to have been instituted as well, changes no doubt patterned on the age-old law of expediency.

How they attempted to resolve the conflict is dimly hinted at in the literature. While it was ultimately agreed, for instance, that males would be allowed to marry ten to fifteen years younger than was the case in the Zulu state, the *umthungwa* ceremony—which conferred the headring (*isicoco*, the symbol of full maturity)—may have been delayed until married juniors had achieved majority, about forty years of age.[61] Second, under the innovations, young men were mainly given access to widows. With regard to the first matter, the data is painfully threadbare; on the last, we will attempt to throw some light.

A number of early observers (among whom were disinterested outsiders) saw anomalies within Natal's matrimonial market, features that they contend diverged radically from marital patterns obtaining elsewhere in the region. In 1868 one commentator, Captain Augustus Lindley, remarked that

> [i]t was only in Natal that we found the value of the young Sable Venuses exorbitant. Everywhere else the average price of a buxom damsel, from fourteen years of age to about twenty-five, was five to seven head of cattle. The first cycle of feminine value seemed to be the ten years after puberty; the elder maiden being considered as inferior stock not worth more than three or four good cows a head. We may safely reckon six fine oxen as the price for an ordinary young and sound wife. . . .[62]

At the turn of the century, A. T. Bryant noticed that young men frowned upon starting married life with a widow, a practice they "regarded as nothing short of self-degradation."[63] But if it was unthinkable (at the time of Bryant's writing in 1899) that widows should become partners in first alliances, such a trend seems to have been rather common in the 1850s and 1860s. The missionaries Lewis Grout and George Mason both spoke of young men "looking forward to earning a widow." The plight of these "old ladies," who, both alleged, were being exploited for their labor, prompted government to contemplate measures to ameliorate their condition. "In fact," wrote Grout, "the English government is just now talking of a law to let the widow go free,—and forbidding her proprietor to require any pay on her second marriage."[64] What is important to understand, if my reading of the evidence is correct, are the forces giving rise to this alternative marriage pattern.

Ordinarily a strong customary obligation existed for the father (or chief) to endow each of his sons (or dependents) with cattle for his first wife. However, when a father disapproved of his son's actions or his choice of a first bride, he frequently disassociated himself from the union.[65] Such scenarios, I think, were common in Natal, where young men openly ignored customs and brusquely attempted to bypass constituted authority in their efforts to take advantage of opportunities presented in the money economy. Repeated warnings were probably issued as to the consequences of their actions, until finally their audacious behavior provoked an equally outraged response. To deal effectively with these challenges, the community patriarchs began to manipulate *lobolo* rates.

Furthermore, any person who persisted in denying his elders their deferential due risked losing the financial, social, and emotional support systems provided by the kraal. In the event of such an extreme occurrence, the youth was left with few alternatives—that is, he could either seek an outside sponsor or furnish the marriage cattle on his own. Yet in the latter instance, it was highly improper, even where young suitors managed to raise the required resources, for the girl's parents or guardian to negotiate wedding arrangements without the backing of the groom's sponsor. This was because a customary marriage was more than a personal alliance between a man and a woman. The transfer of bridewealth gave both the family of the bride and that of the groom a vested interest in the survival of the marriage; for one group invested its resources (cattle) in it, and the other received benefits that might be forfeited should the marriage fail.[66] Thus it was rather unlikely that the girl's parents (or guardians) would waive the matter of sponsorship. Viewed like this, and taking into consideration the economics of the marriage market, the odds against the average young man's first wife being a Natal beauty in "the first cycle of feminine value," were enormous. So it came about that junior men began to marry widowed women. Lewis Grout, in one of his many epistles condemning polygamy, offered further confirmation of this phenomenon when he wrote that "a young man with few cattle, not able to purchase a wife of his own, will purchase some aged widow, or a wife cast off by a man. . . ."[67]

Which brings us to the heart of the argument. One of the inevitable aftereffects of the political and military calamities that wracked Zululand was that a class of dislocated widows was thrown upon the resettlement communities; and, though we can approach not much further than speculation on this, it is entirely probable their condition elicited a collective outcry demanding they be properly cared for. Pressure to alleviate the distress of these women would have suggested a way for the elders to assuage the matrimonial desires of the more boldly insistent young men. But mostly, it seems reasonable to suggest that by sanctioning such unions, senior men were patently trying to preserve the continued loyalty of their youthful adherents while retaining control over the supply and circulation of the most desirable, nubile maidens.

Traditionally, in the case of destitution overtaking a woman, as in the event of her husband's death, she could seek refuge in her father's kraal or receive shelter from an elder son. Another course open to her was *ukungena* (the levirate), a custom whereby the widow consented to marry a brother of her deceased husband. "The principal [was] obvious, never to leave a single, or unprotected female." In the opinion of George Peppercorne, both polygamy and the levirate could be traced back "to the necessity of obtaining protection for the females . . . in a social state which affords so little guarantee for personal security; and thus avoid a condition which would be far worse, and tend to destroy all government whatever."[68]

However, the presumption here is that given the magnitude of their personal losses, access to such social security options were not always available; being unattached and homeless, these "vagrant" women were vulnerable to all sorts of situations and characters indifferent to their welfare. The prospects for these women were made gloomier still if the status of their families was in doubt. Any uncertainty as to whether they had male relations living in Zululand would have made it doubly difficult to find protectors. For while it might have been true that refugees and destitute children were freely accepted and often given full rights, equal status, and so on, it appears that such adoption practices were mostly confined to males. Little or no such help could be extended to females, since in law they were always considered minors and the wards of their husband, father, or sons, whose later claims had to be respected.[69]

Notwithstanding the possibility that male relations might make a future appearance in Natal to reclaim runaway kinswomen, local politics as well as a pervasive sense of anxiety for the security of the corporate whole probably influenced kraal heads, chiefs, and others to extend protection to these women and girls as wards. Once incorporated into these "kraals of refuge," they were generally treated as family members. Girls married in accordance with conventional ceremonies when they reached the age of maturity.[70] In the case of widows remarrying, the amount of *lobolo* was nominal, and payment could be deferred by agreement.[71]

The expectation was that a wife would perform domestic tasks, fulfill conjugal obligations, and procreate, whatever her married rank (first wife, later wife, or remarried widow). The obligations resting upon the husband were to provide shelter, protection, and support for his spouse and her children. For women—especially kinless females—the nuptial contract offered social guarantees, the tangible benefits of which were unmistakable. Marriage gave women direct access to economic resources. With the formation of a customary union, a man created a house for his wife that was endowed with land and cattle. Misstatements of the traditional law (as found in the Natal Code of Zulu Law, 1878), which held that females possessed no legal rights in property, have led to the oft-repeated charge that African women were exploited by despotic husbands who had unrestrained rights to the property earned by their wives and unemancipated children. But as S. M. Seymour rightly points out, if, in practice, the Bantu social system had functioned in this manner, it would not have stood the test of time.[72] On this question, too, Chief Buthelezi contends that "before our law was codified there is not the slightest doubt that women did own property. This is not my view but is also a view held by my mother and some elderly members of the Tribe."[73] As one observer commented, "Zulu men are very much more under female domestic influence than one might have supposed."[74]

It is especially revealing to compare popular notions of African men tyrannizing the women in the kraal with the brief citations quoted above and with the evidence offered by Mr. Howell, who, in testimony given before the 1852–53 Commission, stated that he knew of his own knowledge that "a proportion of Kafir women do 'wear the breeches.' " In 1893 another writer asked Natal politicians who were loud in their denunciation of *ukulobola*, if they were "aware that the poor creature commonly known as the hen-pecked husband [was] frequently to be found among the natives?"[75] Nor was this perception of the uxorious African male confined to Zululand and Natal. Comments in the same vein were made by the Reverend Johannes August Winter, who labored over thirty years in the eastern Transvaal.

> Our native women do not let themselves be compelled by anything. There is no henpecked nation like our natives. The men always fear that the women may put poison into the porridge, make no beer, or bad beer, or run away. If scolded, they take the assegai and give it to their husbands saying: "Here is your assegai, kill me, that is better." And the man eats humble pie.[76]

In presenting this evidence, it is not my intention to supplant one stereotype (that of the aggressively virile male riding roughshod over "his" women) with another (the weak, ineffectual "wimp," nagged and bullied by domineering wives). Rather, it is my belief that somewhere in between the two extremes a more typical, even-handed existence characterized relations between the sexes in precolonial African society.

What, then, were the rights of women?

Each "house" had rights to the fruits of its garden (a woman's garden was called by her name and could not be encroached upon by her cowives), the calves and milk of the cows, the earnings accrued from the labor efforts of the wife and her minor children, and the bridewealth received for its daughters.[77] Furthermore, a fundamental principle was that a husband could not use or transfer the property of one house for the benefit of another without first obtaining customary consent from the wife to whose house the property belonged.[78] Flattery and charm were often the approaches taken by a husband wishing to coax a loan from his spouse for either another wife or for general kraal purposes.[79]

Loans created obligations and required future returns benefiting the house originally making the investment. Such a relationship, for instance, was implied in the arrangement described in 1862 by Mason, whereby a widow recently remarried produced by the strength of her labor a surplus crop, which, when added to his fresh earnings, enabled her young husband to marry again, perhaps another widow, and so on, until "at last the young fellow ha[d] corn and property sufficient to meet the high price set upon a young native woman (which, owing to the enormous demand, ha[d] risen from ten to fifty pounds sterling; and even more in many instances). . . ."[80] What Mason failed to understand was that contributors to the bridewealth had a future claim on the labor of the new wife, and on the *lobolo* received from the marriage of the first daughter born of the new union. Reciprocity or balanced exchange involved whatever individuals raised the marriage cattle—kinsman or patron, man or woman.[81] This is a point of great importance. Neither can it be overstated that where husbands alienated the assets of one wife for use by another, an "interhouse debt" was recognized with obligations resting on the latter to return the equivalent value of the loan.

Ubuntu: The Sacredness of Hospitality

> Amongst the Zoolas each kraal has two head persons who are considered responsible for the good order of the community; one is called the master

[*umnumzana*] of the kraal, the other the mistress [*inkosikazi*]. The latter gets food ready for all travellers and has the care of the household goods; she has also much influence in the kraal with the chief of the kraal. Sometimes the chief's wife assumes the functions of mistress. They are always addressed as mother and much respect is paid to them.[82]

"The Law of Hospitality to Travellers" held that the proper treatment of strangers was an obligation resting on the senior wife of the village, who, if found derelict in her duties, could be expelled from that enviable position of privilege and power. Thus, the Reverend Jenkinson tells us that the *inkosikazi* had to give food, and give it without weariness. If she were churlish with strangers, grudged them sustenance, or turned them out of her house in anger, she was considered unfit to head the village and demoted in rank, and another took her place who was able to fill the role properly.[83]

The wisdom-lore that states "the greatness of an African is above all else a matter of pots" carries two main significations. In the first place, it tells us something about the politics of food—in traditional societies, food was clearly a great social asset. Over and beyond this is the implicit assumption that the contributions of especially the primary wife were critical to the successful social career of her husband. Were it not for her agricultural labor, which provided the bulk of the Zulu diet, her proficiency in preparing food, and her attention to strangers, many men would have been unable to attract adherents or, for that matter, other wives.[84] Clearly, a man did injury to himself when he mistreated his spouse; where relations between the two head persons were based on mutual cooperation and respect, it was more likely that their establishment would prosper.

> Nothing [was] done or discussed of any importance without the Inkosikazi or head wife being consulted. They have their rules of etiquette and politeness, and it [was] certain that on violation of these rules, the transgressors [were] very quickly taken to task by the ladies.[85]

The next source bears out this construction of a balanced relationship and tells us something about the political empowerment of females in Zulu society. Listen carefully to Henry Fynn's remarks:

> [T]o her [the principal wife] is reported all the domestic affairs which she regulates. In the absence of her husband, if a chief, she consults with the chief of the kraal *even in public affairs. Their mutual consent empowers them to have any person killed in the kraal* [emphasis added]. . . . [86]

Fynn goes on to say that when the *umnumzana* or chief transgressed the law, the whole kraal of men, women, and children were put to death. Sometimes young girls were spared, but the principal wife was always deemed culpable, as she was supposed to be privy to all her husband's conduct and, with the people of the kraal, ought to have objected to his faults. In other words, the chief wife was expected by law and long-established custom to play a central role in public affairs and could indeed forfeit her life by being indifferent to such matters.

One might be tempted to conclude from many of the foregoing comments that the efforts of the head wife were directed wholly and selflessly toward making her husband wealthy, that is, rich enough to acquire multiple marriage partners. But the fact of the matter was, as Delegorgue observed, that such increased efforts also opened up for the *inkosikazi* a future of more extensive influence and greater ease. That is, the greater the number of wives, the greater became the ease of their condition and the higher was the consideration of the first wife.[87]

What about the ambitions of the cowives? It was common knowledge that an industrious woman could make her house a strong and important one, even though of inferior rank, by offering hospitality more generous than the other wives. In proportion to her economic and political shrewdness—that is, her ability to augment "house property," to use it to build and cement a continuum of links through loans and hospitality, or to withhold goods and services tactically—a married woman gained proportionally in influence with her husband, sons, and other kinspeople. Nor was this all. For these advantages placed her in a good position to make future claims for assistance; most especially, she could count on the filial devotion of her sons, who were the source of security in her old age.[88] Thus tied to a woman's upward advancement in the production complex and in the wider community were such factors as strength of personality, a combination of practical household skills, and success at domestic diplomacy. Where a woman possessed such talents, the husband learned to put a higher value on her opinion, to listen to her with greater attention, and to treat her with added respect.

Two stories serve to illustrate the workings of women's politics in polygamous settings. They show in particular how the strategies employed in domestic situations overlapped and intertwined with broader political events in Nguni society.

The first tale, a vivid illustration of cooking as a source of power, comes to us from the annals of the Mpondo and is about the San woman, Ntwakazi. It seems that the ancient chief of these people married Ntwakazi as one of his many wives. The story goes that after Ntwakazi was taken as wife, she succeeded in making herself an extremely popular person by her special skills in cooking. By attending to both the quality and quantity of her food, she attracted adherents who flocked to her house when they came to *busa* (i.e., to serve at the Great Place), knowing that they would find plenty reigning there instead of starvation. Many young men assisted in the cultivation of her gardens, and the more adherents she gathered, the larger the area of land cultivated and the more certain her crop. Eventually, Ntwakazi was elevated to great wife; her house, it was said, was not only rich in peace but powerful in war.

It developed also that Ntwakazi's son, Cira, had found ways of ingratiating himself with the people, and when Dosini (the heir by birth) was deposed because of behavior unworthy of a chief, he, Cira, was proclaimed chief in an exceedingly dramatic fashion.[89]

The next story demonstrates how agricultural labor indirectly aided political ambitions. This tale is about Nozinja, mother of Qwabe and Zulu. After the death of her husband, Malandela, we are told, the widow Nozinja found consolation in industrious field work and thrift. The sale of surplus sorghum (*amabele*) brought her a goat, and before long the goats became a cow, which eventually increased to a herd of all white kine. The covetous Qwabe, Malandela's principal son, sought to wheedle them out of his mother but was sharply rebuffed: "No!" was her reply. "And you the heir to all your father's cattle! What then is my child, Zulu, to receive?" Her refusal to yield to Qwabe's pressure apparently produced a rupture that ultimately forced Nozinja to move away to establish an independent kraal near her father's home, together with her son and a man-servant. Zulu, the youngest son for whom Nozinja labored to build an inheritance, was none other than the progenitor of the Zulu people.[90]

This naturally leads us to a consideration of women's labor in the crisis of reconstruction. Contemporary writers seldom failed to notice, though indirectly and invariably in biased terms, the spectacular efforts of female peasant cultivators who raised the family's subsistence needs and produced surplus crops for sale. Mainly, it is owing to these nineteenth-century commentators, among whom can be found some of the most virulent critics of "native customs" and ardent champions of a tougher "Kafir labor policy," that we get the exaggerated claims of female slavery. Their ethnocentric assessments of African women as drudges plodding under burdensome tasks without either emotional or material recompense, was a travesty of truth. Katie Lloyd, a female missionary with intimate knowledge of Zulu customs, wrote in 1868 that "it is easy to sit in the house and moralize or to speak to a few and take their words, but anyone who really mingles with the people to know them can never say women are slaves."[91]

Yet the data do appear to suggest that the "period of the uprooting" took a more devastating toll on female survivors than on males.[92] This being so, one would expect that once these orphaned widows and girls found protection, they would go about their domestic labors, not as drudges, but rather with a single-minded determination to recreate attachments of proven worth. It is in this light that we ought to view their heroic fortitude in the struggle against the refugee ordinance. For these women were acutely aware that kinship connections offered insurance against a precarious future. The following remarks by Henry Fynn make plain this vital point:

> I have frequently known it occur that females so situated as not to know where their relatives were, when rather than not have a claimant [i.e., an individual to receive their *lobolo*], they have secretly arranged with a stranger to declare a relationship. I can only account for this extraordinary proceeding from a natural impression that the husband would have more respect for one who has a parent or relatives than for an orphan.[93]

Survival demanded a cooperative effort; hard work was the collective expression devoted single-mindedly to the object. Women *did* work hard; and the focal point of their labor was the kraal or village economy. But if bumper crops were being produced, as was often reported in the vicinity of the major towns, this would likewise imply that males (young and mature men) were perhaps clearing more land, felling more trees, digging up more stumps, turning the fields with plows, and assisting during the weeding and harvesting seasons.

In addition to surplus crop production, trade in such articles as eggs and chickens brought in a substantial income. Women also intensified their subsidiary activities—commodities were gathered from the veldt, products were harvested from the sea, and there was an increase in manufacturing home crafts; all of these items found a ready town market. Furthermore, early wage-earning women and girls were the predominant group making up the rural *togt* labor force (i.e., the circulating day work force employed on sugar and coffee estates, and on the smaller European farms).[94] But the crucial point here is, *these people were accustomed to working conjointly.* By dint of extraordinary effort, both women and men strove to meet the necessities of life.

The argument put forcefully is that women in northern Nguni society stand out neither as passive victims (the spiritless creatures often portrayed in the nineteenth-century accounts) nor as the effete, static characters suggested in recent writings that impose Western notions or white feminist ideals but that relate little to the everyday realities of the period.[95] Rather, one would expect a range of characteristics, temperaments, and responses within the female population, including personality types that Zulu children, girls and boys, could grow up to respect, admire, and emulate. In addition to those already cited, another notable example of such women were the females of the royal residence who, Paulina Dlamini and Mpatshana kaSodondo tell us, were trained as expert rifle markswomen and served as Cetshwayo's homeguard, in whom the king had greater confidence than in the men.[96] The picture that consistently emerges is of women not only imbued with a spirited determination to protect the integrity of the corporate group, but individuals motivated by personal ambitions as well. Gender roles were not so constricting as to prevent females in northern Nguni society from achieving social, economic, and political power through the strength of their personality, domestic labors, or other specialized endeavors.

Land Shortages

The *voortrekker* Republic of Natalia's reaction to the tremendous incoming surge of black humanity was to propose a scheme to segregate the races territorially. The plan involved the wholesale resettlement of all "surplus" Africans to a reserve demarcated on the coast, a relocation area that was also to serve as a zone of protection between the white republic and the unfriendly Mpondo chief, Faku. Transferring such a large black population, however, required considerable administrative ability and military backup, both of which the trekkers lacked. But even had they had the capability to carry out the design, they were prevented from doing so by Britain's annexation of the district.

Commissioner Henry Cloete was sent out in 1843 to explain to the emigrant farmers their future relations with the government and to settle land disputes between them and the African communities. Friction instantly developed around the question of land registration. The government's position was that only those Boer farms that could prove continual occupation would be recognized as legitimate claims. This turn of affairs precipitated the second great trek. After disposing of their farms to local merchants and other trekkers, with some of the land claims finding their way into the hands of leading speculators,[97] the majority of the *voortrekkers* (emigrant farmers) departed the district.

Thereafter, British Natal was confronted with the dilemma of how to protect white interests, maintain peace, and promote internal security while, at the same time, dealing fairly with Africans in regards to land. The idea of shunting surplus Africans into one reserve was discarded as impracticable. The removal of one hundred thousand black people, who by then had settled over land throughout the district, was deemed an undertaking fraught with danger. And, in any event, the plan, which of necessity required a huge tract of country, implied the future development of a powerful black nation, building up in time to present fresh threats to the white inhabitants.[98] Yet Cloete was inclined to adopt the rationale used by the trekkers to justify their "native policy." The Boers had argued, and the commissioner tended to agree, that Natal had been empty when Piet Retief and his followers first descended the Drakensberg passes; that the great majority of Africans who subsequently entered the district were intruders or foreigners from the Zulu country; and that, according to this equation, only a few thousand blacks had incontestable rights to the land occupied by them. As to the fate of the vast remainder of Africans in Natal, Cloete suggested establishing a series of small "native locations" to be scattered about the district.[99]

Accordingly, seven segregated land areas were designated for African use between 1846 and 1847. In Cloete's view, these locations were to fulfill three functions: they would be mechanisms for dividing and controlling the black population to minimize the possibility of hostile combinations forming against the white inhabitants, they would free up Crown land in order to make it available for future white settlement, and they would ensure a steady supply of migrant labor for the settler community.[100] How was this last to be engineered? Basically, Cloete's idea was to institute "a gate of misery": by placing Africans in such overcrowded, uncomfortable conditions, land hunger and all of the suffering attending the shortage of that crucial resource would compel them to leave the locations to seek work.[101]

It was well known that these locations were chosen from the worst parts of the country, and that they were neither suitable nor large enough to sustain the requirements of a mixed farming economy. Those reserves closely coinciding with the rugged and broken parts of the colony, notably the Drakensberg foothills, the Tugela Valley, and the granite hinterlands, were clearly unsuited to cultivation.[102] The Umzinyati, Inanda, and Impafana locations were especially hilly, stony, and bushy; the sterility of the Impafana, however, was perhaps greater than in most of the others. George Peppercorne, the resident magistrate, testified that not more (and he believed much less) than one percent in every one hundred acres of the soil in the Impafana was capable of agriculture, with the indispensable condition of sufficient water for irrigation.[103]

The three coastal locations—Inanda, Umlazi, and Umvoti—could be similarly described. After these places had been provisionally approved and even assigned by the government to Africans, some of the most valuable portions were cut off and made over to newly arrived white emigrants, while the resident black population were expelled. Quoting from a local newspaper, Lewis Grout stated that "no small portion of these locations is broken, precipitous, rocky, or sandy and barren, suited to the habitation of only the owl and eagle, and baboon and jackal. . . . " From the very first, this was true of Inanda, but in the case of the others, it had become more true after the better pieces of land had been excised.[104] Moreover, it would be a mistake to suppose these areas were generally healthy for grazing and stock breeding: the whole of the Inanda location, with few exceptions, was not. Horse breeding could not be carried on in any of them, except for the Zwartkop and Drakenberg.[105]

Thus it was not long before these people were spilling out of these barren, congested holding sites onto surrounding lands. Numerous groups of Africans anxiously began seeking fertile accommodations by settling on mission-controlled plots, or laboring as tenants on small white farms, or squatting on Crown lands or acreage owned by companies or private individuals.[106] The latter activity became particularly widespread. Colonial officials took action against such wholesale squatting practices with the passage of Ordinance 2 of 1855, which empowered magistrates to remove African trespassers from public and private lands, and laid down that landowners could not house more than three families of Africans on their farms.[107] This law, one of a string of measures that came into being at the urging of the official body that met in 1852–53, had no discernible impact on the "native problem." Daniel Lindley, a relentless critic of the above government proceedings, wrote scathingly of these enactments:

> Three ordinances have been passed, one of which relates to the people who immigrate, i.e., flee from the Zulu chief, Umpandi [Mpande]; another has for its object, the prevention of cattle stealing; and the last was to authorize the removal of native squatting on Crown lands. These three ordinances are now little more than a dead letter. The first two were partially enforced for a time, but no one ever thought of enforcing the last one. I am confident this could not be done, and feel very sure it was never intended to be done.[108]

African tenants were subjected to constant harassment from landlords. To begin with, in most cases they were compelled to labor for the owner of the farm; or they were obliged to pay high rents, which if not paid immediately when due entailed ruinously heavy legal expenses, debts their cattle were frequently seized to liquidate.[109] Moreover, squatters faced threats of eviction for the slightest infractions. Quite possibly what was occurring with regards to Crown lands in the Tugela division in 1860 mirrored developments in other parts of the district. As government alienated large tracts of land and those grants became occupied by whites, Africans moved away and settled in rugged areas near the Mvoti and Thukela rivers to get rid, as they said, of the restrictions imposed upon them, as well as to be out of the white man's way. Such movements created ill feeling, however, and gave rise to innumerable land disputes among Africans themselves, which the Tugela magistrate was finding more and more difficult to arrange amicably.[110]

Given the shortage of land within the reserves and, in many instances, the insecurity of tenure outside, we should not be surprised to find an ardent desire among Africans to gain possession of land through legal purchase and in the form of tribal titles.[111] As early as 1856, we encounter a chief levying a tax, independent of the government hut tax, for the purpose of buying Crown land.

> We are informed, on the authority of the natives themselves, that a chief in this district, who exercises authority over the natives residing in the country south of the Umgeni, . . . has been exacting five shilling a head from his people, numbering, it is said 2000, for the purpose as originally alleged by him, of purchasing land for the tribe; but, since the breaking out of lungsickness, he declares he will keep the money by him, to replace the cattle lost by the prevailing disease. It may be a long time before the hoard is expended in this manner; for, of course, he will wait till the disease has disappeared. [112]

Other communities faced with land shortages applied to the government for permission to buy. In 1860 Ngoza acted on behalf of his people, many of whom were squatting on private farms or inconvenienced by the overcrowded state of their location near Table Mountain, and requested permission to acquire a portion of land available in the location of Matyana, a deposed chief who had recently fled the district.[113] In another instance, Chief Teteleku applied to remove from the Zwartkop location to the country between Fort Nottingham and the Mooi River because his cattle were in frequent danger of being impounded by the many white inhabitants crowding in his neighborhood.[114]

Security of tenure through purchase imparted an exaggerated sense of well-being and independence. This was partly because possession of land through tribal titles enhanced the prestige of the chief and attracted followers, and partly because most Africans never fully comprehended the profound nature of the political and economic changes taking place around them. This was apparent in the case of Sotondozi, a chief who had removed from the unhealthy coastal region to the upper Klip River division in 1869. "I met Sotondozi by appointment last Thursday at Matonkwani's kraal, and shewed him the Crown Lands," wrote the magistrate of Newcastle.

> He seemed much pleased with their extent (I suppose about 8000 acres) and talked of placing his kraals here and there and all over them—I advised him not to open his eyes too wide, as his means are limited, and told him but few white men would be able to pay cash for so much land. He answered that he thought that he was at liberty to live where he liked so long as he paid his hut-tax, and that it was nobody's business where he placed his kraals. He told me also that he could see that the white men did not want him here, but wished his people to work; which they should never do, and moreover, if any white men's cattle came on his ground he would send them to the pound directly.[115]

Word traveled ahead of Sotondozi's impending purchase, spread by runners set off across the countryside. Moving from place to place, the chief's messengers came upon a certain white farm where they met a recently registered refugee who was instructed that "he must not stay with his master a day longer than his time, but must come to them, as they had a fine piece of land, and all comers were welcome." At some point quite soon after these visits, Africans in the neighborhood began to give notice to their masters of their intention to leave, as they were related to some of Sotondozi's people. Even the Klip River magistrate reporting this incident was affected by the movement. Workers who had been with him for seven years refused to supply him with any more labor, "saying they [were] not refugees, and [would] work when they like[d]. . . . "[116] Needless to say, Sotondozi "made himself very disagreeable to his white neighbors."

Sealing the transaction meant a host of practical matters had to be carefully attended to. But Africans were as ignorant of these legalities as they were unfamiliar with the concept of private ownership of real estate. Furthermore, they initially had badly underestimated the depth of white hostility and resistance to their becoming independent landowners and producers. Sotondozi was unable to protect his community against the possibility of the land deal's falling through, which, in fact, it did. In consequence, the chief, with the whole of his people, was compelled to leave the upper Klip River district and return to the coast.[117]

Primacy of the "Firstcomer": The Buildup of New Communities

Tradition tells of a great famine around 1829 in the neighborhood of Port Natal, in consequence of Nqetho's revolt. The Zulu regiment pursuing the runaways laid waste the countryside, driving off the bay inhabitants. In their flight the Europeans dropped a single mealie seed, which was found and planted by Mjozingana, an *umnumzana* (kraalhead) and a follower of Henry Fynn. The seed flowered, dried, and produced a cob. Mjozingana planted all the seed of that cob and the resulting cobs gave enough seed to plant a garden. When this was reaped, he distributed the seed among his kraal, and in this way food increased and people came to *khonza* (pay respects to, seek refuge with) him, or to buy seed there. Mjozingana took in many refugees from Zululand. Juqula, Fynn's great *induna* (headman), and Makokela also received a number of followers on account of having mealie seed initially obtained from Mjozingana.[118]

This anecdote provides a classic illustration of how individuals fallen on hard times turned to those better endowed than themselves, seeking to become their clients. Indigent people had little difficulty finding a person willing to receive them, for a man's prestige was enhanced in proportion to the number of his followers.[119]

Such incidents proliferated in the period when large numbers of fugitives were entering the district unrepresented by chiefly authority, as many of the governing families had been all but extinguished in the wars. One witnesses, therefore, a constant traffic, back and forth, from one chief to another, as refugees found temporary stopping places, only to move on later when more suitable connections could be made. So fluid were these movements that "to maintain useful tribal distinctions," colonial officials tried to discourage the facility with which Africans left one community to join another. Enforcement of *valeliso* (take leave, bid good-bye), a tributary gift or fee (commonly a cow) paid to a chief by a follower wishing to withdraw from his "tribe," frequently had the intended effect.[120]

The essential point is that what appeared at first to be a tangled mess of small and large internal migrations and a confusion of constantly shifting alliances were actually manifestations of new communities maneuvering themselves into being, of scattered groups forging new links, manipulating, being manipulated, and ultimately reconstituting themselves. In the thick of all the activity, during this process of heightened renewal, were men pushing themselves forward with claims to first-comer status. Being the founder of a locale meant having not only "the right to show the place," as Kopytoff points out, but also authority over the inhabitants and all late arrivals.[121] Umkizani was one of those aspirants to emerge on the scene with ambitions to fill the leadership void.

In 1847 a colonist residing at Durban complained about the removal of three hundred Africans from his farm through Umkizani's influence. According to the report, Umkizani had set himself up as head of a kraal and had threatened to report the families to the government if they did not follow him to a place near Pietermaritzburg, where he proposed to locate himself. Evidently, this refugee chief circulated the rumor that if his orders were disobeyed or the people failed to remove forthwith, they would be shot and their cattle taken.[122] Events of this nature were commonplace.[123] The basis on which Umkizani and others justified their actions and urged their claims to chiefship was the universal recognition that a certain distinction and legitimacy was attached to being the senior person or group to enter a locale. George Mason confirms the operation of this convention when he wrote that "all the native population, or the greater part have been refugees in their day; yet these earlier refugees now lay claims to all fresh arrivals, numbering about ten-thousands a year."[124]

Other men gained authority over incoming refugees through their connections with the colonial government. Ngoza's career is illustrative. Originally, he served in the Zulu army under Shaka and Dingane, and had fought against the *voortrekkers*. When Mpande fled to Natal, Ngoza accompanied the prince but remained behind in Boer service. Later he received a colonial appointment, becoming Shepstone's *induna*. He won the confidence of his people, many of whom followed him as their *inkosi* (chief). Subsequently, government placed under his protection all those fugitives who were not prepared to join other communities in the colony.[125]

Mobilizing the Labor of Young Men

Among the heads of kraals receiving refugees were men who legitimately commanded respect and allegiance on the basis of hereditary chiefship. Then there were nonprominent personages—men neither entitled to nor entertaining grand pretensions—who merely hoped to improve their lot by increasing the membership of their personal households. For these individuals, it was deemed a sacred duty to give sanctuary to any clansman or stranger appealing to them for protection. After receiving such distressed persons into their kraals, the chief or family head generally showed them kindness and generosity.[126]

Another class of men took unjust advantage of the fugitives' predicament. In return for shielding them from the apprenticeship ordinance, some of the "refugee chiefs" sent fresh arrivals into the towns on their own account, and took their earnings as they became due, under threat of reporting the illegal immigrants to the magistrate; or, if immigrants were regularly apprenticed to European masters by law, claimed their wages on the grounds of chieftaincy. Orphans and friendless youths were most often exploited in this manner.[127] This element of coercion was not, however, a normal aspect of traditional labor relations.

In Zulu country, labor for the king was mobilized through the army. At about the age of eighteen, young men throughout the land were conscripted into the military. In wartime these regiments served in combat; in times of peace they were required to perform, whenever demanded, a myriad of desultory functions and tasks for the king and others of social rank and power. Twice a year, for example, young soldiers were called from all parts of the nation. The first gathering was for the purpose of hoeing and planting two immense royal fields; the second was for the purpose of reaping. Furthermore, companies of soldiers and cadets were always garrisoned in royal camps to meet any requirements for labor.[128]

Likewise, states Aldin Grout, "the bones and muscles of chieftainship" consisted in the right of chiefs to demand the service of their people to plant their gardens, and harvest them, to make their beer, and bring it to them, as also any food they may require, not simply for their own use, but so that chiefs might have an abundance with which to be royally hospitable. This service was their salary; and such services were rendered by the people as a tax to be used to support the chief.[129] The latter, however, was always cognizant that abuse of this right would drive people away. In all events, such chiefly prerogatives continued to be exercised in Natal. Europeans attacked the usage, for self-serving reasons, and labeled it a form of exploitation. However, from the point of view of the senior men in the community, calling on "boys" to work (even though under altered circumstances, as they were now being sent to labor for wages), was a time-honored practice.

Migrant labor flowed to those areas where high wages prevailed, and Africans were well acquainted with the market trends.[130] Those earnings were then appropriated by the elders for either the benefit of the house to which the junior men belonged or for general community purposes. Government hut taxes (seven shillings per hut) had to be paid, for instance; and wages were used to purchase tribal rights to land, or to reinvest in cattle, a portion of which was set aside for the young men who relied on their guardians for bridewealth. "The only equivalent that I could ever trace to the young man, for the use of his earnings in paying the family tax," wrote Mason in 1852, "was that a nominal ownership was assigned to him of a very certain number of oxen in the common family herd."[131]

White farmers complained bitterly about the interference of chiefs in the labor market. As early as 1848 "a cotton planter" complained:

> I have several Caffer kraals on my farm, one of which belongs to a Caffer who calls himself a captain. This said captain has a perfect control over twenty or thirty kraals of Caffers on the adjoining farms as well as mine. . . . [I]nstead of him assisting me to procure labour, he induces (in fact orders) Caffers in my employ to leave me and go to another farmer who promised him a cow, and etc., if he manages to procure him twenty Caffers. If I order him to leave my farm, he threatens to take all the other Caffers with him.[132]

Another incident involved a chief at Pinetown who allegedly admitted that he could furnish plenty of labor, if he were paid thirty shillings per head, and if a certain high rate was guaranteed to his young men.[133] By the late 1850s the fashion developed among sugar proprietors and other agriculturists of making presents to chiefs in order to procure workers. Traditional leaders were sometimes given several head of cattle or equivalent sums varying from £10 to £40 to secure their influence.[134] However, this feature of the labor question was discountenanced by local government. And when, for instance, Makuta was given money to procure labor, he ordered out his young men, ignoring their protests and fining two "boys" who refused to work, as they were the servants of another white employer. The case was ultimately brought before the magistrate by the master of the two servants involved; the upshot was that Makuta, himself, was fined £5 for his trouble.[135]

Normally *izinsizwa* (young men) were allowed to find their own masters, the chiefs being particularly cautious not to intervene in their right of selection. Even employers recognized in the long run that where they had solicited the "favorable intercession" of the chief, work performances often declined. One magistrate went so far as to state that coercion by chiefs was a major cause of desertions from service.[136] But this opinion was not widely subscribed to, for the system was very often promoted by the resident officials themselves. Inanda's magistrate attempted to support the interest of agriculture in this manner, but was informed by the chiefs either that all the men were out working or that they (the chiefs) had no power to send their people to work, "as they considered their hands their own." Benjamin Blaine wrote that

> In one instance, an applicant for labour offered a large bonus £5 to the chief [Mahlanjana] to send twenty labourers for six months. I conveyed the offer with a request that he would comply with it, and he did so, *but the men let their chief know that it was solely from a desire to present him with £5 that they went* [emphasis added]. . . . [137]

No part of that bonus was ever paid, as the men were dismissed before the expiration of the six months, the planter's being generally dissatisfied with their services.[138]

The weight of the evidence strongly contradicts the above claims of the Inanda chiefs that they lacked authority to send their people to work. For it seems that a kind of labor council of collaborating chieftains may have been called into existence from time to time. This body apparently made decisions not only with regard to where and how labor should be circulated, but also when and under what conditions it would be recalled from the market, especially where working conditions were deemed inimical to the well-being of their people. The following vivid account is of great significance because it comes at the end of the century and shows, among other things, that Natal chiefs still retained powerful control over the services of their young men.[139]

> The news of the treatment natives had been subjected to by the Boers had been disseminated throughout the length and breadth of Natal and Zululand, with the result that *the various chiefs had met by appointment, held an Indaba* [emphasis added] and arrived at the conclusions that the Rand was no place for their men. *Messengers had then been despatched from Natal and Zululand to the Rand to warn all their kindred to return at once* [emphasis added]. These emissaries are now busy all over the Rand, with the result that a panic has set in, and the natives are leaving in the hundreds.[140]

Isibhalo: Government Labor Tax

Finally, the operation of a government mechanism that possibly did more than any other factor to alienate young men from the locations, putting them in direct defiance of customs and ensuring a continuous circulation of labor around jobs in the casual labor market, was *isibhalo*. *Isibhalo*, a tax consisting of obligatory labor, was levied by the colonial government beginning in 1848 on young, unmarried men residing in the locations (which may partially explain their anxiety to marry). Ostensibly, it was meant to enlist labor for certain public works projects, such as the construction and upkeep of the main colonial thoroughfares; it was also used to draft labor for the sugar estates.

Natal Africans hated *isibhalo*.[141] They detested it not only because public work was disagreeable—performed generally in inclement weather or under hazardous conditions—but also because the long contracts of service (six months) were compulsory and paid so little. By working on coastal estates, in the towns, at the Cape, or later on, on the mines, they could earn 25 to 50 percent more in wages. Evasion of *isibhalo* was therefore rampant. Large numbers of young men avoided conscription by entering or claiming long-term engagements with white employers. That is, the young men were protected from call-ups by the superior rights of the white proprietors. In other words, if they moved to private farms, fled to the towns, or went even further afield to the mines, places where their labor sold in the highest markets, Africans were entitled to exemption from *isibhalo* on producing proof of such employment.[142]

This chapter has sought to draw out some of the factors influencing the Africans' orientation to the colonial market economy. Their primary consuming cause, the focus of their collective energy in the early decades of this period, was to rebuild their subsistence base. But this corporate commitment aside, there were other motivations or stimuli capable of rousing them to activity. Life in the new British territory opened the door to a range of unprecedented opportunities. In post-*mfecane* Natal the timing of marriage was no longer either controlled by the Zulu king or strictly regulated according to Shakan practices. This fact alone offered a tremendous personal incentive to labor. And given the prevailing brideprices, this would suggest further that young men worked steadily for many years in order to obtain the required number of marriage cattle. The popular African saying *"inkomo imbiwe ematyeni ku' belungu"* ("an ox has been dug out of the rocks with white people"—that is, it is hard work getting an ox from the white people, one must work hard to get it)[143] seems to underscore this point.

Still, let us suppose for the sake of argument that these indigenous imperatives (the search for status, the need for cattle, land pressures, and so on) were insufficient, to borrow van Onselen's phrase, "to peel [Natal Africans] off the land"[144]—that internal circumstances failed to guide them into wage employment. Of one fact there can be no doubt: the object was most certainly accomplished by means of external impositions such as the colonial hut and labor taxes. The documentation overwhelmingly suggests that Africans were offering their services for hire in very great numbers.

How then do we explain the nineteenth-century parodies of the "lazy Kafirs" (a notion that has had, though phrased in more palatable terms, a surprisingly tenacious and perhaps unconscious hold even on the new crop of revisionist South African writers).[145] That this negative image persists and was so often repeated by contemporaries and with such steadfast conviction, raises an interesting complex of questions, to which answers will be supplied in due course. At this juncture, however, the focus turns to the cultural patterns that governed the responses and performances of northern Nguni speakers who sold their labor in the colonial workplace. These are the subjects of the next two chapters.

3

Traditions of Labor Organization, Prestige Occupations, and White Masters

As critical as the economic situation was, other equally powerful factors helped determine the pattern of black labor trends in nineteenth-century Natal. The most important general point to be kept in view is that the events cited above were not so cataclysmic as to have utterly destroyed the cultures swept up by them. As we have seen, even where core institutions—those that generated customs, established grades of authority, and regulated relations between and within kin groups—did exhibit stress that resulted in some structural adjustments, and even where conditions called for the reinterpretation of traditional beliefs in the new context, such changes only slightly altered the appearance of those institutions; in substance they remained the same. What thus emerges with great clarity is that the cultural integrity of the reimmigrant groups endured; the people, their subsistence economy, and the principles by which they ordered their universe continued on the whole to adhere to northern Nguni forms.

These considerations have a substantial bearing on the present topic, most importantly because they point to the necessity for a historical perspective not only in analyzing questions of cultural retentions, but also in exploring the ways in which Zulu cultural models accommodated conflict, ambiguity, and change. Appropriately, we begin this chapter within the indigenous social setting, where specific institutional structures will be examined for what they might reveal about the persistence of the northern Nguni cultural ethos in the colonial economy.

Preindustrial northern Nguni society was divided into a series of graded statuses based on an age principle codified by custom. Social stratification was expressed in age guilds, associations of individuals of the same sex and approximate age. The central operating assumption resided in the notion that only by virtue of superior age (or high birth) could one be promoted to positions of responsibility and authority in the community. In the days of Zulu military greatness, men achieved majority—a quality synonymous with experience, wisdom, and prestige—when they were about forty, the stage at which they attained full civil rights, including the right to marry, establish family settlements, become members of the chief's council, engage in commercial dealings on their own account, and pursue other sundry professions.

Embedded in the above model is the idea that in northern Nguniland there was a close correlation between age grade, social position, and occupation. This critical concept should enable us—by tracing the continuities in the system of status and formal role differentiation in Zulu social formations and relationships—to work up in far greater detail the cultural profile of African workmen in Natal. Furthermore, by using this approach we should be able not only to reconstruct the broad underlying structure of the African urban work force, but to locate within the matrix of the labor market areas of tension and conflict between elders and juniors and between masters and servants.

Cultural Patterns and Traditional Occupations

At the core of the strongly patrilineal Zulu social structure was the average *umuzi* (homestead), the family kraal, which consisted of one or perhaps two "houses" differing in rank; each hut was occupied by a wife and her children. (Among commoners, the wife married first was generally the senior wife, unless she was a widow.) Presiding over these production units was not only the patriarch or *umnumzana* (husband/father) but the *inkosikazi* (chief wife), both of whom commanded obedience from all household members.[1] All kraal inmates, as Bryant informs us, were ranked, and what they saw and experienced in their superiors they practiced to a lesser degree themselves, demanding from all those inferior in age or position exactly the same measure of deference as was given to those above. Thus seniority, the fundamental rule distinguishing relationships, followed the order of chronological birth or place in the domestic hierarchy. In practice, this meant that small children were subjected to the authority of the bigger children, the bigger children to their elder brothers and sisters; and all were subordinate to the will of their parents. Deference, respect, and precedence were indispensable features of the social order. Strict rules of etiquette on how to deport oneself before one's elders and superiors governed almost every phase of daily life.[2]

The Zulu state was ruled along precisely the same lines—namely, by a gradual ascent in status and power from the common people through a body of superior persons and offices of increasing importance up to the king. So at the apogee of the political structure stood the king and other royals; the aristocracy formed the middle ranks (including men and women of high birth and considerable power and wealth), and the great mass of commoner homesteads constituted the base. Elders of distinction and ability were chosen by the king from among leading clan families as state dignitaries called *izinduna*; they served in civil capacities such as ministers of state or crown councillors, and functioned as military officials as well.[3]

The lowest layer of the social strata, comprising the common folk, will occupy our attention here. Even though this stratum represented the inferior reaches of the social order, there was nothing to prevent individuals of modest background from overcoming their lowly station. Among commoners, status was intertwined with seniority and occupation. Occasionally, adult members of the community could attain high positions by merit or royal favor.[4] One way of achieving heightened status was through martial vigor, for prowess on the battlefield was a virtue Zulu people greatly extolled. As highly esteemed as the military was, however, it would be wrong to overestimate the extent of those promotions or the number of cattle received as rewards for heroism.

The sources demonstrate unequivocally that few opportunities for meaningful advancements were open to young soldiers. Ambitions were thwarted by *izinduna* who feared their own personal status was threatened by others becoming more famous. A prevalent practice was to make it appear as if those already of high rank (like a prince who was a special favorite) had been heroic. The idea was that later on, in gratitude, these princelings would advance the cause of the military leaders to whom they owed their reputations as great warriors. According to Mandhlakazi, many valorous deeds were masked in this self-seeking manner. Soldiers known among their regimental mates to have slain many enemies in the heat of battle were silenced by hearing it said that some other *ibutho* (warrior) had killed a couple of the very casualties claimed, and someone else took credit for having killed the others, thereby leaving the true hero without anything to boast of.[5] Indeed the brave warrior would have placed himself at risk should he decide to contest the issue. It was recognized that some *izinduna*, intimidated by some aspirant vying for recognition, often manufactured slanderous reports to justify scattering the man's forces and "eating up" (i.e., confiscating) his property.[6] Such actions occasionally culminated in the death of the offending party.

Such evidence as we have suggests that local commerce and the skilled and semiskilled occupations were spheres in which opportunities for enrichment, social advancement, and political influence could be realized without the risks involved in establishing a name in the military. Expert craftsmen, persons in the healing arts, and those in other professional careers could amass substantial wealth—and wealthy persons stood above the common folk. Accolades were awarded to individuals of unusual ability and talent who were brought to the king's attention. Special merit was sometimes conferred by incorporating such persons into the body of artisans and specialists who worked in the military towns; still others were admitted to the corps of royal servants who attended the king's household.

Surviving references show that enterprising persons did distinguish themselves in areas outside the battlefield. We are told, for example, of one particular craftsman, Velana kaCungele, who possessed an iron axe *(izembe)* and used it so skillfully as a skin dresser *(impali)* that his reputation gained him a royal promotion to headman over the oHeni kraal.[7] Another celebrated *impali*, Ncwadi kaMnhlonhlo, was frequently called to Mgungundhlovu by Dingane to scrape blankets.[8] The famous woodcarver, Mtomboti kaMangcengeza, made chairs for Mpande.[9]

Women also gained eminence through their skills as diviners. David Leslie describes a "great Natal Doctoress," who, with her entourage, was summoned to prescribe for Mpande and to counteract the spells of his enemies, to which he ascribed his illness.[10] In handicrafts and other trades there were, for instance, Langazana's special calabashes, a beautiful variety she grew for the king, for the ordinary kind were not good enough for him.[11] And Mandhlela, the grandmother of Magidi-gidi, who lived at Noyenda ("the *umuzi* of the goats"), looked after the royal herd of long-haired goats whose skins were worn as clothing.[12] Any earnings women derived from these practices or handicrafts were retained by them to use in bartering cattle, strengthening social ties, acquiring dress and ornamentation, and so on.[13]

The activities mentioned above carried distinctive social rankings. Dohne tells us that the common tradesmen comprised woodcutters and the like; somewhat above them were the cattle doctors. The most distinguished were the master of medicine (*inyanga yokwelapha*), a person who had special knowledge of botany and the mode of applying herbs; and the diviner (*inyanga yokubhula*), an individual (usually a woman) able to obtain information about the causes of evil, sickness, and death, and about the remedies to be employed.[14] In the esoteric professions whole clans sometimes specialized in a particular line of business: the emaCubeni and emaCunwini clans were noted smiths; the Nzuza, war doctors; and the Ntlangwini, rainmakers.[15] Needless to say, it was a great piece of good fortune for a child of undistinguished parentage to enter the apprenticeship of an artisan renowned for his craft or to be admitted as a novice in one of the professions not held by clan monopoly. Anyone who joined these high-ranking branches of trade ensured his or her future social standing, and raised the prestige of his family in the eyes of the community.

A somewhat different approach to improving one's lot was for men of low birth or modest background to become the followers of well-placed individuals, persons of character and considerable influence. Here poverty was often the nudge. But aside from looking to supply basic physical needs, important intangibles could be derived from tendering allegiance to strong men. By basking in the reflection of a "big man" of brilliant reputation, clients stood to gain the respect and admiration of their lesser fellows. We will pursue this subject in more detail later in the chapter. For the moment, our primary objective is to make plain the group that profited most directly from the above ventures by relating access of opportunities to differences in social and economic roles.

Passage from one grade to the next in age class systems was very often marked by visible signs, such as transformation in hairstyles and forms of dress. Such outward symbols proclaimed one's social role and economic obligations. They indicated that in the male journey from boyhood to manhood, both the individual and those with whom he interacted took on a different social attitude each time the person was promoted along the social scale.[16] Because it was overwhelmingly the young and mature men, rather than women and girls, who entered the formal urban wage economy, our analysis will be confined to the social mobility of males.

Samuelson informs us that "the Zulu trained their children, female and male, step by step in the way they should go, until adults."[17] Very commonly youngsters were kept busy every day with light work around the homestead. Little boys from about the age of five or seven, for example, would go out to herd small livestock such as goats, calves, and sheep. At milking time they assisted their father or elder brothers by holding the cow, and in this manner they learned. Play also allowed the little ones to practice roles assumed later on in life. A male child's social birth began, however, with the *qhumbuza* (piercing of ears), a collective ceremony where initiates of the same *intanga* (age set) were treated together. When they reached the age of puberty, the occasion was marked by a series of rituals (*thomba*) accompanied by feasting. During these formalities, the *umfana* (boy) was honored with a new name by which his age mates and all younger than himself called him. His new status was also marked by a change in sleeping arrangements. As a small child (*ingane*), he lived with his mother and girls, but when he arrived at the age of making responsible decisions, he left his mother's hut for the boys' sleeping quarters (*ilawu*). Included among his new responsibilities was that of being sent out with bigger boys to herd cattle for most of the day.[18] Around this time, too, adolescents were elevated to the status of *udibi* (carrier or mat boy). This epochal moment in a lad's life signified he was now strong enough to carry his father's baggage and other travel paraphernalia on long journeys; it further indicated that he had reached sufficient maturity to commence learning by practical experience the family trade.[19]

The next stage in these rites of promotion came with the celebration of *uku-buthwa*, the initiation ceremony, which took place when *izinsizwa* (youths approaching manhood) of similar age were called up by royal decree, enrolled in regiments, and taught the traditional code. Without *buthwa*, we are told, young men could not be full members of the community or know their proper place in the hierarchy of age. In peacetime, conscripts quartered in the *amakhanda* (military kraals or towns) gave labor service to the king, performing a myriad of chores from construction projects to collecting firewood and thornbush, hoeing the royal fields, carrying *amabele* (sorghum grain) when it was being reaped, threshing it, and so on. Small groups of young cadets were constantly engaged in such minor matters as transporting grain, carrying messages to men of rank in all parts of the country, and participating in great hunting parties.[20]

Full social maturation was achieved when the king discharged his soldiers, who by then were middle-aged, from active duty and granted them permission to marry. All previous life experiences were but preparation for this moment of elevation to senior rank—which was announced by the act of *khehla*, or putting on the headring (or *isicoco*). The *isicoco* was a circle of fibre sewn into the hair on top of the head; the hair was then shaved off, both inside and outside the ring. What remained was attached to the fibre, greased, rubbed with charcoal, and polished, till it took on the appearance of a crown of leather. This insignia of high rank symbolized male adulthood; it was the final step by which a man was incorporated into full community life, with all the accompanying responsibilities and prerogatives. On donning the headring, a man became father, teacher, and master of apprentices to the younger members of the clan.[21] Elderhood gave him the power to make decisions in council that affected the entire community.

The normal domestic duties of married men (*amakhehla*) included building the framework of huts, erecting and repairing the various fences of the cattlefold and kraal enclosures, cutting away virgin bush and long grass from spots allotted for cultivation, and managing the stock. The other social privileges enjoyed by married men, by virtue of their high rank, included periodic visits to the king's residence to pay homage, or to seek special offices such as state messenger, or to serve in some other dignified occupation or profession required at the royal military towns. Married men also engaged in itinerant trades on their own account. A member of the professional or artisan class (whether a diviner, a dispenser of medicine, headring maker, blacksmith, stock castrator, basket weaver, or shield manufacturer) was called an *inyanga,* one skilled in any handicraft or profession.[22] As previously stated, expertise in the skilled trades carried the possibility of acquiring wealth.[23]

Several points need to be stressed here. First, not just community expectations but a sense of entitlement were attached to occupations in which elders traditionally engaged. The records indicate that the *amakhehla* possessed prescriptive rights to all professions of social and economic consequence. Second, as Bernardi has pointed out, although the age class system embodied an egalitarian ideal, which distributed power and privileges in turn through succession and thus guaranteed every male mobility through the entire series of grades, passage from one stage to the next did not always occur without tension.[24] The occupational structure was a fertile site of conflict. There the perquisites of rank were challenged by individuals impatient with the limitations set by the norms of their grades. The best proof we have of this comes from the urban areas, where elders repeatedly clashed with their junior competitors over the former's monopoly of the prestige town occupations. This leads us to the final point, which is that northern Nguni institutions were neither abandoned nor swept aside under British rule.

From the colony's inception, indirect rule was recognized as the most viable form of governance for Natal's large black population. This meant that the settler state relied heavily on the African civil code as a method of social control. Accordingly, chiefly jurisdiction was upheld by imperial instructions in 1848. The point is, whatever British influence there may have been on the everyday world of these people, it was not significant enough to displace traditional labor practices. Recent research is beginning to show that the work culture that evolved in the white rural areas and in the two leading townships, where blacks were heavily employed, was largely shaped by deep-rooted African customs.

No one had given greater impetus to Natal's native policy than Theophilus Shepstone, chief architect and principal exponent of African administration in accordance with "native law." Yet throughout his long career (1845 to 1876) as diplomatic agent and later secretary for native affairs, and notwithstanding the apparent success of "Shepstonism," the said policy was never without its critics. In order to achieve a better understanding of the controversy, it will be worth our while to examine the key issue around which the management of "native affairs" was so acrimoniously debated.

Opponents of "Shepstonism" consistently charged, not without reason, that the program actually discouraged segments of the indigenous population from offering labor on the market, which had the pernicious effect of prolonging blacks in their "barbarous state." Others explained that a glaring drawback of the scheme was its tendency to encourage the inegalitarian features of Natal's African communities. Still others were fully persuaded that with government promoting the jurisdiction of chiefs and acknowledging the role of men "whose heads [were] adorned with the manly ring" (men who disdained any labor except those tasks appropriate to their rank), a large number of able-bodied men were exempted from work. These critics likewise noted that the system perpetuated inequality between elders and their juniors.[25] Almost all these complaints make the point that traditional patterns of work taken up in the colonial setting "[struck] a tremendous blow at the labor supply."[26] There are fascinating dimensions to this question, some of the implications of which we will attempt to draw out below.

Adaptation to New Work Conditions

The organizational structure of black workers laboring in the early colonial towns replicated northern Nguni social forms. This is attested at mid-nineteenth-century Port Natal, where African workers were formed in an age hierarchy. Essentially, what this meant was in the urban environment *abafana* (boys) and *izinsizwa* (young men) were forbidden by their social superiors, the *amakhehla* (married men), from independently taking up trades and professions for which their junior status rendered them unworthy.

These ancient conventions held sway when transposed to the new milieu and set the terms under which Africans sought work. Furthermore, from what is known about their customary social behavior, it is possible to deduce the principle guiding workers in their job choices: colonial occupations with analogues in traditional tasks and roles constituted acceptable areas of employment. Or stated somewhat differently, it seems that adult men and male youths originally hired out in those familiar positions that fit their place in the domestic household and wider community. This is borne out in the fundamental distinction maintained by African workmen within the hierarchy of urban occupations, and which grudgingly came to be accepted among whites as town custom—namely, that only young males would engage in areas of domestic service and nonprestigious, low-paying jobs. As an early resident at the Bay wrote about this arrangement,

> Within ten or fifteen miles of the village of Durban . . . there were thousands of Kafirs, the kraals being numerous, and many men and boys working in the towns and on the beach . . . and as to "servants" they were boys so-called, varying in age from 15–25. . . . These unclothed young men nursed the white children and did the cooking and washing in English families. . . . [27]

Yet these early workers were not so tightly bound by inherited customs that they were closed to change, nor did these cultural continuities preclude their capacity for innovations. The amaWasha are a remarkable case in point.[28] The amaWasha guild was an association of Zulu washermen who for forty years (1850–1890) retained a virtual monopoly of the laundry industry in Pietermaritzburg and Durban. The guildsmen are worthy of note because initially they appear to incorporate vestiges of early trade groups of *izinyanga*, who specialized in hide or skin dressing. In Nguni society, hide specialists assumed economic functions of considerable importance—the manufacture of the community's garments and the essential production of raw-hide shields for hunting and war. When members of this artisan group (and other adult males) turned to the towns of Natal, they found that by modifying their domestic skills to meet a growing European need, they could enjoy a prominence similar to that attached to their traditional roles. In the town setting, where these specialists had greater control over their labor, it was in their collective interests to combine, establish rules and regulations, and drive out young competitors. In this manner they became one of the most powerful groups of African workmen in nineteenth-century Natal.

Knowing that age operated as a constraint on an individual's career choices would help to explain the intergenerational struggles observed among the urban labor force. Efforts by the old men to impose their authority outside the traditional context met with unaccustomed opposition from upstart rivals and civic officials who attempted to disregard convention. But as they were bent on retaining the normal order (i.e., reverence for their privileged rank and subordinate behavior in the peccant youths), those elders drew together in a "combination" of patriarchal power. By intimidation, the old men assumed a supervisory position in allocating the labor resources in the town. Similarly, the "ringtops" used their association to counter municipal attempts to curtail their influence in setting town wage scales. The best reported account of their activities is found in this 1856 news item alerting readers to the extensive practices operating among African workmen in Durban:

> We think it right to warn the public against several modes of imposition and fraud now practiced by Kafirs in this town and neighbourhood. . . .
>
> The screw is applied tightly and generally by the more knowing Kafirs to the younger class of native boys who engage in service. They are threatened with severe chastisement, and are often actually punished, if they accept a lower rate of wages than is fixed by "the trade," or if they do certain kinds of work prohibited to them, and specially reserved by their self-constituted taskmasters for their own benefit, such as undertaking expresses to a distance, and similar well paid duties. In fact, there is a widespread concert, or more properly speaking, conspiracy, for keeping up exorbitant rates of wages and regulating the labor to be given. . . . [29]

Seven years later, an aggrieved "working contractor" in Durban contended, "Those who are unacquainted with Kafir affairs will hardly believe what a combination there exists among them about work, and masters, etc. Nor can those whose positions render them independent of Kafir labor form an idea of the worry of others less fortunate."[30] Similarly, in 1873 Shepstone wrote of "a large, but fluctuating native population living in the towns . . . combining to enrich themselves at the expense of the householders by excessive demands, or by directly dishonest means."[31]

The range of possibilities offered in Natal and the opportunity for rising in status were attractions to which many Africans enthusiastically responded. Once they had carved out careers for themselves, these men sought to secure exclusive title and positions for their male progeny. This tendency to preserve craft monopolies and retain mastership in the family has been noticed among traditional Zulu trades and professions. Both Krige and Bryant remarked that occupations became hereditary where the labor involved great skill and where trade secrets were connected with the art (e.g., medical men, rainmakers, or blacksmiths).[32] In addition, there were instances where other trades (especially nontraditional colonial trades) presented fresh prospects for making considerable profits, where appointments to special offices conferred enormous prestige as well as monetary reward, and where, in such cases, members of those occupations attempted to arrogate to themselves *and their sons* the monopoly of that craft or profession.[33]

This preemptive spirit is clearly evident among the amaWasha. However, the principle of privileged entry can best be illustrated in the family career history of Bikwayo kaNoziwawa, a "native messenger" *(isikhonzi)*. The *izikhonzi* were among the well-paid groups belonging to a federation of Zulu tradesmen and professionals organized in Durban. Among the corps of *izikhonzi* sent to the great supply country of Zululand was Bikwayo's grandfather, Mzizima, appointed messenger of all the low country of Tongaland. As king's messenger, he was charged with collecting annual tribute from the Tsonga and neighboring peoples living to the northeast of Zulu country. On Mzizima's death, which occurred during the reign of Mpande, his son, Noziwawa kaMzizima (Bikwayo's father), was made his successor. Noziwawa's elder son, Mnyaiza, used to accompany his father on various missions to the Tsonga but when Mnyaiza died, that position devolved on the younger son, Bikwayo. "I used to go to Tongaland with my father—as *mat bearer*. . . . I was put in Mnyaiza's place when he died." Eventually, following the death of Noziwawa, Bikwayo rose to the position of *induna* over the Tsonga. Under Cetshwayo, and later as messenger for the colonial government, he made frequent official visits to minor chiefs living between Zulu country and Delagoa Bay.[34]

The custom of enlisting young relations as apprentices was practiced among members of Natal's amaWasha community and was also followed by middle-aged Zulu washermen who took their younger sons with them on the long trek to the Witwatersrand.[35] In this manner and ostensibly acting as *izindibi* (mat bearers), young boys learned, as Bikwayo most assuredly had done by observation and practical experience, the family profession.

The following quotation vividly illustrates how a family head hoped to preempt and reserve for his sons entry into one corner of the town labor market. It is significant because it reveals in the worker's own words the *modus operandi* by which he and certainly an impressive segment of the African work force sought to achieve prestige, power and wealth.

> Who says that the native is not ambitious? This week I was told by a member of a big Durban firm employing many natives of one of them who is aiming at dominion. This native has already married four wives, and has many—I forget the number—children. As his boys come to a working age he gets them work with the same firm. He has mentioned to the firm that he is adding to his wives as rapidly as he can, and is looking forward to the day when he will be in a position to supply the whole of the native labor required by the firm from his own family. "Then," he adds with pride, "I will myself stop working, and become their Induna."[36]

Self-esteem Attached to Labor

A further ray of light is shed upon the problem when we consider how European mistresses and masters attempted to cope with the social distinctions prevailing among the African labor force. Wrote Eliza Whigham Feilden in 1855,

> Yesterday Elijah brought home with him a *man* Caffre! Odious animal, as sweet as a wolf! I have always avowed a determination to have only *boy* Caffres, and of this Elijah was well aware, but he did not like fetching water,

and made a merit of bringing anyone when I wanted tambooti grass to be cut.[37]

The mental image that first leaps to mind is of a parody for the countless caricatures of the "lazy Kafir." Ordinarily, we discount such passages as having little or no relevance. But is there something central beyond the immediate import of these words that the author intends to convey? Are we overlooking meaningful clues to a deeper message, and is it not conceivable that, by situating this quotation within the context of the previous discussion, we could reach a profoundly different conclusion? Again we ask ourselves why, in the textual evidence presented above, Eliza stresses the terms *man* and *boy*. Do these idioms hold cultural connotations apart from conventional Western usage? This line of reflection presents a new set of intriguing possibilities from which we are forced to conclude that perhaps we are looking at the passage the wrong way round; that our instinctive reaction to shrug off as racist the settlers' early and seemingly casual use of the term "boy" (when describing their African workers or as a form of address) may have impaired our investigation and concealed vital cultural and historical information; and that it now seems quite possible that what we are dealing with, at least in this particular instance, is not so much a matter of white ethnocentric disdain but rather a case in which an early pioneer settler attempted to accommodate a social world vastly different from her own, a world predicated upon the indigenous peasant ethos.

The conventional portrait of Zulu domestic roles as being rigidly drawn along gender lines is in need of serious qualification. For in practice, the sexual division of household labor in northern Nguni society was not nearly so inflexible as the literature suggests. Just for the moment, however, let us assume the validity of the accepted model. On surveying the range of tasks imposed on females, our immediate reaction is that those tasks could hardly have been efficiently performed solely by women and girls, especially not in households of limited size where male labor was available. Even if such chores were normally reserved for the womenfolk, these categories had little relevance in daughterless households or in situations where female children were too young to undertake heavy tasks; in these cases, it would not have been unusual for boys to perform those jobs instead. The explanation that such an expansion of social roles could only occur under adverse demographic conditions is unconvincing. Life in the real world dictates otherwise.

Wit and flexibility were skills critical to the survival of preindustrial communities the world over. People in northern Nguni societies were no exception in this regard. They possessed both a pragmatic resourcefulness in coping with the vicissitudes of the physical environment and a capacity for modifying and altering patterned ways of behavior to meet basic needs and carry on essential functions in the ordinary course of everyday life. Where standard household labor was concerned, rules were not so impossibly rigid as to disallow "youths" of either sex from performing such monotonous tasks as fetching wood, cutting grass, drawing water, and so on. This is not just a hypothetical argument; this picture finds remarkable support from information gathered on child-rearing practices.

For instance, stark inconsistencies immediately crop up when the generic ethnographic descriptions are read in conjunction with what our sources have to say about child caretaking, an area where one would least expect to find role sharing or gender role reversals. Nevertheless, among the responsibilities of *abafana* (boys) in Nguni households was that of child nurse. Admittedly, our knowledge is rudimentary about multiple child-rearing systems in traditional African societies and the full significance of male nurses in the socialization of younger children.[38] Nonetheless, the available evidence points unswervingly in one direction—namely, that there was considerable participation of southern African males in this and in other areas generally subsumed by Western writers under the rubric "female sphere."

Majuba kaSibukula "use[d] to nurse" Ngwanaza, chief of the Mabhudu, when he was a baby and knew him well.[39] Ngqengelele kaMvulana of the Buthelezi people "was literally a hewer of wood and drawer of water to Tshaka's people, also a nurse." Among his duties was that of taking care of babies in the Zulu royal kraal when their mothers happened to be absent.[40] Further, we know from the testimony of Melapi kaMagaye, who attended Mbonisa and carried him around on his back, that boys were involved in infant care while their mothers were in confinement or occupied with more pressing work.[41] Lunguza kaMpakane tells us also that "boys were put on to taking care of babies prior to herding calves, about 8 or 9 years of age." Melapi, however, declares that he was ten or twelve years of age at the time he attended Mbonisa, "old enough to herd cattle."[42] Ngqengelele's case is significant because it clearly demonstrates that nursing duties were not consigned solely to preadolescent males. According to tradition, Ngqengelele was a commoner who quickly rose from menial servant (*isigqila*) in the royal household to a position of prominence under Shaka and Dingane.

Thus all the hard evidence suggests that child caretaking was not inconsistent in their gender system with male behavior. As noted above, it was customary for older boys to serve as baby tenders (i.e., to assist in the supervision and socialization of younger children, particularly of their younger brothers). Their small charges, from about five years of age, were allowed to accompany the bigger boys (or their fathers) to the cattle pen to "help" with the milking, and so on. Buttressing the argument that no stigma was attached to males enlisted in child-care services was the emergence of a class of "Zulu nurseboys" in the colonial towns of Natal and later on the Witwatersrand.[43] It is common knowledge that in these urban centers, young Zulu males actively sought jobs as servants to European children.

In like manner, we can eliminate any confusion surrounding the evidence of Mkando kaDhlovu, who states quite plainly that in Shaka's day in times of war, "girls used to carry mats as carrier-boys (*izindibi*)."[44] A man who had produced no sons relied on his daughter to carry his baggage and essential supplies on military campaigns as well as on peaceful expeditions. Ndukwana kaMbengwana says, "Our mats had always to be carried by girls, no boys being available."[45] The *izindibi* also performed various domestic duties. As soon as they arrived at military headquarters, for instance, they swept out the hut, smeared the floor with cow dung, fetched water, collected firewood, put the pot on, and cooked.[46] Boys undoubtedly learned these household skills and chores while living in their mother's hut.

Let us finally note that while practical as well as symbolic considerations may have been attached to labor given to the king, it is nonetheless significant that young warriors also performed a myriad of menial tasks at the royal kraal, duties that again one would most commonly associate with women's work.[47] Indeed, we are told that King Dingane plied a hoe in the fields to set an example for his subjects; and that Zulu monarchs appeared personally to supervise the warriors harvesting corn in the royal gardens.[48] Another image that seems glaringly incongruous with their warrior status is that of soldiers smearing Shaka's hut floor with cow dung.[49] Smearing floors, if we rely on information found in the ethnographic accounts, was a job preeminently associated with females.

All this may appear to be an unnecessary digression, but it brings us full circle to a very simple point, it seems to me, and one so fundamentally basic to Nguni cultural logic that it is rather easy to overlook: *all* unmarried Zulu males, being in a state of protracted marginality, were customarily referred to by their seniors as "boys." Obviously, this is a very touchy point that I am anxious not to see misrepresented, though I know it will be distorted anyway.

Writers repeatedly stress that the concept of hierarchy, with its differentiation of power and roles, was an abiding feature of African society. This principle permeated the whole of the social structure, shaping and defining every aspect of its character. Within this construction, seniority had especial value, and elders were revered. Laduma Madela pertinently states that it was a sign of respect if someone who was old was attended by a "boy," and it was an honor for the young person as well; to be a servant (*inceku*) of the aged was a sign of trustworthiness.[50] Taken in this sense, the word *umfana* (boy) could never be interpreted as derisory. Only later, when Europeans debased the concept, reducing it to a racist cliché and using the vocative "boy!" to summon all males, irrespective of age or social position, did Africans come to relate the term with a loss of dignity and respect. We should be aware, however, that not every white person employing this style of address was motivated by bigotry. At least, that is the inference to be derived from the literature, where one sometimes finds that the idioms "man" and "boy" have been set in quotation marks or underlined to inform the reader of the borrowed usage, and perhaps also to distance the writer from rhetoric loaded with racist assumptions.

Support for the argument presented above comes from the Reverend Joseph Shooter, who informs us that "the Zulu army . . . consists of two classes, namely 'men' and 'boys'—the former being those entitled to wear the head-ring, and the latter all others." He goes on to state that both classes were divided into regiments, and that the Hlambehlu, a junior regiment in Mpande's army, included "boys" thirty-five years of age.[51] It is worth recalling, too, that the "boys" working on the beach and in the town of Durban were reckoned by Holden as between the ages of fifteen and twenty-five.[52] Since within the Nguni social construct, jobs of a servile nature generally fell to *abafana* (boys), and whereas the province commonly appropriated by the elders were the trades and a variety of specialized professions, it makes perfectly good sense to view from this internal vantage Eliza Feilden's "avowed . . . determination to have only *boy* Caffres" to work in her domestic establishment.[53]

Still missing, however, is a fully satisfactory explanation for why Elijah, Feilden's African servant, brought "a *man* Caffre" to perform feminine chores. This brings us back to our starting point, that is, to the events discussed in Chapter 1; but here it should be kept in mind that while the post-*mfecane* era opened the way to expanding opportunities for people formerly kept under rigid controls, for many the experiences of these years were full of uncertainty and devastating effect. One example of this was manifested in the resolve of the elders to resist the dissipation and dispersal of their status and power. If it were possible to make a detailed inquiry into the fate of those hardest hit by the crisis, notably the aged and the disabled, we would be enlightened even more on this matter. From what can be figured out from the sources respecting such marginalized groups—old and/or crippled people *who were suddenly without communities* and barely able to survive—their chances of starting afresh or altering their position of dependency were practically nil. Becoming a dependent, especially under the roof of a nonkinsman, generally implied loss of social status.[54] Such persons were not only made to suffer the stings of condescension and scorn of their superiors, they were further humiliated by being forced to perform menial jobs around the village homestead.

Now, the Reverend Shooter disputes this last point. He believed subordinate men only performed such tasks as were "appropriate to their class."[55] But in reality, one finds this was not always so. When the fugitive Dingiswayo first left home, for example, the story goes that he fled to Hlangabeza's people, where (significantly) he was "picked up" or sheltered by an old woman, who gave him so much work to do, however, in the way of collecting firewood and other domestic duties (he also had to thresh *upoko* millet) that he became greatly dissatisfied, and so ran off to live under Chief Bungane.[56] Mvayisa states that at the place of the Langeni (Nandi's people), Shaka was treated like an outcast, made to thresh *unyaluti* millet, and given a louse-ridden blanket, "even though he belonged by birth."[57] We learn too the reasons Mamfongonwa, the Qwabe chief, left Zululand in Mpande's reign: "He left because of the indignities he had to put up with; he was, for instance, made an *inceku* [an attendant in the king's household] *responsible for milking and had to extend both hands like an inferior, to receive curds* [emphasis in original]."[58]

So far as one is able to tell, these incidents cannot be made intelligible by relating them to fashionable concepts of the present day. There are no allusions to gender relations in the aforementioned texts; nowhere is there a discussion delineating jobs that fell within the purview of women's work. To insist, then, that these incidents were somehow linked to gender issues would grossly misinterpret the passages, assigning to them a meaning never intended.

The best explanation for the above protests is that they were one way of saying (as Levine reminds us) that "the allocation of work, and especially menial, burdensome or servile tasks, *reflects the distribution of status* [emphasis added]: the higher one's status, the less work visibly performed and the greater the tendency to delegate tasks to inferiors."[59] In this sense, the preceding passages resonate the theme of the entire chapter: the message that seniority was the very essence of social interaction—a principle that intersects Western notions of gender in very significant ways. Let us state this another way: only in terms of breaches of the "hierarchical etiquette" can we account for these otherwise unremarkable events being preserved in the archives of remembered history. That is, the above episodes were communicated to posterity *only* because the individuals spoken of were *not* lowly commoners; rather they were Nguni worthies, who should have been above such mean occupations. Yet one finds them being scandalously ill-used, treated like inferiors and outcasts, an especial outrage in Shaka's case as not only was he a lad of rank, "he belonged by birth."

Perhaps we can now return to the original proposition with a better sense of what might have motivated Elijah in his actions. Might this have been a question of class, Elijah's way of distinguishing rank? Is it not conceivable, for example, that the "*man* Caffre," who probably assumed the mien of a pauper, was Elijah's social inferior, one of the many set adrift by events described in earlier chapters? Or shall we interpret this occurrence as simply representing nothing more or less than an astonishing display of conduct in direct opposition to Nguni laws and customs? In the latter case, one surely would be moved to say that the incident speaks poorly for Elijah's upbringing, reflecting, as it were, upon an individual in contempt of those carefully nurtured values of deference, respect, and precedence.

Of course most colonists, far less discerning than Eliza Feilden, had not the slightest inkling of these cultural nuances. They seemed to lack the necessary awareness and sensitivity to appreciate the distinctions and interconnections between age and occupational categories. Here and there amid the sources, we see how their European centeredness—their failure to adapt to critical features of the culture around them—deeply affected master-servant relations.

The evidence at our disposal indicates that in colonial Natal very many whites, some with a kind of unwitting perversity, repeatedly violated custom by assigning to their maturer African laborers jobs that the latter felt degraded their rank. Knowingly or not, this was a bruising insult to a people well known for their prideful arrogance. Of the available sources, none was found to be more revealing than the following complaint lodged by a master against his farm servant, Usamo.

> He returned late and disobeyed my orders when I told him to secure the calves; he further said he had nothing to do with the goats when I told him to put them in the kraal, nor would he fetch a bucket of water on account of it being too dark. I then asked him through another Kafir (Booy) what was the matter with him, and he said he would not stop any longer with me on account of my calling him constantly for nothing and that I had stolen an assagai from him. . . . [60]

Viewing this vignette more closely, one can plainly see not only the employer's confusion over and bewilderment with Usamo's conduct, but also the fact that the servant himself was the victim of recurrent humiliations and insults. Consider first the implications of being ordered to perform tasks (herding calves and goats) fit only for *abafana* (small boys) and then being told to fetch water (another menial chore) after sunset (*shona langa*, the relevance of which will be seen in the next chapter). Finally, and probably most grating of all, Usamo's staff of manhood—his assegai (spear) was taken from him.

Another master-servant dispute may be instanced here. It is important because it allows us to hear more directly the African's testimony for withholding labor from the market. A fieldcornet investigating a land dispute in 1849 reported:

> I saw Majone and five other caffers who have kraals in the vicinity of Mr. Nel's farm, they all confirmed the statement made by Golala; and further stated they are averse to engaging in the service of white men, some of whom have deceived them with respect to wages. *They do not like engaging as cattle herd because they usually employ their boys in such work* [emphasis added]; they do not like being leaders of the wagons of farmers to Pietermaritzburg because they are afraid of being run over by the wagons and they suffer cold in the roads. . . . [61]

So much for the African male. The next question is whether the voice of African women can be invoked to speak forthrightly on this issue. Earlier we saw that it was not only desirable but possible to bring the perceptions of African women to the discussion. We surveyed women's roles in the household economy, and we gave some attention to missionaries and other adversaries of African culture who were among the first to let loose charges of "female slavery." Significantly, Aldin Grout, a staunch foe of polygamy, was forced to admit in testimony given before the Kafir Commission that not one female in a thousand would feel or express gratitude if relieved from what he and others judged as being a life of "daily drudgery."[62]

The fact was that prerogatives attached to age, rank, and occupations were just as fiercely defended by African women as by their menfolk. The unsolicited "philanthropic" campaigns against *lobolo* ("their national sin No. 1; Polygamy No. 2")[63] were regarded by most African women as unwelcome meddling, as an assault upon their position in the homestead, and as an attempt to degrade the status of their husbands, with whom they shared a partnership in the production unit. What perhaps was a typical traditional female response to this question was recorded in the late 1860s by a visitor to Natal who frequently made "a point of studying the habits, characters and peculiarities of the people amongst whom he travelled." His observations deserve to be quoted at length:

> [A]t a Mr. Besley's sugar plantation on the Ifafa river, I saw a Kafir made to relieve his wife of a huge pot of treacle she was carrying balanced on her head. He did as the white people ordered him without the slightest symptom of ill-will or disagreement . . . but . . . as soon as they . . . were out of sight of the mill . . . the lady called to her spouse . . . and in peremptory tones ordered him to put it down. At this point I appeared upon the scene, when the wife pretended to have no desire to take the burden, until I asked if the man was her "umfazi" (wife). *Then she at once fired up, and asked what the "umlungas" (white people) at the mill meant by the insult upon her? Was she an "ingane" (infant)? Was her "indoda" (husband) a boy? No, he was an "ibuto" (warrior), and she was his head "umfazi"* [emphasis added]. Whereupon she indignantly vindicated her outraged rights, by seizing upon the treacle pot, . . . elevating it upon her head, and bearing it off in triumph. . . . [64]

Another incident recounted by the Reverend Joseph Jackson while on a tour of villages near Verulam in 1861 suggests what African women must have thought about the Western ideal of womanhood, again—most importantly—in their own terms. Jackson recorded his disgust on finding young women at these homesteads in a state of almost entire nudity. But when scolded for their "immodesty of fashion," the women laughed shamelessly, then flatly told the good reverend, "we are not white people."[65]

European Masters in the African Servant's Perspective

[T]his you will find to be the great difficulty, that the Kafirs will pay honor to one only of the missionary body; all the others they will regard as subordinate. With the Kafir, everyone is either *inkosi* (chief) or *inja* (dog); and many, who think they ought all to be placed on terms of perfect equality, cannot brook that others should receive this distinguishing honor, rather than themselves or their husbands.[66]

Aside from defining the individual's position in the colonial workplace, similar archaic codes and values bound African laborers in their selection of employers and strongly prejudiced them against accepting instructions from any but their own master. White employers motivated by pragmatic concerns acknowledged that if they were to retain the services presently being offered, they had either to give way to the idiosyncrasies of their peasant workers, or alternatively make do without indigenous labor supplies altogether.

No adequate account would claim to analyze African perceptions of European masters while neglecting the related subject—the estimation in which blacks viewed themselves as people. For whatever the extent of psychological damage inflicted by the system of apartheid, there is no getting round the fact that preceding the period of subjugation and institutionalized racism, Africans thought they were the greatest people in the world, and this was especially true of the Zulu. They possessed a tremendous sense of self-value and confidence, a measure of which can be seen in the personal characteristics noted by whites, who were impressed by the Zulu's dignified bearing, the haughty demeanor of the king's warriors (the same "impudent airs" noted later in the male population in Natal), the meticulous care given to their personal appearance, and the overwhelming pride in the blackness of their skin. This last calls to mind a conversation that took place in 1824 between Henry Fynn and the Zulu king, about which the former related:

> Shaka went on to speak of the gifts of nature, or, as they term it, *uMvelingqangi*. He said that the first forefathers of the Europeans had bestowed on us many gifts by giving us all the knowledge of arts and manufactures, yet they had kept from us the greatest of all gifts, such as a good black skin, for this does not necessitate the wearing of clothes to hide the white skin, which was not pleasant to the eye. He well knew that for a black skin we would give all we were worth in the way of our arts and manufactures.[67]

When declaiming his attributes, the people routinely saluted the king with the praise, "Hail! Thou who art black (or awe inspiring)!"[68] Such praises were more than deferential expressions of royal adulation. That the average Zulu shared the same self-image of beauty and special worth comes across vividly in Mrs. Shooter's description of Natal Africans. She writes, "their colour is a dark brown, almost like old mahogany; and of this shade they are very proud; and consider it the perfection of beauty." She goes on to state how it amused her to taunt the "lighter-coloured Kafirs" by telling them they were "quite like white men. Sometimes they became angry," she wrote, "and protested vehemently that they were not white." Shooter's own workers, "who were the regulation colour, used to stand by grinning and enjoying the others' mortification."[69]

From the foregoing one naturally would expect that the notion of superiority based on skin color negatively impinged on master-servant relations. It did, and with irritating certainty. The issue, however, is whether this matter was viewed differently by Africans and whites. We know that to the former, dark skin was aesthetically valued, but other than that no overriding significance was attached to one's pigmentation. Europeans took the matter to perverse extremes. Color differences profoundly shaped their cultural ideologies and constituted a "natural" social barrier to normal human interactions. Moreover, their aberrant ideas about the "aristocracy of skin" made them feel entitled to the deference, submission, and service that Africans were accustomed to bestowing only upon their great women and men. Not only did Africans hold to a different view, but initially a profound sense of disgrace was attached to working for white people.

The celebrated philologist Wilhelm H. I. Bleek tells of his servant, Umayamane, whom he had hired in Zululand, but who ran away because "he could not bear to be called the kaffir of the *umlungu* (white man) by the other fellows."[70] The swear word *ikhafula* in Zulu country referred to a Natal African under the yoke of whites; free Zulu served none but their king.[71] The ignominy of being associated with the *umlungu* had little to do with the latter's genetic misfortune in being born white; rather, the attitude may largely be explained by the fact that British Natal had yet to demonstrate valor and military qualities worthy of Zulu respect. So of two things we may be sure: first, though many factors encouraged intercourse between Africans and Europeans in Natal, frightened reverence or awe of the white man was not one of them. Second, and this should not occasion astonishment, the settlers' overbearing attitudes stemming from their own racism tended to exacerbate an already difficult situation and caused incalculable injury to master-servant relations.

In the discussion to follow we will touch upon the personal qualities and material incentives that attracted workers to European employers.

"Praises Give a Man Personality"

Almost every adult male in Zulu society was possessed by the ambition to achieve a measure of greatness outside the domestic complex. Only a few, however, had sufficient means or sufficient personality to inspire the confidence required to accomplish such a goal. One became an *isikhulu* (a "big man," a person of some power and respectability), or an *inkosi* (chief) by gathering a retinue. Followings were built up in several basic ways. An individual came by adherents either as a birth right, or because he possessed sterling qualities or special abilities, or as a result of having control over a special set of conditions from which others could derive benefits in exchange for their subordination. Various oral accounts describe in detail how these situations evolved. Among the many anecdotes, for instance, is the testimony of Mahaya kaNongqaba, who relates how a man of junior rank wishing to gather a following usually made a point of treating old men and old women hospitably; such open-handedness induced his elders as well as others to follow him to set up independently elsewhere.[72] Then there is the renowned case of Nqina, whose generosity was legend. Nqina entered Zulu country a stranger but in possession of a large herd of white cattle that he lavishly slaughtered to gain favor with his neighbors. By popular acclaim his homestead earned the name *abakwaHlabisa* (the people who entertained well with meat feasts). As time passed the Hlabisa rose to great prominence and eventually married into the Zulu royal clan.[73] Another classic way in which this social dynamic found expression was for a kraalhead to come into possession of either a healthy, well-watered stretch of arable land (a region "where calves did not die") or a place where there was room for many gardens and a plentiful supply of firewood and then invite others to join him. And because of his claim to firstcomer status, the people *khonza*'d (submitted themselves to) him, whereupon they were guided to the new settlement.[74]

Under pressure of extreme want, individuals, distressed family groups, and so on, were impelled into relations of dependency. The need for physical protection from ill-disposed neighboring chiefdoms and dangerous marauders motivated others to enter relationships of subordination. But apart from obtaining subsistence security and a safe haven from wanton attacks, people unburdened their grievances to the holders of power and authority and looked to them to intercede peacefully in conflict situations arising in their everyday lives. A person of chiefly rank was looked upon as the "nurse of the land," the source of all things required for one's total well-being. In addition, then, to feeding, sheltering, and providing health care for his followers and propitiating the ancestors, it was the duty of the chief to listen to the grievances of his people and, when necessary, treat with higher authorities on their behalf. These were the qualities of *ubukhosi* (the highest state of goodness, kindness, and mercy) which made an *inkosi*.[75] Thus, whenever an ordinary person entreated a man of rank to show compassion or generosity, he did so by reminding him, "but you are an *inkosi*."[76] The other side of these reciprocal relations binding chiefs to followers and patrons to clients was the dependent's unquestioning devotion and obedience given in loyal service.[77]

The reader should experience no surprise to learn that both Africans and Europeans sought to establish similar attachments with each other.[78] We need only instance the extraordinary careers of Henry Fynn, George Ogle, Nathaniel Isaacs, and other Port Natal traders who set themselves up as "white chiefs" in Shaka's time to make this point. Other examples, perhaps less spectacular, are seen in the colonial period.[79] Would-be clients were ever on the lookout for a man of position and limitless hospitality, as well as such other inducements that "stopping at" the *isikhulu's* homestead might offer. Likewise, non-African patrons were forever contriving ways to draw labor onto their farms, plantation estates, or mission stations. Etherington shows, for example, that it was those missions with the best land that attracted large bodies of adherents (i.e., squatter kraals).[80] In the same way, white farmers often ploughed pieces of land especially for the use of any Africans who might come to work, and as an inducement for them to settle. The cost of ploughing was usually repaid in labor on the farm.[81] The point is that any one or all of these factors favorably inclined the prospective worker in his selection of a master. On the other hand, the decision about "where to stop" could, and often did, hinge on much weightier considerations than those cited above.

For returnees it always came back to the same vital issue—that of finding a guardian for the entire family unit, an employer who could be persuaded to maintain all the surviving group members, rather than indiscriminately scattering the women and children throughout the several districts of the colony. Other apprehensions had to be allayed as well, such as whether the refugees would be allowed to retain the few head of cattle secreted into the district, or whether their livestock would be reported by the farmer and turned over to the authorities as contraband. Alternatively, if the family were destitute of livestock, would loan cattle be provided for the children? Would a sufficient amount of land be allotted for family cultivation? and so on.[82]

Major attention was given to securing a shield of protection against induction into *isibhalo* labor gangs. Weighing heavily on the minds of young men going out in search of work, sometimes overshadowing all other issues, was the question of whether the *umlungu* (white man) would be amenable to apply on the young man's behalf for relief from the oppressive labor tax.[83] Thus the choice of whether to enter into, or continue in, the service of any one master depended largely on a combination of the following considerations: the general character of the employer (i.e., did the *umlungu* exhibit compassion, as well as other sympathetic qualities of an *inkosi*?); his willingness to guarantee immunity from government impositions, especially the onerous labor tax; and the material advantages offered by the particular job.

How then did these peasant workers go about locating masters?

Rarely did Africans enter work engagements without first reconnoitring from a distance the farm or household they had taken a fancy to and, then, before coming to closer quarters, carefully ascertaining from the gossip of the neighborhood the general conditions of labor and the treatment they might expect.[84] Complained one farmer in 1866,

> [The applicant] reverses the position of master and servant in Europe, brings no character with him when he seeks employment.... [H]is first enquiry, whilst snuffing and chatting with others of the same colour, idling in their work under the shade of a convenient tree, is—What is the master's character? Is he indulgent? Is he easily deceived?—and if the replies are not to his satisfaction, he takes up his bed and proceeds further on his journey, until he has found an employer sufficiently loose in his management to satisfy my Kafir gentleman's ideas of comfortable service.[85]

Traditionally a special functionary called the *imbongi* (praise singer or poet) chronicled all the notable as well as disreputable feats and exploits in the king's and his ancestors' lives. According to Mafeje, the main function of this individual, the South African bard, was and is to articulate the sentiments of the people. Thus the topics emphasized were generally determined by contemporary social events. Being concerned mainly with the welfare of the nation and as the leading public critic, the praise singer not only celebrated great battles and recited royal genealogies; in addition, he expressed the "people's conscience" when he criticized the king's abuse of power and neglect of his responsibilities. Another role of the African bard was to uphold the moral norm by exhorting the general populace to obey the laws and respect the ways of their forefathers. Dread of public censure, fear of the "power of the word" should one stray from community standards made the *imbongi* a powerful force for social control.[86]

Anyone in Nguni society could become an *imbongi*, a composer and reciter of poems.[87] In like manner, every person, whether of high birth or modest station, was commemorated in praise poems or songs (as were certain species of fauna and even some inanimate objects). "Praises g[a]ve a man personality, indicated the esteem in which he was held by his people, and showed his value to the community." Every Zulu, Bryant tells us, possessed a string of praise names, each *isibongo* (name) being awarded at those stages in life when rites of passage were performed. In addition, cognomens were appended either in recognition of some heroic achievement or in remembrance of some disgraceful or cowardly act; individuals were also given descriptive monikers to highlight quirks in character, and so forth.[88]

Everything about the African seemed to irritate and annoy the white man. On the other hand, the biggest challenge confronting the African was trying to figure out what, within reason, would satisfy "master." So it is no wonder that those laborers who came into contact with the European, if for none other than defensive purposes, took up the habit of scrutinizing the latter's personality and alien ways, searching for comprehension, seeking out the white man's redeeming traits, yet noticing every blemish and flaw at the same time. From the settler's perspective, of course, it was aggravating to know that when "their blacks" were sitting closely huddled around the evening fires, they conversed earnestly upon these matters and in the most irreverent and graphic details imaginable. Usually it was here at such gatherings that the employer came to be commemorated in traditional verse or infamously branded in satirical songs.

This genre of verbal art still has entertainment value and great practical uses as well. Nor is it difficult to see how the concept of expressing the "people's conscience" through the oral art of praising came to be adapted to the new socioeconomic conditions of the nineteenth-century workplace. Such an idea suggests an important area of focus for comprehending the early stirrings of worker consciousness.[89] Certainly, contemporary whites were aware that potentially damaging information contained in some of the poems and satires was disseminated among all the people by migrants returning from employment, and that these forms of communication had a subsequent impact on determining the direction of the flow of labor.

The system worked something like this. Once minute observations of the employer had been made, the next step was to give the mistress or master a nickname derived from some singularity of character or manner. These nicknames or descriptive phrases were so carefully thought out and so sharply accurate in detail that it was often possible to recognize a stranger when he or she visited their kraals. The remarkable thing is that in consequence of this practice, as one settler in 1846 informs us, the name of a good or bad master or mistress was made known from one end of the colony to the other.[90] This cultural form represented not only an obvious medium for transmitting information respecting jobs and employers; it was an ideal channel through which the migrant work force could assess general market conditions and broadcast their grievances. We will have more to say about this institution in a later chapter.

The main point to be stressed here is that this informal communications network (which some writers have interpreted as "hidden forms of labor protest"),[91] was in operation long before the white man came. The decision of where and to whom to subordinate oneself was an act of enormous import requiring serious thought and calculated reasoning. Operating from intelligent self-interest, Africans contemplated well the merits and drawbacks before making such a move. Stated somewhat differently, their efforts to discover working conditions on European farms (or later at the diamond mines or at the gold fields), as well as their attempts to become acquainted by repute with the master's or mistress's character, were the same commonsense strategies traditionally employed before one made the decision to *khonza* (to enter service) at the place of some locally based "big man."[92]

To briefly sum up this section: such evidence as we have suggests that masters who judiciously managed their laborers, who understood the more subtle aspects of chiefship, and who played the game had less difficulty in maintaining a reliable work force.

The important thing not to lose sight of is the fact that ordinary people accepted the hierarchical ethic. As Henry Callaway noted in his journal in 1860:

The Kafirs have their gentlemen and nobles as well as ourselves and can detect high and low breeding as quickly and perhaps more so than the generality of white men.[93]

For this reason, I have endeavored to show that of the set of factors directing their social behavior, advancement to rank (which enabled one to establish a family settlement and raise "seeds" to perpetuate the clan), was the prime *raison d' être* of the common man. Kraalship, "the inalienable possession of manhood," indicated one's economic independence, and civil and social place. "Greatness of house" was determined by the number of one's wives and children, the size of one's herds, and the quantity of one's grain stores. The social ideal was to become a member of the propertied class.

A logical presumption following from this is that poverty-stricken individuals, people not living in their own kraals or those of close kin, lacked social weight; moreover, so long as these persons remained in a degraded state, less respect was accorded them in the community. This knowledge gives us a place to stand, so to speak, in order to gain a perspective on the ways in which Africans might have conceptualized whites. For it seems likelier still that the qualities they praised and admired most in themselves—the criteria by which northern Nguni-speaking people recognized status—were also the measures by which they evaluated individual Europeans, and that very probably these criteria were used as a yardstick to determine the acceptability of whites as masters. Hard evidence of this is not altogether lacking.

Many of the settlers who arrived in Natal under the auspices of the Byrne colonization scheme (1849–1851) failed miserably as pioneers from want of spirit, ignorance of farming, and lack of capital to carry out enterprises they had begun. Destitution drove most of these emigrants to the towns, where some became temporary servants in households of the more well-to-do. Others found farm employment as supervisors or overseers of groups of African laborers. Such information as we have on these poor whites comes mainly from the diary of Eliza Whigham Feilden, one of the more prosperous settlers.

Eliza, who arrived in Natal with her husband in 1852, was, as previously noted, an individual of competent observation and remarkable good sense. During the five years they remained in the settlement, Mr. and Mrs. Feilden (later Sir John and Lady Eliza) employed a number of Africans and whites in their Durban home and on their farm, Feniscowles, located four miles from town. As Eliza was directly involved in the domestic management of both establishments, it became possible for her to acquire a firsthand knowledge of her African laborers. The chief value of her diary lies in the fact that she managed to capture and faithfully record rare insights into the class biases, job attitudes, and *modus operandi* of these nineteenth-century black workmen. The diary is practically a running commentary upon the issues that seem to have created the most tension between her black and white workers.

One learns immediately that while their African laborers liked Mr. Feilden as a master and worked well with him, that same group did not work well under the supervision of the white overseer, for "they felt no respect for the man."[94] In fact, Eliza discovered that they obeyed her better; thus when her husband was away she occasionally would "go and stand by them, which they [did] not dislike."[95]

In another place we are informed that two Africans "[had] struck work under Davenport at the farm, they don't like the man, telling him there is enough for them to do over here in the garden. . . . "[96] These tedious, seemingly endless, petty conflicts punctuated the workaday routine at Feniscowles; and a root cause of at least some of the hostility being directed at Feilden's white servants can be found in these intensely revealing remarks by Eliza:.

> Poor Ginger is very handy for a Caffre, but growing quite lazy with Mrs. Welsh, *upon whom, and all of her class, he looks with extreme contempt* [emphasis added], and when squatted on the ground will ask her to hand things to him. She is rather fearful of exercising the authority I tell him she has. *He says to her, "you are poor people, but me is a gentleman* [emphasis added]; me have plenty of mealies, and plenty of oats. When me in craal me do no work; me wife make fire, gather wood, cook food, and she say "Now you come eat."[97]

With a twinge of exasperation she writes three years later:

> These Caffres are a queer set. The little oxherd told Mrs. Smith to-day that she and Smith were servants, and so was he himself, but his *father* was *not* a servant. This is the second instance that has come to my ears in which our servants have been told this. The Caffres are really more free than Englishmen.[98]

These two excerpts need no comment beyond stating that the fundamental conflict was conditioned by the African peasant worker's perceptions of social rank. As a general rule, what gave a commoner status was the social and economic weight that inhered in the kraalship itself. Poor whites who possessed none of the prestige symbols of a successful social career (land, cattle, and so on) were viewed with as much contempt as kraalless black menials. By one route was it possible to rise to "gentlemanly position": a man became an *umnumzana*, his wife an *inkosikazi*, when he acquired an *umuzi* (kraal, a family settlement) and the material wealth that title implied.

We can take this a step further. Early observers frequently made a point of telling us that the African worker "serve[d] the white man quite as much because he is an 'inkosi,' or chief, as because he is a payer of wages."[99] In traditional society, Africans had a great sense of obedience and gave loyal service strictly to their lawful chief, although the latter often delegated authority through *izinduna* (headmen), who themselves were selected for qualities the common folk were bound to respect. The evidence bears out the view that migrant workers, especially the "raw" recruits, initially perceived themselves not so much as being in a pure wage relationship with European masters, as being in a classic patron-client arrangement. This explains why some laborers stoutly refused to take instructions from anyone but their (white) *inkosi* or *inkosikazi*. (With experience and accumulated knowledge, however, African notions matured and their actions became increasingly sophisticated.) We revert to the words fitly spoken by the Reverend Allison at the beginning of this section, the point being that Africans adhered to an uncomplicated code, which allowed them to honor only one of the missionary body, and to regard all others as subordinates.[100] His remarks support those made by others in entirely different contexts, of which William Baldwin provides an excellent illustration.

Baldwin embarked on a hunting expedition to Zululand and wrote, "near the Umvoti [river], forty miles from Durban, we each hired a kaffir to attend upon us individually, it being strictly prohibited to order another man's kaffirs to do anything for you, as they have a great objection to wait on any but their own master. . . . "[101] On more than one occasion, masters and mistresses spoke candidly of the "strong native stubbornness of disposition," for African servants did what they believed themselves bound to do, and then no more. Again, we are permitted to see this in the following extract taken from the pages of Eliza's journal.

> Ginger refused to clean the boots of a gentleman who was staying in our house, saying they were not his master's boots. I made him clean them, but again he declined cleaning Mrs. Brenton's when she stayed with me. He eyed them all over, as if measuring, looked at my foot, and shook his head. I told him he must clean them, and I believe he did, but I was not strict to inquire, and after a struggle of this kind for mastery, though I succeeded at the moment, I did not generally try it again, lest I should come off the loser.[102]

Thus far this book has focused on the forces guiding and shaping northern Nguni performance in the colonial work centers. More specifically, I have tried to identify and analyze regularities in their behavior, patterns that could be said to be in conformity with principles governing African work habits. As the preceding discussion has shown, the cultural logic that intertwined status, seniority, and occupation played a critical role in both facilitating and impeding interactions and performance at the workplace. Outside their internally sanctioned environments, cultural traditions about work and masters continued to be passed along. Jobs in which Africans hired out in the European areas were prescribed by rules of precedence and hierarchy in much the same way that task assignments were dictated in northern Nguni society. Very similar rules greatly influenced workers in their selection of employers, and also caused them to manifest a degree of feeling amounting to class prejudice against subordinate agents, poor whites who had been assigned to supervise their work.

Underneath this layer of explicit assumptions ordering their day-to-day lives, there existed a deeper strand of implicit beliefs, which, though seldom expressed in words, were nonetheless unquestioningly obeyed by every member of the society. These unspoken assumptions exercised a powerful influence on people's behavior and the ways in which they experienced the world. This "unconscious grammar" is the main focus of the next chapter.

4

"Kafir Time," Wage Claims, and Other Sociocultural Antecedents of Togt, or Day Labor

A curious irony is that the "lazy Kafir" myth crystallized in Natal at a time when Africans were dramatically responding to the commercial economy. But as spectacular as their involvement was, whites were almost uniformly unsparing in their ridicule. Why was this? To start with, it is important to recognize that colonists who had invested capital in the country felt vexed because the labor needed to bring returns on their investments was not forthcoming. After several years of failed enterprises and building frustrations, colonists regarded with disfavor any display of African industry that did not involve their undertaking extended work engagements in European employ. Independent black initiatives were acknowledged only grudgingly, their advances often disparaged as desultory and primitive. Indeed, the popular rhetoric was so interwoven with facile assumptions and racist mythology that the imagery became increasingly confused in the colonists' minds until it was difficult to discern reality from fiction.

Weighing up the evidence objectively, even a disinterested party would be pressed to explain the great body of data that lent verisimilitude to the critics' charges. Viewed superficially, there seemed little in the African's behavior towards wage employment to contradict the perceptions of the "lazy Kafir." Africans either could not or would not fulfill the terms of their contracts, often absconding from service requiring steady manual labor. Even more confusing was the tendency for peasant workers in the towns and in some sectors of rural industry to insist on marketing their labor for the briefest of terms—that is, by the day or even some fraction of a day.

In other words, Natal's internal labor market looked very different from the way we imagine it should have been. Whatever else could be said, it was totally unex-

78

pected to find workers being drawn in the above direction. If the returnees were indeed attempting to recover from a series of wrenching crises, as has been demonstrated above, why were they apparently withholding the commodity that could have hastened rebuilding their crippled economy? Great as their distress was, how do we account for the litany of complaints that Africans would not work, and what possible construction, other than the "lazy Kafir," should we ascribe to this state of affairs? These issues are much too large to ignore, and giving attention to them will expand our understanding of Natal's labor problem.

The state of the colonial money market, the seasonal nature of colonial industries, and the long debate over municipal housing for African workers were partly responsible for shaping the labor situation. Together these factors provide plausible explanations as to why and how day labor developed into a system embodying a set of rules and regulations sanctioned by government proclamation in 1874, and much later by an Act of Parliament in 1902. The trouble with this rather unextraordinary confluence of ingredients is it adds little to our understanding of the nineteenth-century African workman, who, after all, is the focus of this study. As such the aim here must be to ascertain in some concrete ways what *togt* (or *itoho*, day labor) meant to the black participants in the casual labor market. Who were these "*togt* men"? where did they come from? how was this large body of urban casuals organized, if indeed they *were* organized; and why the great popularity of *togt*? are some of the questions I propose to address.

It has often been suggested that *togt* appealed to Africans as much because it suited their "irregular working habits" as because of the considerably better pay received in day service compared with wages received in monthly employ. "Jobbers" averaged 2s. 6d. per diem, while the earnings of general laborers and domestic workers under master-servant contracts was anywhere from ten to twenty shillings per month. We shall return to the problem of wage earnings, which is fundamental to any study of this nature. But first we should consider the possibility that employers intent on imposing a work discipline had somehow infringed upon traditional practices, and that the mischief this caused led to an increasing disaffection of workers from long-term engagements. The sources leave little room for doubt on these matters. A systematic examination of the documents will reveal the nature of those violations.

As in E. P. Thompson's article on the temporal reorientation of the English working class,[1] so this section of this chapter seeks to examine basic cultural phenomena ordering and coordinating the daily activities of the Natal Zulu; it aims to explore changes in time perceptions—the shift from peasant to industrial time—as they were experienced by these northern Nguni speakers on coming into contact with a society undergoing early stages of capitalist growth; and it concretely demonstrates how Christianity aided the transitional process. This analysis, however, must be understood in the context of a settler-based colonial regime, in which the master and servant represented totally different social worlds and operated from systems of logic that eluded mutual comprehension. The friction caused by this state of affairs was considerable and may be seen as one of the potent factors blocking Natal's advancement along industrial lines. We begin with comments made in 1846 by the planter "H. W. L." His remarks are important because they put the problem into immediate perspective.

I am not one of those, who, when they arrive in a settlement, because they see a number of blacks infer that they have a right to the labor of those persons, and that if they will not work for them they are set down as lazy scoundrels. But I am one of those who maintain that *if a number of Kaffers come voluntarily and offer their service, and accept service at a given rate of money wages, and for a specified time, that I have a right to the services of those persons, until the time expires* [emphasis added].[2]

A basic tenet of economics states that labor, like any commodity bought and sold, is purchased by measure. That is, a certain quantity or number of units is obtained for the price paid. For example, land is purchased by the acre, meat by the pound, cloth by the yard, and so on. The measure for labor is based on *time*, and a man may contract to buy or sell labor by the year, the month, the day, or by the hour. (One could also engage by the job, piece, or gross.) Generally, this form of exchange operates smoothly enough *unless*, and this is the crucial point, the buyer's and the seller's modes of measuring the commodity differ.

Put simply, time was at the nexus of the "Kafir labor problem." No sooner was a work agreement made than confusion arose from the disparate notions of the white employer and his African employee regarding the computation of time. In other words, the record of persistent desertions from service was in very many instances related to the fact that the terms of master-servant contracts, which were based on European units of measure, did not accord with the African mode of temporal reckoning.

"Inyanga Ifile! Siphe Imali Yethu!"("The Moon Is Dead! Give Us Our Money!")

How is the moon at present? [asked the master.] It is the new moon (the first quarter; full moon; the last quarter) [replied the servant].
    Listen, now, to what I say, and don't forget it [instructed the master]. When the moon becomes just as it is now, then say it is one month.[3]

Like most preindustrial people, the Zulu used the moon and stars to keep track of time. The season of cultivation was announced by the *isilimela*, the star cluster called the Pleiades. Early stargazers observed also that the evening star, *isicelankobe*, appeared when men were asking for boiled maize, their evening meal; and that *indosa* rose before the morning star, *ikwezi*, when night was advanced.[4]

Inyanga, the word for moon, was also the name by which the Zulu called their "moon period" or lunar month. They computed time by the phases of the moon and the annual cycle was divided into thirteen "moons,"[5] each associated with ecological changes and social activities that represented time indicators for holidays and seasons. For example, *uncwaba* was the new grass moon, the month in which the land took on a rich, dark green hue; *umasingana*, the moon of the new season's food, was the time of the annual rites of the first fruits; and during *untlaba*, the red flower of the aloe came forth, hence "moon of the aloes."

The circuit of the *inyanga* was about twenty-eight days. *Inyanga ifile* ("the moon is dead"), that is the interlunary period, "the moonless day when every one paid respect to the darkness," was traditionally observed as an unlucky or sacred day of abstinence from work and pleasure seeking.[6] Certain diplomatic enterprises, for instance, fell under this avoidance. Miss Colenso reports that the deputation of Zulu leaders on behalf of the exiled Cetshwayo could not conduct business on the day of the new moon. The resident magistrate told the chiefs that he could not hear them because it was Sunday, and they must therefore come the following day. The chiefs reminded him that "the morrow was their own (Zulu) 'sacred day,' " on which the chiefs might not enter upon a new undertaking. "We had no Sundays in Zululand," recalled Mpatshana kaSodondo, "what we went by was the waning of the moon."[7] When the new moon made her appearance important undertakings were commenced with confidence of success.

Coming as they did from a culture that had adopted and adapted precision instruments and other convenient methods of timekeeping—watches, clocks, and solar calendars, which contained months of irregular and capricious lengths (e.g., twenty-eight, twenty-nine, thirty, or thirty-one days)—whites contemptuously referred to the lunar reckonings as the "Kafir month." The complications arising from the two systems of time notations were enormous, as this agitated correspondence from "C. P.," dated (and this is the pivotal clue) 29 October 1846, attests.

> This afternoon, because I would not pay a Kafir *whose month is up on the last day of the month, I was abused like a thief* [emphasis added]. He shook his stick at me, and was so violent that if I could have got assistance, I would have sent him to the tronk [jail]. . . . [8]

The following observations made in 1855 by the missionary Alfred Rivett carry more evidentiary weight.

> The month of service (their wages are paid monthly) begins with the new moon, but often before it is quite completed, they will come to their master, asking for their money, and although the month is not ended they will declare it is by an appeal to the fact that the moon "inyanga file" is dead. *They cannot understand there being more than 28 days in a month. It is impossible to make them believe there are 31* [emphasis added]. . . . [9]

Confusion surrounding this issue led to notable incidents such as the 1858 strike among "Kafir mail carriers." This involved ten men who had been hired for six months (from 2 July to 2 January) to carry mail between Durban and Pietermaritzburg. Evidently, "by some process of their own," the postmen "arrived at the conclusion that their engagement expired on the 28th December." The situation was made all the worse because of the strikers' stubborn insistence on their "unwritten and ignorant system of computing time in opposition to the statements of the Postmaster and the interpreter." To ensure the incident would have no imitators, severe punishments rather than fines and light jail sentences were recommended.[10]

What stands forth most clearly is that resorting to summary punishments (including such draconian measures as floggings and extended stretches in jail) to discipline preindustrial workers around the question of time had the effect of driving labor from the market. Yet employers seemed astonishingly slow to learn this lesson, and were slower still in taking constructive steps to rectify what would prove to be a long-standing problem. Years later, in 1894, a colonist was prompted to suggest that provision be made for "the boys in town [for] a lecturer or teacher who would, say, once a week, impart free instructions on the European method of computation of time." This perceptive individual pointed out that

[i]f it could be explained to them that they are not engaged by the lunar month, it would save much difficulty. *At present in very many cases, either the master or mistress must give way to the ignorance of the monthly servant, or the native thinks he has been cheated of his time* [emphasis added]. . . . Many a score of good, hardworking boys found themselves landed in the gaol in consequence of disagreements with their employers, caused in the first instance by their inability to reckon their own time, *and then the case is frequently aggravated by the employer being unable to explain matters in the native language* [emphasis added]. . . . [11]

Several details arising from this passage merit attention. First, it makes clear the workers' attitude regarding efforts to impose a foreign system of reckoning time: they saw it as an attempt to cheat them. Second, to mollify servants, employers had either to submit to indigenous usages or to risk the workers' precipitate withdrawal from the market. Another point made explicit was the quality of labor—"Many a score of good, hardworking boys"—alienated from wage employment in consequence of such disputes. Finally, the last-raised issue, namely, recognition that the mutual inability to communicate needs was a major factor aggravating master-servant relations, will be examined in depth.

The Reverend C. W. Posselt's prefatory comments in his Zulu–English phrase book, published in 1850 "to facilitate intercourse with the natives," catch the blatant mood of cultural chauvinism prevailing in the settlement. Posselt's conviction was that "mistresses and masters [did] not want to know the barbaric dialect of their servants beyond the small circle of subjects which [had] an immediate reference to the kind of labor wherein natives were employed. . . ." [12] The sentiments evoked by these words no doubt helped to perpetuate a general contempt for Zulu culture. Particularly noticeable was the almost total ignorance of Zulu and the indifference as to acquiring it exhibited by the white colonists. [13] Settlers deigned only to learn a hybrid version of the language, called Fanagalo. [14] Rarely was the effort made to master proper Zulu so as to obtain a clear sense of Zulu terms and phrases. The word *inyanga*, for instance, was translated as "month" to conform with European time units; it was not seen as expressing the lunar seasonal phenomena of the Zulu *inyanga*. Yet such deliberate perversions or "mistranslations" led to the most serious consequences, as Carl Faye, an interpreter in the Native Affairs Department, cautioned:

It is not advisable, when interpreting, to give the name of an English calendar month as the equivalent of a Zulu lunar month; the two do not begin together, nor do they end together, and besides the Zulu name is expressive in a way peculiar all to itself: then again the seasons themselves are not always identically the same each year, and a mistake in interpreting may have a very important bearing on some question or other and lead to serious consequences. *It is advisable therefore to give the original Zulu name given by a Native, and if the meaning of it be required, to ask the Native himself for it and then give it up in that way* [emphasis added]. [15]

Problems also arose owing to the absence of a concept in Zulu to denote *year*. Take the word *unyaka*, or *umnyaka*. A. T. Bryant tells us that Europeans "quite mistakenly" assumed this term signified "year." However, to the traditional Zulu, the word had quite another meaning. Their annual cycle was divided into two seasons of which both had approximately six "moons"; *unyaka*, the rainy or field work season; and *ubusika*, the dry or winter season. The point is the two *were entirely separate and distinct*.[16]

Two things seem fairly evident. First, it was no accident that the word denoting the time of greatest activity and importance in the Zulu work schedule was redefined to correspond with the Western calendar. Second, few individuals were better suited to corrupt the Zulu language systematically than were missionaries, who pioneered publishing works in the vernacular, including phrase books, dictionaries, and grammars.

Religion is a vehicle for disseminating culture and, in carrying forth their civilizing mission, the "soldiers of Christianity" sought, among other things, to inculcate industry, the moral of steady work. "Our natives will not be anything," the missionary Charles Kilbon observed, "if they do not feel the propriety and necessity of forming habits of industry and frugality, as their easy going ways do not furnish favorable soil for the Gospel."[17] Thus we find early missionaries such as the Reverend Henry Callaway resolving "to make the Kafirs around [his mission station] feel as much as possible the value of time, labor and skill."[18] With this plainly being a directed objective, it must have seemed entirely appropriate to stretch the bounds of the preindustrial *unyaka* to incorporate the notion of a more stable, continuous duration of labor.

How did this exercise in cultural engineering work itself out in practice? Consider a work seeker being told by a settler-farmer, *"Ngiya kukuthola umnyaka wonke."*[19] Such verbal contracts in fact were constantly entered into if found mutually agreeable. A translation of the arrangement, however, reveals the rub: "I shall hire you for the whole year [twelve moons]," was the farmer's version of the contract. But, and this is an important qualification, to the traditional Zulu the above sentence, loosely rendered, translates: "I shall hire you for the whole of the field work season [six moons]." This discrepancy makes more meaningful the following statement by the magistrate of Alexandra in 1868: "The period of six months continues here to be the maximum term of service, and it seems as if the Kafir was unable to [perceive] the idea of a longer unbroken term of exertion."[20]

In other words, masters and servants would often be working at cross-purposes without their being aware of it. But sensible employers requiring a year-round work force managed to avoid labor difficulties by adopting the relay method. This involved a private arrangement between a colonist and the head of a homestead, the latter agreeing to provide a continuous, circulating supply of labor.[21]

"Kafir Time" Versus the Rhythms of Commercial Agriculture

"Abantu basebenza ngelanga." ("The people work by the sun, or day.") While there are Zulu expressions indicating the various divisions of the day, it should be noted that only the lighted portion of that "twenty-four hour" period, from the rising to the setting of the sun—the Zulu day—was called by the same name as the sun, *ilanga*.[22] Peasant notions about the length of the working day thus provided another area of contention. The crisis was most noticeable in commercial agriculture where "Kafir time" had a profoundly adverse effect on the development of sugar plantations.

Aside from the daily passage of the sun across the sky and the natural rotation of the seasons, Edward Hall suggests that the fundamental tempo and rhythms of life are dictated by a foundation of unspoken assumptions (primary-level culture), accepted as unquestioned reality, which control everything we do.[23] Hall's fascinating discussion of this "other dimension of time" leads us to a wider consideration of northern Nguni cosmography.

Zulu society provides an apt setting for this kind of analysis because their universe was filled with frightening phenomena over which they exercised little control. The belief in unseen and evil influences was intensely real and universally prevalent among the people. They were habitually occupied with fear of being attacked by *abathakathi* (witches or evil doers), who went about at dead of night, causing sickness and death.[24] To avoid meeting these dreaded objects, the Zulu conducted their affairs in the safe light of day and refrained from going abroad at night, which, we are told, was a great consolation to the small settler community that lived among them.[25]

Along with sinister spirits, natural hazards in the physical environment posed added constraints on traditional societies. In times past, to secure immunity from fever the Zulu retired to their huts before sundown, emerging in the morning when the dew was off the grass. This adaptive response most probably originated in regions where malaria was endemic. Force of habit and continued belief in the efficacy of the custom may account for its eventual spread outside Zululand. But notwithstanding similar preventive strategies, homesteads in the more tropical colonial districts continued to suffer sicknesses thought to be environmentally related.[26]

It is important to appreciate some of this background because it helps us greatly to understand how the conventions or protective measures taken to deal with these natural and superhuman forces may have operated outside the traditional context and may ultimately have interfered with the industrial work regime on commercial sugar estates. Starting in 1849, the whole coastline of Natal was taken up in cane production. During its formative years, the plantation economy was essentially a decentralized system, which incorporated two productive processes within the ownership of one unit. One such operation was agricultural, based on the cultivation and harvesting of sugar cane. The other was industrial, involving the crushing of cane and the boiling and treatment of juice in the mill.[27]

Observations made by the successful planter Edmund Morewood raise an important point about the availability of local labor that should not be lost to view. Except at crop time, Morewood asserts, the cultivation of sugar required very little hard labor, and then, as it happened, the best time for taking off the crop fell in the slack season (*ubusika*) of the Zulu calendar, when hands were most plentiful.[28] Another point well worth noting is that, insofar as the agricultural side of the operations was concerned, no substantial readjustments were required in the temporal bearings or the labor rhythms of the work force. Where difficulty arose was around the industrial aspects of the plantation, which introduced a time routine that ran counter to indigenous conventions. These different interpretations of work time were critical. For the pressing concern of Natal planters and other early employers of African labor was *not*, as commonly assumed, "will the Kafirs work?" Rather, the big question was *whether Africans could be persuaded to submit to an extension of work hours beyond their customary active work day.*[29]

It seems few cane growers understood the rationale behind the peasant notion of a fair day's work, yet most agreed that the Africans' diurnal pattern of "late" rising and "early" retirement had a ruinous effect on the nascent industry. Robert Babbs, proprietor of the Umlass Plantation and an individual reputedly possessing "extraordinary skill in managing Kafirs,"[30] provides invaluable details regarding the peasant's disinclination to discard their traditional chronology.

> It is generally known that the Kafir looks to the sun's course to regulate his hours of labor; that "puma langa" with him, commences about an hour after sunrise, and that "shuna langa" begins with the same time before sunset. It is difficult either to induce or compel him to work either before or after those periods of the day, which have received his arbitrary definition of sunrise and sunset.[31]

Essentially the difficulty was this. The value of time fluctuated as the cycle of sugar production passed from summer to winter season. In summer there were sufficient working hours (fourteen hours of daylight) to perform routine operations such as weeding. All the heavy work, however, came at one time of the year—in winter with the harvesting and crushing. Once the cane was cut, it was important to convey it to the mill as rapidly as possible, and then carry out the crushing immediately. Neglect at this stage could ruin the quality of the sugar.[32] At the height of the manufacturing process, from June through September, when the bulk of the crop should be secured, the average of the sun's course was ten and a half hours. Allowing the peasant's definition of a work day (as between sunrise and sunset) meant the loss of two precious daylight hours. According to Babbs, ten hours of "good efficient labor without including meal times" were needed to perform only a "moderate day's work"; were laborers left to persist in their habits, a day's work could not be performed and a great amount of produce would be jeopardized, if not spoiled. Nor, he contended, was it unreasonable to demand ten working hours per day, for in Mauritius fourteen and fifteen hours were not infrequent, and similar working hours were customary in the West Indies.[33]

Sobering lessons were drawn from the experience of the Springfield Estate. Writing of the problems plaguing that new operation, the *Natal Mercury* reported:

> The proprietors have secured for the present a sufficient number of Kafirs for *day work; but it is essential to the perfect success of sugar manufacture that the operations during the season, should proceed night and day, without interruptions* [emphasis added]; and for this purpose, it will be absolutely necessary to obtain labor of a more settled and suitable character. *The aversion of our natives to night work*, and to any work in cold weather, *as well as their peculiar social habits will for a lengthened period render it impossible to rely on their labor alone* [emphasis added].[34]

Three months later in September 1855, the *Mercury's* lead article announced "The Springfield Sugar Mill [had] been closed for more than a fortnight for want of labor," forcing the proprietors, Messrs. Miller and Milner, to pay a considerable sum as compensation, as they had been prevented from manufacturing the whole ripe crop as required in terms of the agreement with the lessees of the estate. The very fate of the colony, continued the article, hung on the labor question; and it further warned that, unless the government resolved the matter by securing external supplies of labor, planters would lose heart and a great waste of capital and labor already expended on sugar and in other estates would take place.[35]

Babbs's interpretation of Springfield's misfortunes stood at variance with the editorial view. Indeed, he entertained strong objections to the "erroneous impression" conveyed in the *Mercury* account:

> Though apparently true [the article] does not convey a fair idea of the circumstances of the Springfield Estate. It is a well known fact that Kafirs would not, and will not work with the managing proprietor. It is not for me to unravel the causes, or to assign any reasons, whether it be attributable to infirmity of temper, or to unpleasant reminiscences of the past. . . . In this individual case the want of labor was the proximate cause of suspended operations; but you err, in my opinion, in drawing general conclusions as regards the future.

More illuminating still was his assessments of the state of Natal's labor market.

> Facts will not bear out what you assert; and you will find that tropical agriculture is not the forlorn hope which you represent it to be. I do not doubt that a portion of the growing crop of sugar will not be manufactured next season; but the want of labor will not be the only cause. The want of capital, and the absence of judicious and necessary arrangements will be important elements of failure.[36]

This, then, was the crucial lesson to be drawn from the difficulties experienced at the Springfield Estate and by extension, commercial agriculture in general. That the industry was undercapitalized (i.e., unable to purchase up-to-date machinery, for example) and lacked the necessary organizational and managerial skills to cope with the cultural idiosyncrasies of the work force were all potent elements in its early failures.

Mention should be made of the sugar plantations' attempts to impose an industrial discipline by apportioning piece work. As early as 1852, hiring by the job rather than for stated periods of service was recommended for cane cultivation. The chief argument for such an arrangement was that parties undertaking tasks worked more satisfactorily and got through much more in less time than the usual day labor. "It was no uncommon sight," recorded the Inanda magistrate, "to see the laborers under this system returning from the fields by noon, or shortly after, having completed their tasks for the day."[37] But despite such efforts to increase efficiency and attract labor onto the market, the response of Natal Africans was negligible.

From Peasant to Industrial Time: The Urban Context

> The eclipse on Thursday caused great consternation among the Kafirs. Some slippery togt boys tried to make out that their day was done when the darkness came on, just after 4 o'clock; and when it lightened again came back and demanded a second day's wage.[38]

The situation developed somewhat differently in the urban areas. This, however, should not be taken to mean that migrant workers completely discarded their temporal identity or that no traces of it survived in the town milieu. Even in the major European centers, Africans "succeeded in their usual stolid fashion of establishing the custom of a day's work as between 'sun up' and 'sun down.' " The "Kafir month" also continued to be problematic throughout this period. As Russell wrote in 1895,

"Our initial difficulties in regulating their hours of labor have not yet been overcome, notwithstanding a half a century of experience acquired in prisons, garrisons, railways and mining camps."[39]

Neither should one infer that the reaction of town workers to the new set of temporal boundaries was uniform. Quite rightly one would expect attitudes to vary from period to period and from one group to another. Hence, in centers like Durban and Pietermaritzburg, it is possible to discern both strenuous resistance and quite remarkable adaptive responses as well.

On coming to town, the fluctuating work force found itself caught in (to borrow Le Goff's phrase) "a chronological net,"[40] a complex fabric of merchant time, church time, leisure time controls, and so on. Along with new work routines, for example, came the regimentation of organic functions: monthly workers were obliged to alter their meal patterns to authorized intervals of breakfast, lunch, and supper, a practice contrary to the traditional custom of eating twice a day, that is, around 11:00 a.m. and 6:00 p.m. or dusk. Yet they did not readily yield to these efforts by management to coordinate job schedules. Strong attachment continued to be shown for the custom of taking meals in common. Laborers steadfastly opposed attempts to rotate mealtimes, refusing to eat till all their work mates assembled "to share in the pot."[41]

As these people came into contact with more industrialized societies, they became isolated from time cues in the natural environment. For example, mornings in Zululand were ushered in by the rising of the *ikwezi* star, around 4:00 a.m. when "the sorcerer turn[ed] back rapidly from the place where he [was] going."[42] But individuals actually awoke to a chorus of sounds: the music of beasts, birds, and insects engaged their immediate attention, for the singing or calling was kept up throughout the whole twenty-four hours constituting a day, by various animals, in turn, as their time for performing came round. From the habits of the *umngcelu* bird (pl. *imingcelu*), one of the earliest to chatter in the morning, derived the expression "*Ngiya 'uvuka imingcelu ingakakhali*" ("I shall be up before the *imingcelu* begin to chirp," that is, very early).[43] Zulu folktales also turned the singing and calling of birds into language. Thus the large black owl, called *umandubulu*, was said to say, "*Vuka, vuka, sekusile.*" ("Get up, get up, it has dawned.") About the same time the *inkovana* owl would be heard to say, "*Woza, woza, woza ngikubone.*" ("Come, come, come that I may see you.") And at Zulu homesteads the common rooster entered the vocal competition shouting, "*Woza la! Silapha!*" ("Come over here! This is where we are!") The first cockcrow announced the small hours of the night; the second crowing saluted the dawn.[44]

Man-made signals replaced this natural performance and aided town workers in determining their temporal bearings. Though public clock-time was established at Durban in 1860,[45] it is perhaps valid to say that many years would pass before the migrant population truly developed clock consciousness. Devices of a more utilitarian character, the most familiar being the time bell, regulated work and various aspects of nineteenth-century urban life.[46]

"True local time" was first recognized in 1854, when the mayor semiofficially began the practice of hoisting a flag on his tall flagstaff at five minutes before nine o'clock every morning and lowering it at nine in the evening. Burgesses questioning the accuracy of the time flag led to it being given up. Under alternative arrangements, the corporation undertook to ring St. Paul's cathedral bell every morning, "precisely at nine o'clock solar time." The bell began to chime at the hour and continued for two minutes.[47]

The practice at Pietermaritzburg, the administrative center of the colony and headquarters of the military, was to discharge a cannon at eight o'clock every morning—the hour when all African servants and laborers were expected to be at their work. Presently, the hour of gunfire was altered to nine but, as local lore has it, workers experienced difficulty phasing their inner timing mechanisms with the new starting hour of labor. Bertram Mitford recounted the familiar tale in 1881:

> [He] still persisted in sticking to the old hour, and from sheer force of habit would go to his master for his daily task. The "baas," however, would put him off: "Don't bother me now, come by-and-by when the gun fires!" "What does he say?" would be the inquiry of an expectant group when their spokesman returned. "He says 'come by-and-by.'" Directly the expected detonation was heard nearly every native throughout the city would exclaim "Haow! Ubain-bai!" and betake himself to his work. The expression stuck, and forthwith the gun became ubain-bai! among the native population of Natal, extending thence to Zululand.[48]

From Russell's historical ruminations one learns further that, "all good niggers were supposed to go to their respective places when the camp bugles recalled the military to their quarters at 9 p.m."[49]

Decisive progress towards an industrial regimen came with the imposition of the seven-day work/rest rhythm,[50] a custom transmitted throughout a large part of the world by Christianity. Africans coming into contact with missionaries were first taught the Fourth Commandment;[51] thus Sabbath observances made it incumbent upon mistresses and masters to teach such useful notions as the "week," the "week-end," and the proper time sequence of "workdays" (euphemistically termed "week-days"), for which there were no words in Zulu. Hence Monday came to be appropriately known to servants as "the turning out to work-day" (umsombuluko), Tuesday, as "work-day the second" (umsombuluko wesibili or olwesibili), and so on till Saturday, which became "the filling up or completing day" (umgqibelo). Sunday or "church day" was isonto, the name by which the "week" was also known.[52] From Ndukwana kaMbengwana we learn that

> [n]ames of days of the week came into use after [the battle of] Ndon-dakusuka [1856], and long after missionaries had entered the country [Zulu-land]. In the earlier part of Mpande's reign no names of days were in vogue. . . . There had previously been no division of time into weeks, no such thing as a week (isonto). N. knew nothing of words like Msombuluko or Mgqibelo. Time was divided into days and months, the moon being the basis for calculation. Men reckoned so many days after the moon's appearance, so many before full moon, and so many after. There was no division of time into seven day periods. Nor, as all days were alike, was there any day of rest or Sunday—it was unknown.[53]

Influences of the weekly rhythm ran shallowest in remote country districts. Employed labor on small white farms often took advantage of the Sunday proscription to earn a few additional pence working on land occupied by Indians.[54] One group of Sabbath breakers, reproved for not keeping the Lord's day, summed up their sentiments with the query: "Why did not the Lord command the monkeys to keep holy the Sabbath and not on that day to rob our gardens?"[55]

The reverse of this can be seen in the towns where the growing experience was toward an outward conformity to these new points of temporal references. There are, of course, notable reasons for this. The urban centers presented stimulating environments, challenged traditional assumptions, and fostered change. But perhaps of even greater significance were the complex nature of the urban economy and the conditions of urban labor. To generalize broadly, Africans found a number of practical advantages in recognizing the established workweek pattern, the public holidays, and other structured time intervals encountered during their town sojourn. All of this and more is indicated in the fact that at least by 1872,[56] and perhaps well before that date, segments of the cities' black laboring population were perceiving time in discrete market as well as noneconomic terms—namely, regular work time, overtime, and leisure time.

People in the urban areas were encouraged to explore a variety of choices. In this connection it is noteworthy that many young men could be found who had learned to "mark time" spent on chores, so as to attend the one-hour's school each evening in the week with master's permission or at their own insistence. At Pietermaritzburg, St. Mary's seven o'clock bell tolled the start of classes; and a "native" service was generally held twice on Sunday—one in the afternoon at three o'clock and the other in the evening at seven.[57] Attendance fluctuated very considerably, however, owing to various causes, a leading one being the migratory character of the work force, which was a bar to early mission churches having any real lasting influence.

Observance of traditional holidays regularly interrupted the flow of labor, and natural rhythms continued to have an impact on work patterns and social customs. The "moon of the new season's fruits" (*umasingana*) was widely celebrated among Natal Zulu. While this annual festival officially opened the season of plenty, the actual abundance of foodstuffs came with the gathering-in of the ripe grain from the fields, about March and April. Therefore, the common practice during the first three or four months of the year was for large numbers of Africans to withdraw to their kraals to help with the harvest and eat green mealies. This practice lessened the amount of labor in the towns and threw extra work on those who remained.

> We were told that at this season we were most unlikely to meet with a Kaffir wanting work, and that therefore we had better reconcile ourselves to the idea of doing our own work for at least two or three months.
>
> The cause of this unusual dearth of domestics is the celebration of a ceremony which, for want of another name, may be called the "Feast of Firstfruits."[58]

Before the advent of electricity for general consumption,[59] seasonal differences in the duration of daylight affected the length of the workday and other areas of social life. Missionaries frequently remarked that school attendance fell off with the brightening of days in summer, when the general practice with householders was to put off their tea an hour or more to take a walk, or engage in some outdoor occupation while the daylight continued, a custom that kept servants on the job until between eight or nine o'clock. With the return of the colder season, school attendance increased.[60]

Another factor directly contributing to irregular trends in colonial commerce was the weather. Labor demands at Durban and Pietermaritzburg, for example, fluctuated with the overberg trade, which came to a standstill in winter. Yet notwithstanding the erratic nature of town occupations, we are told that in slack spells "time was by no means frittered away." One wholesale firm managed to maintain discipline by occupying "boys" with the job of "wheeling sand from the billowy heaps in Smith Street to fill up the hollow at the back of the store."[61]

Port employment was especially at the mercy of the seasons. A busy day at Port Natal usually commenced at 7:00 a.m. and ended at 5:00 or 6:00 p.m. From the 1880s, and with improved shipping facilities, the industry grew more labor-intensive. During periods of increased trade, operations proceeded round the clock and on Sundays. By 1895 tiers of electric globes illuminated the wharfs and permitted workers to carry on with their tasks after dark.[62] Such conditions not unexpectedly gave rise to labor unrest. That dissatisfaction is vividly seen in the rich record of industrial protest among dockhands, of which time disputes were a major grievance. More than anything else, the sources convey that it was through the process of defining time as well as other concerns central to their daily existence, and in the course of struggling around these issues, that Africans gained not only a new time sense but a greater understanding of their role in the workplace. Specifically, the principal disputes were centered on demands for both the weekend and Sabbath rest days.

A usage that crystallized into town custom was the Saturday half-holiday. It came to flourish in full favor at Durban in 1856, when wholesale merchants agreed they would close their places of business at two o'clock on Saturday afternoon.[63] Subsequently the hour was pushed back to one o'clock. With the early cessation of weekend business activities came the separate social timing of organized entertainment. The whole of Pietermaritzburg, for example, men, women and children, black and white, turned out for the great weekly festival conducted by the military band in front of Government House; similar Saturday concerts were offered by Durban's Volunteer Band on Market Square.[64] African workers also made use of the leisure period tending to personal needs or simply relaxing in the company of friends. Of course, it would become a source of provocation when deprived of this, their "rightful season of rest." *Togt* men, that is, the day laborers who were heavily employed on the wharfs and who frequently were compelled to work through the weekends including on Sundays, raised the loudest protest. From 1881 on, it is common to come upon references such as the following:

> Employers of Kafir labor experience great inconvenience frequently on account of togt natives refusing to work after certain hours. They seem to be impressed with the idea that they ought not to work after one o'clock on Saturday, six o'clock during the remainder of the week, and not on Sundays at all. Masters are placed at a great disadvantage by the refusal of togt natives to work at these specified times. . . . [65]

Since the laws regulating daily workers did not state what number of hours constituted a day's work—especially with regard to Saturday—or how much pay laborers were entitled to for Sunday work, strike action around these questions was significant. Although generally conducted on a small scale, several major strikes did occur during this period. In 1895, for example, some two hundred Union Co. workers, "led by one over 6 ft high . . . marched in a body on Saturday afternoon to the residence of Mr. T. S. Alston, the Company's Durban Agent," demanding overtime pay.[66] Four years later, nine Africans appealed the magistrate's ruling that forced them to work after one o'clock. A higher court deciding for the appellants concluded that as the

"Togt Regulations" were silent with regard to the hours of Saturday labor, daily workers were entitled to follow town custom.[67] Clearly this was an important victory for labor—employers were now obliged to pay black workers for half-holiday overtime.

One remaining observation must be added to the arguments and illustrations presented here. But first it is helpful to recall how the Zulu were deterred from participating in labor and other affairs after sunset by fear of the *abathakathi* (witches). Consistent with this aversion was their resistance to night work on sugar estates. Thus it is most intriguing, given the imposing magnitude of this belief, that town workers appear to have overcome their terror of the powers loosed in the night. What special set of circumstances or modifying influences justified the risks implied in breaching this proscription? How did urban laborers reinterpret the ancient norms to suit their altered behavior?

Two broad categories of nighttime engagements were recognized in the municipalities—those considered socially permissible and those characterized as antisocial. Subsumed under the former was night-shift work made necessary to accommodate periods of increased shipping at the point. Large monetary inducements tempted servants, those employed monthly as well as daily workers, to hire out nightly on the docks. From these efforts by blacks to maximize their earnings, we get complaints from masters that "some of their boys after working in town till 5 o'clock went to the Point and worked till 9 o'clock or 10 o'clock, receiving something like 4 or 5s. for the night and, thus, instead of having a full blown native in the morning they had a half dead one."[68]

Besides the immediate need for extra money to meet subsistence requirements or government impositions, there were other motives inducing workers to supplement full employment with part-time engagements. Young men, whose monthly salaries were usually handed over to their fathers or chief, may possibly have wanted to earn some extra *imali* (money) to fill their pockets, or to expedite the accumulation of bridewealth funds, or to pay evening school fees, the latter activity and expense being wholly disapproved of by their elders. Nevertheless, by 1867 the demand for education was so great among workers in Pietermaritzburg that church schools were being supplemented by educational entrepreneurs. White storekeepers also picked up money by teaching young men for a fee of 2s. 6d. per month.[69] In addition to this "craze for education," overtime engagements must also have been undertaken to satisfy material wants created by contact with Western culture—such as the desire to purchase ploughs, sewing machines, concertinas, bicycles, or other items admired in the location or town trade store.

It is also possible that working at the seaport held an attraction all its own. Under normal business conditions, the established practice seemed to have been to exclude young Africans and "men of the houseboy class" from taking out *togt* licenses.[70] This meant, of course, that only the more mature males were employed as "togtmen" on the docks. Yet it is very apparent from the spate of complaints from householders that this prohibition was relaxed considerably in boom periods when the port's demand for labor exceeded the available supply. One can imagine, then, that these busy times at the point occasioned great excitement not only because the opportunity was present to earn additional money, but because male juniors may have deemed it a privileged to perform labor ordinarily reserved for older men. The important thing is to appreciate the complexity of levels to this question. A wide range of factors and motives were in operation, any one of which could have accounted for why these men chose to put in labor time in excess of the conventional work day.

In other respects, the enlargement of the day to encompass late-night activities constituted a problem of growing proportion. Whereas an early Durbanite could write that initially curfews were unnecessary, for "as a rule superstition and custom operated favorably in restraining Africans from being abroad after dark,"[71] by the late 1850s the migrant population had summoned the courage to engage not only in legitimate nocturnal pursuits, but also questionable ones. Recurring throughout the documentation, decade after decade, are reports of loiterers and vagrants who nightly roamed about the towns' residential areas and suburbs. The one huge irony in all this is that the conditions creating this situation were largely of the towns' own making. To satisfy their basic physical requirements for food and lodgings, day workers were forced to deviate from custom and to modify their ideology in a way that allowed them to retain familiar institutions while adjusting to a starkly new experience.[72]

We do not as yet possess direct African testimony regarding these matters for this period; but it may quite possibly be, as Philip Mayer found much later in his East London study, that migrants rationalized away ancient fears with the explanation that the evil power of witches was largely associated with the community at home, that in the European centers they were safe from the witches' pursuit.[73]

Whatever the combination of circumstances that "let loose" these men upon the towns, the municipal response was to pass legislation that in effect attempted to colonize the worker's leisure time. The nine o'clock curfew bell sounded in Pietermaritzburg officially for the first time in 1871; three years later similar measures were instituted at Durban.

The Laborer's Tally of His Time

Preliterate societies kept time count by means of mnemonic aids such as tally sticks, which were in wide use among the Zulu and which can also be traced to the Ngoni, Venda, Sotho, Xhosa, and Khoikhoin populations of southeastern Africa.[74] The idea of writing or numbering (*ukubhala*)[75] in Zulu society was that of representing things by simple figures, such as notched or marked notations used to record taxes that had been paid, to register livestock and other personal property, and to recall historical events. For example, while giving evidence in courts of law, witnesses kept a finger on a notch that had been previously scored on a tally stick, the different notches serving to recall the different points of experience or fact. Marks incised on the post of granaries furnished a record of inventory of the quantity of sacks stored within.[76]

Keeping count by tallies was observed in the time of Shaka and Dingane. Both Andrew Smith and Henry Fynn noted that Zulu warriors made their bravery public by wearing battle strings with pieces of wood round the neck, each wooden bit reckoned for an enemy slain.[77] Presumably Sotobe, *induna* (army officer) at Intontela, who reputedly was excused by Shaka from going on campaigns because he could count the king's cattle "at a glance," employed similar memory devices.[78]

Tallies purportedly were made for both sexes. Knotted strings were used to memorize what needed to be purchased or what messages had to be delivered.[79]

While there is no direct information for the Zulu, pregnant women elsewhere in Africa (as among the Cokwe) tied knots in a "string calendar" at each new moon in order to know when their delivery was due.[80] In Zululand during Cetshwayo's reign, Ludlow saw in one kraal a calendar rod "with notches on it, which served to show the date when cows were due to calve."[81]

Notched sticks (or "nicksticks") and maize seeds were used to determine the length of journeys, such as hunting or military expeditions, and for settling transactions as units of measure or price. Between 1850 and 1855 settlers regularly sent trusted servants, on foot and with a bullock cart loaded with blankets, calicos, beads, and other items into Zulu country to barter for cattle. Barrett sent his "stalwart Zulu" in charge of a trading expedition with three assistants. After about four months they returned and recounted their experiences.

> Of course I had in my books a detailed account of goods they had taken, and the cost thereof. During the whole of the day following their arrival, he and an assistant were making up their accounts, and I was astonished at their wonderful memories. As touching the 350 heifers and young oxen, they told me the price given for each. By the aid of notches on sticks and maize corns to represent each one the number ten, they satisfactorily accounted to me for every article they had taken with them.[82]

Most important for the purposes of this study, these devices were used for recording labor time, one notch representing a day's work.[83] "In this way count your moons [instructed the master]. Cut your days on a stick, and show it to me on every Saturday."[84]

The best account of the nearly infallible working of the calendar rod, however, comes from the Cape colony, where some indigenous groups, particularly members of the Khoikhoin population, appear to have mastered European temporal concepts quite thoroughly. Writing in 1812, William Burchell reported that several people in his employ always carried notched tallies about them on which they kept a careful account of each day. When the tally was filled, the amount was transferred to another on which the notches represented weeks, or months. In this way he observed that his Khoi workers were able to mark accurately the lapse of time for short periods. Among his men, Speelman was regarded by all as the "grand Almanack-maker." Burchell was continually surprised, on putting questions to him relating to past occurrences on the journey, at the accuracy with which Speelman was able by means of the tally to recollect when the events happened.[85]

No observant traveler stopping at the Cape in the seventeenth and eighteenth centuries could fail to note that the daily routines at the Dutch fort were models of exactness, method, and order. This fact prompted Mentzel in 1784 to state, "For a man who loves method it is a veritable joy to observe the excellent order maintained in the Castle. The whole work of the day is mapped out by the clock and performed with the utmost punctuality." He further added that, because of the violent winds that frequently raged at the Cape, no clock could be put up in the open, so the hours were struck by hand upon a bell that hung in a little tower over the castle gate.[86] The point to all this is to suggest that, owing to a prolonged interaction with Dutch people at the fort, those Khoi who had become used to a life of punctuality, successfully acquired skills for measuring Western time.[87] On the other hand, where the period of racial and cultural contact was less protracted, as in Natal, masters found it difficult to teach their laborers how to keep accurate count of the days from one monthly period to the next.

Barrett recorded that "the working Kaffir, every morning on waking up, ... makes a notch in a stick; and when the twenty-eighth notch is cut, his money is due.... "[88] Imagine, he continues, "how a Kaffir will think himself cheated out of two or three days' work every month by not being paid according to the moons."[89] To add to the confusion, very many servants had the fixed idea that they could demand their wages when four Sundays had expired after the beginning of their engagement. Others cut a notch in their stick every day but, if they became anxious to obtain their wages before they became due, they were known to cut two notches for one day, "in order that their days may tally with the 'death of the moon.' " [90]

Want of an adequate system, argued one colonist, was the cause of Natal's labor crisis. And he felt strongly that all time disputes could be avoided if master-servant contracts were registered.[91] M. Joscelin Cooke engaged the matter squarely in 1863 when he advocated that a day's work be officially defined as from sunrise to sunset; that there be instituted a morning, midday, and evening bell to regulate the movement of workers; and that an enactment be passed to eliminate the ongoing problems caused by the variations in the length of the calendar months.[92]

Only belatedly did government attempt to legislate a remedy for this last problem. For the purposes of Act 40 of 1894, the Master and Native Servant Law, an official calendar was devised wherein the twelve months contained an equal number of units of thirty days.[93] In this, it should be pointed out, they were following a precedent observed by white employers generally, of obliging workers to keep a tally cane and when the notches numbered thirty, they were paid. Thus as the system remained basically unaltered, the official calendrical reform had only a minimal effect on the recurrence of time disputes. On the other hand, the law functioned to the great advantage of the major employers, whose primary goal was to extract as much labor as possible from African workmen under the thirty-day ticket system.

At least by 1871 certain employers had begun to issue distinctive "service tickets," a method more efficient from their standpoint than allowing each individual worker to keep his own personal record of days worked. Such tickets were issued daily and, at the end of the month, the presenter was paid a number of shillings corresponding to the tickets held.[94] An updated and perhaps more effective version of this system came into vogue at the port at the turn of the century, where work tickets were issued with thirty squares; each square bore the date and signature, and was marked after a day's work was finished. When the ticket was full, after the expiration of thirty days, it was taken from the laborer and a "month's" wages were paid.[95]

In the final analysis, the problem of teaching laborers to "properly" compute time resolved into the fundamental question of cultural conversion. A few town missions had by 1862 informally included as part of their teaching matters of common knowledge, geography, and explanations of natural phenomena.

> Occasionally we lengthened the visit, after the service, by explaining simple astronomical and geographical lessons; and I need hardly say there was quite a shout of exultation when I showed them how to account for sunrise, noon and night, by means of a suspended pumpkin to represent the earth, with a tiny insect on it to represent man, and the globular lamp for the sun!

But when, on another occasion I illustrated the changes of the moon, I established a lasting reputation amongst these quick and keen-witted children of the wilderness.[96]

Earlier at Lewis Grout's mission, formal examinations in basic astronomy were conducted;[97] and at Springvale on the upper Mkhomazi, as has already been noted, Dr. Henry Callaway determined it would be "best to make the Kafirs around [the mission] feel as much as possible the value of time, labor, and skill."[98] Farther afield at St. Matthew's Station in Keiskamma Hoek, more ambitious efforts got underway with the publication of a *Kaffir Almanac* (commenced in 1863), which was printed entirely in Xhosa and which contained astronomical and meteorological data arranged according to the days, weeks, and months of the given year.[99] Despite such efforts, the conversion process was slow among the mass of the population. This was because, as Hall explains,

> [o]ne of the principal characteristics of PL [primary level] culture is that it is particularly resistant to manipulative attempts to change it from the outside. The rules may be violated or bent, but people are fully aware that something wrong has occurred. In the meantime, the rules remain intact and change according to an internal dynamic all their own. Unlike the law or religious or political dogma, these rules cannot be changed by fiat, nor can they be imposed on others against their will, because they are already internalized.[100]

Workers' Wage Claims

In the magistrate's court on Thursday, while a native was claiming for wages due to him by his master, he informed the magistrate in reply to a remark of His Worship that overwork would never kill a Kafir, but not being paid for it might. The sable logician also added that if overwork would kill a Kafir there would annually be great loss of life in the colony.[101]

Often it happened, as one old informant related, that a person in some way procured a lump of iron and proceeded with it to the king with the hope of bartering it for cattle.[102] Iron, the "primary metal of war and peace," was greatly prized and had status value in mixed farming economies, which is why we are not surprised to hear that in the early days of the settlement's history wages were paid in precious iron bar currency. Three months' labor was originally paid with a bar equivalent to about nine inches, which the boy or man carried home in triumph to be welded into a hoe by professional smiths.[103] Africans also labored for blankets, knives, hatchets, cloth, or brass wire. In 1846 women and girls could be employed for six days on cotton plantations for "two ells of coarse unbleached calico" [an ell being a measure equivalent to 45 inches]; "boys" engaged for either 2*s.* 6*d.* a month or for a heifer a year.[104]

While Natal's black population may have been, relatively speaking, slow in converting to imported time practices, no corresponding level of resistance was shown toward the adoption of foreign currency. As early as 1849 African women trading farm produce in the towns invariably refused any payment for their goods and services "that did not bear the impress of majesty."[105] (Presumably this also obtained for the black workmen employed in and near the major white settlements.) Interest in a standard trade currency quickened in 1849, the year the hut tax was inaugurated, the payment of which was encouraged in hard specie. One "indirect benefit of the lung-sickness" epidemic of 1855 was the hastening of an appreciation for the inherent utility of British sterling as a medium of exchange and as a convenient store of wealth. Yet some of the views as to the epidemic's immediate and lasting impact were more expressive of wishful thinking than a reflection of reality.

> We hear, on good authority, that the Kafirs are generally coming to the con-viction that they must change their currency from cattle to coin and work for the latter for hire, or in productive industry. They say it is no use work-ing for years for that which may die in a day.[106]

Acquisition of cattle continued to be a primary concern. One need only recall how Africans "hoarded" their wage earnings to make land purchases and to recover livestock when ravages of the lungsickness abated.[107] Nevertheless, the cattle scourge opened a hole in the gate through which this innovation passed into their society. By 1859 even Mpande was expressing interest in the uses of *imali*:

> He wished to see money, and made a number of inquiries about it, what use we made of it, and etc. "We could eat mealies, and oxen, and make *utywala* [beer] and *amasi* [sour milk], and keep ourselves warm with blankets; but what could we possibly do with money?" [he asked.] I told him, "If I wanted to buy things worth an ox, I should carry this little coin (a sovereign) with me, and not drive about an ox, as a Zulu must." "Then we kept these coins as people here do cattle?" William gave him some idea of the use made of money by himself and others, by borrowing and trading with profit. Several people came to ask to see *imali*, and expressed their admiration of it—"And this is *imali*?"[108]

Part of their eager acceptance for hard cash had to do with the Africans' practi-cal discovery that silver and gold represented a uniquely reliable measure of value, a standard against which their goods and services would be more fairly remunerated. For the documents speak on many occasions of employers who engaged "boys" for a heifer a year, "forcing them to accept when their time was out a calf or a toothless cow"; or when they were hired for a woolen blanket, being given a paltry rug instead.[109] Yet experience would come to show that the introduction of specie into labor and other financial dealings hardly guaranteed protection from perpetrators of fraudulent practices and other unprincipled men.

> One pound has twenty shilling. Half a crown is like two shillings and six-pences. A shilling is just as much as two sixpences. Don't fear that I would cheat you. Believe that two threepences are one sixpence. Ye stupid people, when will you understand that two sixpences are like one shilling?[110]

Before Africans became fully acquainted with its workings, their attitude towards metallic currency was naturally that of wary skepticism. In addition, their confusion as to the relative values of the coinage exposed them to the false represen-tations of con artists and swindlers. For example, a man named Beckham was charged by two Africans before Durban's magistrate in 1851 with having passed them a medal of no value, as a genuine sovereign.[111] But of the many such incidents, one anecdote about a florin found its way into popular lore. At their first introduction into the colony, "a canny Scotch farmer" paid his Zulu workers with a florin (a two-shilling silver piece), a coin with which they were unfamiliar, and which he paid to them as half-crowns. When the deceit was discovered, Africans christened the florin *isikotshimane* ("Scotchman"), by which name it was known ever since.[112] Thereafter they generally spurned small change, that is, low-denomination coins of less than a florin or half-crown (especially the bronze three- and sixpence series).

Extracts from Posselt's phrase book indicate better than a thousand pages of documentary evidence could the vulnerability of black workers in securing a guarantee for the fair payment of their wages.

> Boy, I am tired of you.
> You are obstinate (bad, lazy, saucy).
> You are dirty (a fool).
> You are quarrelsome (you have much anger).
> I have warned you enough already.
> I now threaten you.
> If you do that again I shall dismiss you without payment.
> I shall keep part of your wages.
> I shall take your blanket.
> I shall make you pay.
> I shall put you into prison.
> I shall have you flogged.
> I shall stint you in your food.[113]

It came down to this. Whether or not servants received their earnings very often depended on the vagaries of the master, a fact that reveals yet another critically important strand in the labor question. For next to time disputes, wage grievances were perhaps the second most prolific cause of master-servant litigation in the colony. An apt statement of the problem is expressed below by a contemporary sharply attuned to the issues.

> Provision is not made whereby justice between the white man and the Kafir can be unfailingly secured in the matter of carrying out engagements to labor and engagements to pay for that labor. *But a bargain is a mutual affair . . . and we are persuaded from lengthened observation, that the latter cause has much to do with the unwillingness of Natal Kafirs especially, to work* [emphasis added]; he feels he has no security for payment of what is due to him, and he has learnt by too many bitter experiences, that he is found fault with in some way, thrashed, or kicked off the place where he is working, when his employer finds it inconvenient to pay when due, which in the Kafir's case, as he has no security for payment at all, he is very unwilling should be deferred longer than a month. . . . [114]

It must be added that this propensity of certain employers to avoid paying workers wages that they had fairly earned was seen as one of the causes promoting the evils of *togt* or day labor.[115]

A Question of "Desertions" or a Matter of "Turning the Tables on Them"?

> It is . . . a too common practice with masters, when their servants go to court for the purpose of making a complaint to follow them and give them in charge at once, either for desertion or some other offence, thus turning the tables on them.[116]

The subject of Africans "absconding" from labor service has exercised the attention of other writers to the extent that we cannot pass over the subject in silence. Some authors have used the analogy of North American slavery to explain the phenomenon, and have further interpreted these desertions as manifestations of a reflex reaction to bad working conditions or forced labor. Others see in this mobility an early unsophisticated stage in the evolution of labor protest, or a strategy of class action particular to the migrant situation, one that demonstrates "the pervasive influence of the rural economy on the character of resistance."[117] Neither the slavery model nor the latter constructions fit our situation. In the first instance, Africans in Natal were *not* slaves, nor generally as a group did they perceive themselves inferior to white men. They were the "queen's children." As such, when grievances were felt their first recourse was to the courts for due process of the law, a familiar practice in their own society. It may be useful to point out that more often than not, the servant was the initiator of court proceedings. From the servant's perspective, it was master who had breached the original terms of the contract by cheating him of his time, his wages, or both. Furthermore, looking at it from the standpoint of the "more mature" laborer, master was again at fault if he failed to make the best use of the worker's time and skills, instead of constantly "calling him for nothing," that is, calling on him to perform unsatisfactory work tasks—chores not consonant with his rank, which would cause him to lose the esteem of others.

Though he first applied to the court, the servant usually discovered to his horror that the employer could forestall the process, and obstruct the wheels of justice by having him hauled into the dock for desertion! Many a complainant found himself in Umbaza's predicament. Charged with misconduct and refusal to obey the "reasonable commands" of his master, this "dull and heavy headed boy" was sentenced to a fortnight's hard labor and twelve lashes, and the *sjambok* (whip) was vigorously employed "to quicken his apprehension."[118]

The use of the lash seems to have formed part of every judicial sentence as a matter of course, especially in the country districts.[119] Indeed, we are assured by one colonist that every white man with a sense of justice would have readily admitted that, as a rule, the black man in a court of law in Natal was at a disadvantage from which no European could possibly have suffered. The tendency, he stated, was to believe the African a rogue (and the administrators of justice were imbued with this racial prejudice), and it merely required the necessary formality of taking evidence to cause punishment. Instead of encouraging workers to look to the magistrate for protection and fair play, this situation drove them to actual desertion as the most effective means of ending the disputes.[120] From time to time, these questionable proceedings drew attention. At least one critic urged the higher courts to investigate the decisions made at the magisterial level, "so that at all events there might be some check upon Justice's justice."[121]

The operation of these biases in the courts naturally raises grave questions about the reliability of the surviving records of civil and criminal cases. We learn from one contemporary court watcher, for instance, that the returns of criminal cases were sent regularly to the attorney general, but those returns stated merely the charge, the plea, and the sentence, and therefore were generally of little use in monitoring magistrates. Then, again, judges often found the simple record "plea Guilty" in cases where the plea ought to have been "Not Guilty." In one civil suit, for example, a worker charged with desertion said that if leaving his work without permission to complain at court was desertion, then he was guilty of desertion. That was construed as a plea of guilty, and no other record was made.[122] It was therefore concluded that the only effective check on the whims of magistrates was to give full publicity to their court proceedings, a practice of rare occurrence, however. Moreover, in the outlying districts pursuing such a policy would have been impossible. Back-country magistrates had things pretty much their own way.[123]

Inevitably, then, cultural conflicts, time disputes, chicanery and deception with respect to wage payments, and injustices in the legal system were leading contributors to the workers' alienation and occasional withdrawal from long-term labor contracts. Taken together these factors make the *togt* phenomenon more comprehensible. Broadly speaking, *togt* meant many things to many people. Each *togt* man no doubt could have told his own unique story. Still from the point of view of a great number of Africans, *togt* represented a safeguard against ill-tempered masters, insecurity of payment, and an unsympathetic judicial system. For the vast majority of these casual workmen, the underlying attractiveness of day labor resided in the fact that people who engaged by the day could by and large avoid the numerous grievances that rankled monthly servants.

In no way is this to imply, as we will shortly see, that the day worker's circumstances were ideal. Yet there is no gainsaying the fact that there was a palpable degree of independence and flexibility inherent in the *togt* system. "Jobbers" did exercise a broad range of choices regarding where and for whom they would work, and were entitled to receive their pay immediately upon finishing the day's task. Moreover, *togt* men determined not only the duration of their contracts but negotiated for increases in wages and employed such tactics as boycotts and strikes to achieve their goals, when they were in a position to do so. Urban laborers and domestic workers channeled their grievances through organized guilds and "kitchen associations"—networks that linked craftsmen, jobbers, and monthly servants. Through these organizations, they acquired the capacity to defend their rights to receive amenities in the form of board and lodging. They also successfully resisted municipal attempts to put a halt to their organized activities. It is to these and other issues that we now turn.

5

The Evolution of the Togt Labor Market Within the Political Economy of Natal, 1843–1875

This is an appropriate place to broaden the analysis to incorporate questions regarding the manner in which the *togt* labor phenomenon was tied to the wider political and economic forces unfolding in nineteenth-century colonial Natal. In a sense, this is a theme familiar to the writings of some South Africanist authors who have drawn a correlation between the limitations within settler politics, the region's sluggish economic growth, and the level of autonomy experienced by the indigenous black communities.

The conventional picture of white Natal is of a small settler community thinly spread out, and profoundly torn into competing interests groups with opposing views as to what constituted an effective "native policy." On the one side were the commercial farmers, agitating for far-reaching measures to keep wages down, restrict the mobility of labor, and maneuver Africans into lengthy contracts of servitude; on the other were individual landowners and land companies (such as the Natal Land and Colonization Company) promoting the squatter system, which involved profitable schemes of renting land to Africans at hefty yearly rates paid in cash or crops. To these two leading factions must be added the position taken by the metropole: the outstanding canon in its policy was economy, which is simply another way of saying that the Colonial Office effectively blocked any proposition having to do with the African population that might eventuate in costly wars.

These contradictory currents in colonial politics have been held up to explain Natal's lack of success in controlling the labor of its black population. It has been argued that these rival tendencies not only undermined the effectiveness of white authority but also strengthened the position of the indigenous population with respect to the particular kinds of economic transactions in which they were willing to engage, and, furthermore, directly enhanced the Africans' capacity to withstand efforts to force them off the land and into steady wage employment.[1] There are a few problems with this interpretation. First, such a formulation tends to detract attention from the spectacular achievements of labor during this period (i.e., African gains are minimized when juxtaposed against the inadequacies within the white power structure). Second, whether the argument is valid or not, it is irrelevant for understanding the rich pattern of cultural nuances underlying Natal's chronic labor problems. A major failing, then, in the above line of thinking is that it distorts our efforts to comprehend the substance of black proletarianization.

Beyond a doubt one of the defining features of these years was the breadth and diversity of economic choices available to the indigenous inhabitants. They could choose to remain in the "native reserves," or move to mission lands, or onto white-owned farms as labor tenants; or alternatively, they could become squatters in private Crown areas, paying an annual rent. In connection with this latter category, it has been estimated that by 1874 five million acres belonging to private individuals or land companies were occupied by Africans. Far more appealing than the above arrangements was the option of pooling their resources to purchase land under "tribal titles." The wherewithal to make these land purchases often came from the accumulated earnings Africans received in temporary service on commercial estates and in the towns.[2] Furthermore, recent research has shown that from 1868 through the mid-1870s, well over ten thousand Africans were diverted from Natal's labor market (by wages paid in firearms) to the newly opened Kimberley diamond fields.[3]

This more or less shows the manner in which the relatively open internal market conspired against the development of capitalist agriculture, and ultimately forced planters to turn to Mozambique and India for labor supplies. Despite their recruitment efforts, the number of foreign workers imported under the various contract schemes never seemed fully to satisfy the requirements of commercial farming. Which brings us to a contradictory proposition: with few exceptions, colonial enterprises were incapable of supporting a large work force year-round. Yet for some unexplored reason, this did not diminish the perennial cries (except during periods of economic troughs) for steady and continuous supplies of labor.

Economic activities in the colony, as in the inland Boer republics, were centered upon seasonal industries—farming, raising stock, hunting, and trading. Further, so long as capital was scarce, expertise limited, and regional communication systems rudimentary, these areas would remain undeveloped and the volume of seasonal products insubstantial. Owing to these circumstances, and the fact that the nearest seaport was Durban, European-imported commodities purchased in the Transvaal were extremely costly. All stores had to be brought to Pretoria in ox wagons by a long and tedious land route of some four hundred miles.[4]

In Natal, crucial sectors of town employment were deeply affected by vagaries in the weather. Labor demands fluctuated at Durban and Pietermaritzburg with the above overberg trade, and at the port, with the movement and number of ships. Year after year, prior to the coming of the railways, trade with the interior came practically to a standstill during the dry "moons" of winter. Drought, frost, and grass fires destroyed the pasturage on the high veldt, making it impossible to work the oxen along the dusty roads.[5] The main highways were also difficult and precarious to negotiate in the rainy season. During this time, the business of the merchant middlemen was subject to accidents of wagon transport caused by heavy downpours that rendered roads impassible and prevented delivery of goods into the towns.

Nature was both generous and cruel to the port establishment and other small waterfront industries. Violent winter gales (the "dreaded black South Easters") stirred up raucous seas, caused numerous wrecks on Durban's back beach, and were severely felt among the shipping concerns. Just as influential in shaping the seasonal demands of the market was the general state of the harbor. Facilities at Port Natal had a notoriously bad character. One reads constantly relative to this period of vessels left riding at anchor in the roadstead, of goods prevented from being landed because shifting bars and sandbanks blocked entrance to the harbor.[6] Posselt portrays in descriptive phrases the meteorological factors hampering dockside work.

> There is a ship coming.
> The wind is against her; she cannot enter today.
> The wind is favourable; she will enter on the floodtide.
> How the sea is roaring. The waves run very high.
> The rain has ceased; it is clear weather.
> She is landing her goods.
> Go, boys; carry the goods out from the boats.[7]

At a future date a properly constructed breakwater as well as other modernized facilities would minimize some of the problems outlined above. But until such improvements were instituted, nature continued to pose a formidable obstacle to increased shipping. The English social historian Gareth Stedman Jones notes that by the 1880s, technological advances in shipbuilding had a positive impact on London's dockside industries. Likewise, it may be that seasonal interruptions at Port Natal would have slackened by the late nineteenth century with the gradual substitution of steam for sail.[8]

Building construction was another area subject to climatic hardships. Trades such as stonemasonry and brickmaking, for example, were busiest in dry months, when bricks and tiles could be produced in bulk and left to bake in the sun. The building industries and the question of seasonal production will be more fully explored in the discussion to follow on rural and urban employment practices in vogue within Natal's internal labor market.

Rural Parameters of *Togt* Labor

Farms in Natal were devoted either to agriculture (and worked with the plough or cultivated by hand) or to the grazing of cattle, sheep, and horses; in some cases the two land systems—arable and grass—were combined. In the coastal counties of Durban, Alexandra, and Victoria, arable farms were chiefly owned or occupied by cultivators of cash crops—cotton, sugar, coffee, arrowroot, tobacco, and other tropical products. In the midland divisions of the country, Umvoti and Pietermaritzburg, European farming operations combined growing corn with rearing stock. In the upper districts, pastoral husbandry was the prevailing character of farming—cattle, sheep, and horses formed the chief wealth of the inhabitants in Weenen, Klip River, and Newcastle. Labor needs varied according to the size of the farm, its geographical location, and the character of the enterprise. Throughout these several districts it is possible to distinguish, by duration of contracts, three basic patterns of employment.

First, there was tenant labor, which, broadly speaking, was regularly employed on standard chores related to the industry and general upkeep of the farming establishment. Next were seasonal engagements subject to swings in nature and the intensity in the demand for labor, which, in turn, were governed by the organization of the industry and the market. For example, during picking season coffee growers and cotton planters hired extra hands to work off their crop; and, as we have already seen, temporary work gangs supplemented permanent labor pools in the peak manufacturing season on sugar estates. The third pattern of agricultural employment, overlapping the second category, was defined by daily or weekly engagements. Our earliest reference to rural day labor is dated 1843.[9] Thereafter, the sources reveal that this form of contract was distinguished by a preponderance of female laborers.

All the rural districts employed women and economically productive children for light work. From the very early years and throughout the period of this study, wage-earning women and girls from the locations were engaged on adjoining European farms to weed, hoe, and reap mealies; pick cotton; gather coffee berries; and so on, the usual agreement being that they would return to their kraals the same day. Significantly, many of the tasks on which they were employed dovetailed neatly with the end of the traditional agricultural calendar. Picking coffee berries may have been considered not an onerous task because the work (described as light and clean), undertaken at the time in which the coffee beans were due to ripen, occurred after the women had harvested their own gardens, generally in the month of May.[10] The prevalent feeling among white employers was that female *togt* labor was quite efficient. One Alexandra farmer, who employed their services in clearing and hoeing his fields, drew such a picture, asserting that, he "averaged about twenty ["a different lot"] every day, and really it is astonishing the amount of work we get through."[11] The value attached to the services of these women may be further gauged from the resultant outcry of farmers against the Native Identification Act of 1901, a law prohibiting Africans from offering themselves for hire and masters from engaging them unless the latter produced a pass. The principle objection to Law No. 49 was that it would interfere with the supply of rural *togt* workers. Agriculturalists were fearful of suffering loss and inconvenience, as a great deal of work was done by women and children, who, the farmers believed, would not trouble to attend the magistrate's court for a pass when they only turned out occasionally to work.[12] Their clamor persuaded government to revise its instructions for magistrates in the country districts, where the law was waived with respect to female casual labor.[13]

To secure local labor at times when it might not otherwise have been forthcoming, many colonists offered various forms of encouragement to Africans to settle on their farms. For example, we saw earlier how northern farmers extended protection to refugee families in exchange for their services.[14] On upland farms in Weenen in 1858, the condition of tenancy involved arrangements whereby the right of pasture and cultivation was secured to heads of families, who, on their side, were bound to supply the labor of their young men and children of either sex at the monthly rate of 5s. and 2s. 6d., respectively. Skilled laborers living on the farmer's land, such as African wagon drivers and ploughmen, earned eight to ten shillings a month; workers with similar skills who resided on their own farms hired out at one shilling per day. Other arrangements included the understanding that married men would give their labor gratuitously at harvest time, or on extraordinary occasions such as erecting or repairing cattle kraals, clearing out a watercourse, or branding cattle. Another version of the contract stipulated that such extra services would be paid for at the rate of 3*d.* per day. General laborers were supplied with rations, and house servants with clothing as well.[15]

Official wage statistics compiled during this period must be read with discrimination. The impression conveyed by these figures is that the wages offered in the midlands and coastlands were either compatible with or did not greatly exceed rates paid in the north. However, the unofficial sources are quite conclusive on this matter: more favorable wages could be obtained in the lower districts. Indeed, these higher earnings were responsible for promoting considerable migration from the upland "tribes" coastward to the plantations and to other parts of the colony.[16] Such a movement was visible, for instance, around the mid-1850s, when a boom in the sugar market and the concomitant increase in acreage given over to cane production led to escalating demands for labor.

The allure of the sugar estates in the early days of the industry was threefold: the offer of high wages may be seen as an obvious boon; another and perhaps more potent enticement was gang work, which was preferable to the isolation of the upland farms; and the third seductive factor came in the form of molasses, a byproduct of the industry.[17] Molasses was freely or very cheaply obtained on the estates. Regrettably, it was insidious in its effects when fermented into the intoxicating beverage popularly called *isishimeyana,* after the "machine" that crushed the cane and left behind the thick residue or treacle.

As far as labor needs were concerned, we are left with the unmistakable impression that the sugar industry without exception began on a tenuous footing. Yet not all cane growers were in this unenviable position. A handful of planters who were sensitive to the cultural needs of their black work force, and who inaugurated a judicious system of labor management, seldom had cause to complain of labor shortages. This small group of capitalist farmers maintained that "Natal Kafirs" (as workers) ranked far above Indian and other foreign labor imports.[18] In the end, mainly owing to the general lack of positive experiences encountered on the commercial estates, plantation work lost the appeal it originally held for Natal Africans.[19]

In Chapter 2 we saw how it had long been the practice for agriculturalists to make presents to chiefs (in cash or cattle) in order to obtain their influence in supplying the labor of their young men.[20] Moreover, large numbers of planters, perhaps most, as the magistrate for Lower Umzinto reported, "rather than be known to their neighbors to exceed the average wage gave additional amounts under the head of good conduct money."[21] Therefore when these sums—above and beyond the usual compensation paid to their African workers—are factored in, it may be concluded that wages in the sugar belt doubled, sometimes trebled, those offered up-country. Obviously, the ability to pay the extra costs gave coastal farmers the edge on rural labor supplies. Yet it would be wrong to try to adduce from this that local pools of labor met prevailing needs along the coast. Just as the remote, economically stagnant northern divisions were deprived of hands primarily in consequence of their inability to compete with labor prices reigning on commercial estates, the midlands and the coastlands, in turn, were markedly drained of labor by even more lucrative prospects held out to black workmen by the towns. They were also hurt by the extra incentives that railway contractors offered, and the personal satisfaction and economic advantages that the African derived from becoming, say, an independent producer supplying the export market. In addition, the public works department and other government projects made demands on local manpower, through *isibhalo* call-ups. Subsequent years saw a steady outflow of African males to the Kimberley mines and the Rand goldfields.

Commercial farmers detrimentally affected by these trends turned to unsound practices with the hopes of solving labor deficits. Almost all tried bribes and bonuses, in one form or another, with meager results. Finally, desperation drove them to further extremes. They were not bound by compunction of conscience to abjure the use of threats, nor had they any scruples about violence. Excerpts from Charles Barter's journal (Barter was a member of the 1852–1853 Kafir Commission) give a clear idea of the kind of methods reverted to in order "to induce the Kafirs to work." On September 21, 1852, a meeting took place (at which Lt. Governor Pine was present) between a group of Umgeni farmers and the principal African chiefs in the neighborhood, about which Barter reports:

> [T]he Umgeni farmers, who had spoken out boldly told him (Pine) the real truth that unless something was done and done strenuously and in earnest, to compel the Kafirs to work . . . farming would be at an end. Pine had assented to all they said, and promised to set matters to right; but now with his usual inconsistency, he was falling back upon "Philanthropy" and talking Exeter Hall to the assembly of black ragamuffins before him. Luckily, his interpreter "pro tem" Joe Archbell, was an old hand and knew what he was about; and not a few of Pine's promises of protection, and threats of punishment to their white oppressors, etc. etc., were converted by him into threats of severe visitations in case of refractory conduct. When this farce was over, at which the farmers smiled, many of them went their way, having drawn up a petition to Government on the subject, for Pine to take with him to the Cape, whither he was shortly going, which I signed.[22]

Prior to this meeting, official objections to just such underhanded tricks were circularized. Magistrates were urged to use their legitimate influence to promote labor supplies. But while they were being cautioned not to threaten chiefs or to sanction their using threats or violence towards their people, coercion was the order of the day, as the above passage appears to demonstrate.[23] Again, another particularly well documented incident comes down to us of an agent, allegedly representing sugar interests, sent to Durban in 1859 to circulate rumors designed to whip up fears and drive out the "unproductive" groups of Africans idling there. That the ama-Washa were targeted is highly significant, as will be seen shortly.

> A panic is at present rife among the class of Kafirs known as washing Kafirs, supposed to have originated from some evil disposed white man, who has succeeded in impressing these necessary evils (the washing Kafirs we mean) with the notion that the authorities intended very soon to put them apprentice in the same way the refugees were. The public will therefore be put to much inconvenience. It has been said that the object to be attained was the withdrawal of a number of Kafirs from the town, to the sugar plantations, where their services are just now required. . . . [24]

Such ploys had unintended consequences. By 1860 it was painfully obvious to commercial farmers that their situation was worse than ever before. There followed a growing refusal of African males to hire on to sugar estates as monthly workers. Instead, they now exclusively demanded day engagements; and what is more, they were beginning to be "paid so much daily, according to the precise urgency of their employer's needs.... "[25] At least one individual saw advantages in this alternative system of employment. The Reverend Walter Baugh had reason to believe the population on his mission station would increase as a result of it.

> This kind of engagement quickly became most popular with the natives and comparatively few will now consent to work otherwise than by the day. The introduction of the new system, I think, will be the means of inducing natives from a distance to apply for permission to reside in our village so as to engage in this daily work, for all who so labor go to and return from work morning and evening.[26]

The custom, however, was decried as "vicious and disorganizing" in an editorial appearing in the *Natal Mercury*.

> It is easy to comprehend how this ruinous plan has got to be established. Desperate men adopt strong measures for their own relief ... but ... let those who encourage that system remember that they deprive themselves of ever permanent guarantee for the future; that they help to perpetuate an excessive standard of wages, and that they are implanting an irregular disposition amongst a population that needs ... to be inoculated with ideas of fixed organization.[27]

This new feature of the labor scene is not to be confused with the trend discussed in the preceding chapter of monthly servants resisting nighttime work on sugar estates.[28] What we see here appears to be an entirely different phenomenon, blurring what had been a rather neat distinction: until the 1860s the profile of the *togt* work force was identifiable based along lines of sex and locale. That is, hitherto rural *togt* labor had typically comprised female workers, apparently because of social prohibitions against womenfolk's residing unprotected on white farms; whereas this same category of urban workers predominantly comprised the more mature class of African males.

This pattern of agricultural employment becomes significant for yet another reason: it brings out the manner in which Africans themselves were shaping the conditions of labor. Of course, one might argue that the indigenous population was already prejudiced against written contracts, which were perceived as instruments of entrapment, and that being frequent victims of deception disposed them to the loose arrangements day work afforded. Nonetheless, we should consider the idea that positive forces were also operating here. There is no getting away from the fact that as early as 1846, Durban workers were evincing signs of independence and a developing awareness of their worth on the market.

Something else strikes me as worth mentioning here. It is related directly to the argument and has to do with traditional perspectives and structural forces that were being imported into the colony. I have in mind the practice of African males assembling to take counsel and receive advice in matters of general importance to the community. Customarily, audiences were summoned by the chief to discuss the proposal of any public undertaking, or on occasion of celebrations, or disasters, or simply to hear the news of the day. In Zululand, for example, trial cases were actively followed in order to listen to what was happening on the local as well as national level, and to participate in discussions that generally preceded those meetings and court hearings. Attendance at these open forums offered an education in law and oratory, and in the methods of investigation and reporting facts. Suits tried in Zulu country were prosecuted by able men, who had acquired their knowledge and skills chiefly by attending such local hearings and sitting in on proceedings at the royal kraal, where issues of fact and law were first determined.[29] The opportunities to meet together and publicly engage in discourse regarding contemporary and past events was a critical indulgence that the worker continued to pursue, particularly in the urban areas.

That Natal Africans were not just passively adjusting to a new set of realities but were giving "very intelligent attention to public [colonial] matters" is substantiated by reports of their deep interests in the proceedings of the Kafir Labor Commission. During the sitting of that body, they daily made enquiries to whites as to what new things had transpired in the examination of witnesses. Workers who "understood English became the ready interpreters of those views to their fellows." In fact, Africans proved themselves capable of such astute observations, and they expressed such a lively interest in learning the conclusions and recommendations reached by the impaneled group, that their conduct occasioned alarm. Indeed, from several quarters special applications were made to local news editors and to government officials, requesting they suppress publication of the official report and certain other documents pertaining to "Kafir affairs," "in order that the natives may not come to the knowledge of their content."[30]

An episode reported seven years later may be taken as expressing African workers' maturing class consciousness. A rumor was circulating among Africans in the Lower Umkhomazi District in 1860 that the government intended to fix the rate of the next year's hut tax at fourteen instead of seven shillings. This created much conversation on the subject when one individual, described as a "half-coloured native," addressed a group of assembled Africans in the following manner: "Don't you see that the Government are meeting you on your own terms? They never talked of increasing the hut tax until you increased the amount of wages for your labor."[31]

The weight of evidence also favors the view that the preference for daily contracts over long work engagements during this period was as much as anything a manifestation of the workers' attentiveness to market trends. Coinciding as it did with those buoyant years from 1860 to 1864 when both sugar and the general economy were in an upswing, the new labor development is indicative of a practical awareness of prevailing economic forces. That is, it shows the black workers' grasp of the fundamental principle of supply and demand, a rule that they most certainly saw at times placed their services at a premium.

In 1865 and 1868 the economy experienced sudden slumps. Four years later, however, the colony was prospering once more, and its recovery stimulated demands for cheap labor. The ensuing decades resonated with the responses of previous years—an expansion of the *togt* market and an escalation in workers' demands for pay raises. In short, we are finally in a position to see what experience had taught Natal employers very early on:

The Zulu Kafir exhibits, as we all know, a very lively apprehension of his own interests, and has acquired with a readiness that seems intuitive, a knowledge in all its practical bearings of the world wide philosophy represented by £. s. d.[32]

Nature and Scope of Urban *Togt* Labor

Though our earlier sources happen to be silent on this point, it nonetheless seems plausible to suggest that the day form of casual engagement was a practice contemporaneous with the original Port Natal settlement. A wide range of opportunities was available in both agricultural and nonagricultural spheres; moreover, the pull of high wages and the possibility of acquiring irresistible "high tech" items found in the settlement—the splendid knives, hatchets, picks, and steel traps, as well as brass wire, beads, and blankets—whetted African enthusiasm and acted as inducements "to accept service by the month (lunar)."[33]

Durban county was the most dynamic of all the divisions, as the extension of commercial intercourse had given a powerful impetus to every branch of business. By 1846 cotton cultivation (Natal's first earnest attempt at cash-crop production) and shipping were very active industries.[34] Hence the greatest percentage of Africans desirous of entering labor service were drawn to the port, because of the abundance of "jobbing" work to be had there, and to the towns and surrounding farms. Large numbers of laborers could also be found gravitating to Pietermaritzburg, the seat of government, where in the same year one reads "from the first to the last house Caffres [could] be seen at work, making bricks, tending tradesmen, cultivating gardens and serving as domestics."[35]

Essentially *togt* labor relations represented a form of minute contract in which Africans hired out by the day and were paid a wage upon completion of the task, although arrangements varied between individual employers and employees. The following scenario is reconstructed largely from Durban records. Initially, refugees enticed by the security they met at Port Natal established themselves extensively in the area and began to cultivate large tracts of land. By 1835 they were producing quantities of mealies for export to Mauritius.[36] A further measure of their continuing prosperity is indicated in a report twelve years later of an African peasant producer by the name of Fernai, living near Durban, who had bought a wagon and a span of oxen on the same day with Indian corn of his own growing, and who was now "desirous of engaging a European driver of sober and industrious habits."[37]

The towns were developing faster than their burgeoning needs could be met. The white residents could neither produce enough to feed themselves nor supply the growing population of migrant workers. From nearby African homesteads came an energetic and enthusiastic response. Every day starting in the early morning, a constant stream of peasants (both female and male) began to pass in and out of the white communities, to hawk not only farm produce (milk, eggs, chickens, mealies, and pumpkins) but veldt products (honey, wild berries, thatching grass, firewood, and game meat) and domestic manufactures (pottery, wooden bowls and utensils, grass mats, etc.) in exchange for beef, tobacco, cloth, blankets, and cash. Concurrently, some of these peasants were drawn into the town labor market. African males responded first by bartering then selling their labor services for money wages.[38] (The evidence shows that with the exception of a few mission-trained girls, only males hired themselves to work in the port town during these early years.)

For a length of time this circulation of labor followed the established migration routes laid down by the large class of hawkers and traders. Taking well-trodden "Kafir paths," the narrow footways leading to the European center, workers entered Durban after dawn where they engaged their "rough talents" in various odd jobs; then, about sunset they returned to their family kraals on the outskirts of town. Some of these establishments may have been situated on the heights near the Mgeni River.[39] Other African craftsmen and workmen, such as laundrymen, brickmakers, and dockworkers, settled nearer to their places of employment. Hence derives the Dutch word *tocht* or *togt*, which pertains to a trip or journey,[40] or an itinerant trader such as the Jewish *smous* or *togtganger* described by S. Daniel Neumark in his study of the South African frontier.[41] In Natal the phrases "*togt* labor" or "day labor" were used interchangeably to describe any persons who undertook such daily tours and who were *not* contracted by the month to a white employer. This definition amends the notion that commonly associates *togt* almost exclusively with dock work and allows us to extend it to include a variety of other enterprises. Furthermore, a mid-century account provides the first detailed glimpse of this class of urban workers, and dispels any remaining confusion on the subject.

An exhilarated city editor boasted in 1855 that daily workers at Pietermaritzburg were indispensable assistants to European artisans, and in that capacity were making a valued contribution to the development of the city and its immediate environs.

> A growing feature in our social state, seems to point also to the fact that a class of day laborers is being trained, who are gradually coming out of their native customs, and who promise to form a most useful acquisition to the inhabitants of the city.
>
> The tradesmen in town require, and generally take into their employ, more natives than are necessary for mere domestic purposes. These are undergoing a very salutary training, and are gradually acquiring habits of industry and skill which fit them for a higher social state than the barbarism of a native kraal.
>
> Evidence of this is seen in the fact, that all the streets of the city and the new road over the town hill, are mainly the result of native labor. . . . No one . . . will deny the fact, that every sawyer, mason, builder, carpenter, and, indeed, every tradesman, finds it necessary to his successful operation to employ natives.[42]

With the growth of the white population after the 1850 arrival of the first batch of Byrne immigrants, building operations exhibited an extraordinary burst of activity. Inhabitants were given every encouragement to substitute safer building materials for the inflammable wattle and thatch of which the early townships largely consisted. Thus manufacturers of bricks and tiles as well as bricklayers occupied a central place in the periods of prosperity enjoyed by the construction industry. May through July was the building season, and during this period heaps of stones, stacks of bricks, and the laying of new foundations spoke of the progress of the times.

Demands on Durban's brickmakers were met by employing numbers of Africans at several sites located at the Mgeni River, Greyville, Currie's Fountain, and the Brickfields at the back of the Berea. Bricks were fairly expensive, averaging when delivered about one penny each. They were sold at the yards either burned or green (i.e., sun-dried), the latter being in demand primarily for inside work.[43] We know African laborers near Pietermaritzburg were already involved in the industry as early as 1846.[44] Essentially the job required very little skill—by means of simple wooden molds, one or two bricks could be turned out at a time.

> Make bricks.
> Put them into rows when they are a little hard,
> then turn them on the other side.
> Set them up into heaps.
> Burn them.[45]

Mason built a commodious brick workshop in 1855, and provides a more detailed description of these operations.

> It was in the middle of May when we commenced brick-making on our last-purchased land. The weather was favourable in the extreme for our under-taking, whole weeks passing over without a drop of rain. The number of hands, too, made the work comparatively light; for some dug the clay, others carried water, some again tramped in the treading-pit, and all sang merrily as they applied themselves right heartily to their daily tasks. I and my brother took the moulding and laying down part of the process; and, by directing the labours of our Caffres, rewarding them when they specially deserved it, and feeding them well, were able to manufacture from two to three thousand bricks per diem.[46]

At Durban in 1859 the price of these items rose due to the scarcity of labor, the "exorbitant" wages demanded by Africans currently employed in the business, and the difficulty the proprietors were experiencing in procuring wood for the kilns.[47]

Besides heavy involvement in the building trades and on municipal projects, daily labor was prominently employed in other areas as well. Since harbor work fluctuated seasonally with the movement and number of ships, it naturally suited the purpose of landing agents to pay Africans day by day as they needed them, rather than to keep a large staff who might periodically have nothing to do. Africans worked as nonspecialized dockhands, as well as lightermen, boatmen, and so forth.[48] They were extensively involved in porterage and cartage—that is, ship-to-shore activities and waterside and warehouse traffic. And as the sandy streets of Durban did not admit the use of handcarts, African porters either shouldered burdens or balanced parcels on their heads, or two workers carried articles on a handbarrow. Heavier items, such as bulk goods delivered from the point, were transported by ox-drawn carts and wagons.[49] Products flowing into Durban and Pietermaritzburg from the interior occasioned an intense flurry of activity. Gangs of laborers were hired by town merchants to unload wagon trains laden with wool, butter, ivory, skins, and other products for export. For the return inland journey, each vehicle was then reloaded with merchandise and provisions from the warehouses and stores.[50]

The above may be considered merely an index of how pervasive the minute casual labor market was. To the list must also be added self-employed workers such as the firewood collectors, washermen, and hawkers. In short, *togt* was perhaps even more a part of the urban labor scene than it was a feature of the rural economy.

What follows is a somewhat fuller account of the latter category of day laborers, the self-employed "*togt* men." The ubiquitous wood merchants and washermen featured prominently in the informal processions of Africans who circulated around the boroughs in daily pursuit of their various trades and specialized callings.

Self-employed *Togt* Men: Fuel Merchants and Laundrymen

Household fuel for both cooking and heating in Durban and in Pietermaritzburg consisted mainly of wood. There were municipal injunctions against tree cutting, so town dwellers were in the habit of drawing their supplies of dry branches and twigs from the corporation's bushlands, or alternatively, they relied on vendors (often women) who brought in quantities of wood from areas outside the municipal boundaries. The "kitchen boys" usually were sent to the bush on alternate afternoons for the family's fuel supply.[51] However, domestic establishments that could ill afford the expense of a monthly servant ordinarily relied on independent Africans who traded in firewood to come round offering bundles for sale. Fuel wood was a scarce commodity, and prices accordingly rose in rainy seasons and during the cold winter months when demand was greatest. The standard-sized bundle—a small quantity that lasted only a day—cost sixpence.[52] This particular line of trade was thus very attractive to many Africans because it offered lucrative returns. Anyone taking up the occupation earned 2s. to 2s. 6d. per day by selling a minimum of four or five bundles.

Significantly, contemporary accounts credit Zulu washermen with popularizing *togt* labor practices.[53] And as the documentation is fullest on these craftsmen, we will relate in some detail how colonial women perceived laundering chores and the manner in which African males came to predominate in the industry.

A growing body of literature on the history of nineteenth-century and early-twentieth-century household labor agrees in one essential: housewives universally deplored doing laundry.[54] What this meant, prior to inventions that lessened that and other household duties, was that women in both Europe and America who were in a position to employ general or casual help delegated washing and ironing to a live-in servant or alternatively hired out the family wash. Similarly, in mid-nineteenth-century Natal, diaries, letters, and newspapers indicate that colonial women were consistently disinclined to do hand laundering.

The best expressions of the prevailing sentiment regarding this sphere of women's work are recorded in a series of letters written between 1850 and 1888 by the early Byrne pioneer woman, Ellen Mcleod.[55] The following letter to her sister, Louisa, established the tone: "The raining season is now set in . . . and we generally have one or two fine days in the week and then I set to work washing which I still find one of the worst things I have to do." Disconsolate, she related in a letter dated 28 September 1851, "I wish I could get my washing done for me, for I find that the worst work of all and I cannot get the clothes clean. One of our gentlemen settlers who has left here gave me an iron so that I continue to iron a few things such as shirts and collars, but my starch that I make of mealies I cannot say is very good."

Relief for a brief spell prompted Ellen in 1856 to record wistfully: "I miss Bessie very much in the nursing department, but I have the Kafir one day a week to wash for me, which is a great assistance. It makes me wish we could always afford to keep one." Inability to pay adequate wages was among the reasons modest households, such as the Mcleods', experienced difficulty in retaining general farm workers as well as domestic helpers. Government attempted to alleviate labor shortages in 1856 and the Mcleods were among a number of settler families to whom African refugees were apprenticed for a three-year period at five shillings a month. About this arrangement Ellen wrote in 1859, "George has the assistance of a Kafir, a refugee. . . . " And then she added, "His wife also comes to assist me in my washing one day a week, of which I assure you I am very glad."[56]

So from the beginning the laundry dilemma was a major cause of anxiety and worry to the white immigrant wife, who, when unable to do it herself, either put it out or left it undone.[57] Another clue to the importance attached to this category of additional household help is that during difficult economic times, the washerman's regular weekly visits were cut back rather than dispensed with together: "As we cannot afford to keep any Kafirs but one herd boy, we have to do everything ourselves. Once a fortnight a Kafir comes to wash the clothes for a shilling."[58]

Seasonal shortages of clean water only added to the frustrations of Natal housekeepers. Cooking and bathing water was preserved in private tanks, and large vessels were turned into receptacles to collect downpours during the rainy seasons. However, this method of storage was inadequate and scarcity was acute in dry winter months. Conveying village water by pipeline was not an option until the late 1880s. So inhabitants of Durban had to send barrels about four miles to be filled at the Mgeni River, or be faced with the alternative of drinking brackish water from the town wells.[59] Pietermaritzburg was supplied with pure water from the Dorp Spruit, which, in Dutch fashion, was led in open sluices or ditches along the edge of the street.[60]

Despite seasonal water shortages, well-to-do housewives in and near the towns were not as harried by weekly laundering chores as their rural sisters. From Feniscowles, Durban, for instance, Eliza Feilden could blithely record in her diary of 9 June 1855: "Saturday's work began. The clothes were counted and sent off with Bonnet to the wash. . . . "[61] "The wash" was either the Mbilo or Mgeni River, and it was at those sites that all the clothes of Durban were cleaned. Likewise, for many years in Pietermaritzburg the only laundry was the Msunduze River where, as Barbara Buchanan recalled, along its banks "on Mondays were lined stalwart natives vigorously belabouring the stones with the family wash."[62]

Sending the "kitchen boy" or African domestic to the river with a bundle of linen, soap, brush, and a board was originally the common practice. But assigning the task to the general domestic frequently met with uncertain results.[63] African domestics in one-servant households were charged with a wide variety of functions: from gardening, fetching firewood, lighting fires, and cooking to cleaning boots, polishing floors and silver, setting table, and grooming horses. In short, the African servant, like his American and European counterparts, was expected to be a general factotum and put his hand to anything. From the outset, mutual inability to communicate their needs exacerbated mistress-servant relationships; long hours, isolation from community and friends, ill-treatment, and poor wages encouraged an apathetic response to on-the-job training. The dismal conditions of domestic service resulted in a reluctance by Africans to hire themselves out. Whenever services were sold, it was done with an unwillingness to engage for long periods, and even short-term labor contracts were frequently breached. Constant turnovers in staff militated against workers acquiring competence in housework, including hand-laundering. Before long, however, this pattern gave way to an entirely different organizational structure.

To fill the demand created by a worrisome domestic situation, Zulu men began to specialize in washing clothes and to hire their services on a daily basis. (It is worth remembering that laundering recalled the specialist craft of dressing hides, in which Zulu males traditionally engaged as *izinyanga*, a prestige occupation that paid handsomely.[64]) Eventually, this development led to the removal of the bulk of clothes washing from the home. Furthermore, the occupation of laundering was elevated to guildlike status. Within the guild, working conditions were regulated, the craftsmen were disciplined, and work standards were upgraded by the membership.

As professionals, the washermen maintained a regular round of customers and schedules of employment. Depending on how industrious the individual was, he might work anywhere from one to six days a week, with each weekday possibly devoted to two customers. Clothes sent out were usually inventoried the day before washday by the householder. On the following morning a washerman made the pickup call, taking away a *muid* sack (the measure, equal to about three bushels, of a week's wash) packed tight with soiled linen. From the beginning, some laundrymen declined certain articles of underlinen at any price; intimate apparel, therefore, had to be attended to by the housewives themselves. Customers provided a large bar of yellow London soap, a bucket, and two or three balls of thumb blue (a fabric whitener).

The washerman soaked dirty clothes in the river and took care to avoid their being carried away by the current. He then selected a stone, a stranded log, or a board, soaped the clothes well, kneaded them a little in his hands, then flogged them on the hard surface, rinsed them in the flowing river, blued them, and wrung them out to be hung on the neighboring bushes or spread on the hot sands to bleach and dry in the sun. Towards the end of the day, the articles were collected, the washerman refilled his sack, and returned with his load, for which he received a wage of one shilling, with possible liberty to sleep in the "kitchen boy's" hut and share in the evening meal. Over the years the price of laundering increased to 3s. 6d. and more per bagful.[65]

By 1856 the washermen were remarkably well organized in a combination that punished young competitors attempting to enter the trade and lower the price of labor.[66] Because their "exorbitant" fees provoked loud criticism, we are able to trace the activities of these craftsmen. Yet in spite of the bitter outcry leveled at the "washboys," their "excessive" demands were nonetheless met. To the vast majority of white town-dwellers the amaWasha were engaged in a service crucial to maintaining the health of nineteenth-century European households.

Despite their worthwhile services, almost all the descriptions left to us of the doings of these traders and craftsmen have been written from the point of view of their detractors. What we know of the firewood collectors (variously referred to as "day Kafirs," "wood Kafirs," "unemployed natives," or "vagrants"), for example, comes primarily from negative reports of their alleged operations: that they lived on earnings received from pilfering bushwood, and that far from confining activities to scavenging, their practices entailed the wholesale destruction of young and old trees. According to one account, their mode of procedure was to go into the bush in pairs, one serving as lookout while the other chopped, and if a suspicious character approached, the alarm was given, affording both "wood Kafirs" the opportunity to decamp.[67]

Farmers near the villages and towns also complained of wood thefts perpetrated by African women. It seems no owner of a farm allowed his tenants to cut firewood for sale for their own benefit; and yet what often happened was that women, not wishing to carry bundles too far a distance, loaded up from the most convenient farm proximate to that town. The practice was seen to encourage laziness: "I have known them refuse a shilling a day wages when they can make their 2s. 6d. a day by wood stealing," someone signing himself "Two Miles from Town" wrote in the *Natal Witness*. To rectify this situation it was suggested that no African woman should be allowed to offer firewood for sale unless she could produce a permit to do so.[68] Eventually, in 1874, a system of firewood licenses was initiated whereby a householder, on payment of 1s. 6d., was able to obtain a badge that was worn by his monthly servant and that permitted the latter to cut firewood on the town lands.[69]

The amaWasha were the focus of much earlier complaints. The apparent incongruity of the "warlike Zulu's" involvement in this line of feminine work engendered numerous comments. To the European way of thinking, washing clothes was an "unmanly" profession as well as an unproductive use of sorely needed labor power.[70] Partly on this account, partly because of their "excesses," and partly because of their alleged evil influence on monthly workers, washermen became prime targets for attack. Off and on, then, for a span of over sixty-five years, town dwellers and civil officials conducted vigorous campaigns to rid the boroughs of the *togt* menace. It is a remarkable story more especially for its lack of success. In retelling it, we go back to the historical events that shaped the environment in which this struggle would unfold—namely, to the year 1843 when Henry Cloete, Her Majesty's commissioner, was sent to Natal to disentangle land claims in such a way as to prevent overt clashes between African interests and those of the *voortrekker* farmers.

6

Emergence of an African Work Culture, 1846–1900

Resonances of the *togt* labor problem surface in 1846, three years after Henry Cloete's ill-considered pronouncement that the future government should establish "in several districts of the colony, six or more locations, keeping them, if possible, a little way removed from the contaminating influences of the chief town and the port." Accordingly recommendations were made for the removal of Dr. Adams's mission station situated on the Mlazi near Durban (a settlement of ten to twelve thousand inhabitants), as well as the relocation of Reverend Grout's temporary village on the right bank of the Mgeni near the port.[1] Government deferred to Cloete's suggestion and gradually, as the location boundaries became fixed, large groups of Africans were evicted from the now unauthorized lands.

The actual task of relocating the African population fell to Theophilus Shepstone, diplomatic agent and later secretary for native affairs. Beyond the Africans' physical resettlement, however, Shepstone was charged with drawing up a plan for the management and efficient control of these new sites. For instance, he envisioned these areas would serve primarily as centers of rehabilitation, places where Africans could be effectively contained and "civilized," molded into white men in black skins. As originally conceived, the reserves were to be staffed with powerful magistrates whose role would combine legislative, judicial, and executive functions, with power to punish summarily all minor offenses and decide civil disputes. Their duties would also entail registering all Africans—women, men, and children—executing contracts between masters and servants, and recording those as well. Shepstone saw these agents as having a salutary effect on the people in that they would encourage agriculture and industry, while discouraging polygamy, bridewealth, and witchcraft. Further recommendations provided for the spiritual elevation and industrial development of his charges. Missionaries would be assigned to the several locations, and model "mechanical schools" erected to help promote and assist the mission endeavor. Direct British involvement, then, was to be the keystone of Shepstone's proposed "native policy." But convincing the Executive Office to commit sufficient funds for the program's effective implementation was altogether another matter. As things turned out, government was hesitant to incur the added expense of such a scheme. The plan subsequently urged by Shepstone and formally adopted for the administration of Natal's large black population was based on the concept of indirect rule.[2]

What is often lost to view is that the principle of removing the peasant working population from the town lands and their immediate environs was taken up without first determining its acceptability to those white commercial farmers and other key employers directly affected by the measure. Nor, apparently, was any investigation conducted into the best mode of executing the scheme to avoid doing injury to local enterprise. Needless to say, Africans were last to be informed of their imminent removal because sale of land near the port town was contemplated by the government. The upshot was that acreage near Durban was sold while African communities were still in actual occupation of it. Quite suddenly, these people were reduced to a class of squatters.

Accounts of this episode assert that the implementation of the relocation policy went smoothly under Shepstone's guidance—by all admissions, an amazing feat—an accomplishment usually attributed to the diplomatic agent's unique influence over the "native mind." Such statements are, of course, in direct contradiction to the actually observed facts. Confusion reigned, and the signs are plainly there to read. Local papers speak of communities being told to remove themselves or to hold themselves in readiness to move, while others were counseled to quit the land immediately (by men who took advantage of the confusion by representing themselves as government officials) without being told where they were to go. Repeatedly, but in vain, Africans implored government to confirm their residence. Meanwhile, overt speculations and wild rumors produced a situation of near-uproar. Stories circulated to the effect that if Africans did not go to the locations, they would be burned out, or worse, shot. Their anxiety was reflected in reports that women and children were being removed to places of greater safety, carrying with them as much as possible of their belongings, in anticipation of being attacked. Feelings were thus running high. And in the midst of the commotion one Durban farmer, thoroughly disgusted by the developments, angrily asserted: "I don't know what the government are about. They appear to be determined to make everyone discontented, and to do the place as much injury as possible... [The Africans] appear strongly prejudiced against Mr. Shepstone, and call him _____, how this has arisen I cannot imagine."[3]

In 1846 the *Natal Witness* noted:

> While the location system seems to be giving general satisfaction, an apprehension still exists in the minds of some, that much inconvenience will arise, both to the natives themselves, as well as to the other colonists, from the absence of an allotment of ground near the village of D'urban, *on which caffers engaged as day labourers might squat* [emphasis added]. . . . A matter of this kind may easily be managed while land is yet indisposed of.[4]

A cotton planter relying on the day labor of African women to cultivate his farm urged that "*a native location*, however small, [be placed] *on the Umgeni*, or in its neighbourhood." For, as he pointedly stressed, "*The women* will work at the land *if they can sleep at their homes*, but not otherwise."[5]

The following year brought more complaints. The original expectation was that when the location system was first announced, colonists would be glad to rid themselves of the kraals of squatters on their grounds. But now, in some important instances, at least, the reverse was found. One knowledgeable observer warned that unless an ordinance was speedily passed, government would find it impossible to carry out their plans, as both Africans and planters would oppose them. Africans would not cheerfully move to a place where they could not get money, and the planters would resist the withdrawal from their land of the families who provided labor.[6]

Failure of the "Native Town" Scheme

In December 1847 the Survey Commission, which was impaneled to report upon the division of the Natal territory into separate magistracies and the selection of sites for towns, proposed that each established township have a portion of its lands appropriated for the use of Africans in the service of inhabitants as daily laborers.[7] Charles J. Gibb, a lieutenant in the Royal Engineers, drew up a plan on the subject, with which Shepstone and the other members of the Native Location Commission were in full concurrence.[8]

Several considerations presented themselves in support of Gibb's scheme, a little-known document entitled "Memoranda proposing the establishment of a Native Town to be attached to the Towns of the District of Natal, particularly of Pietermaritzburg and Durban." First, it was felt that day laborers and their families would enjoy the same facilities for improvement as the planners hoped to see enjoyed by those in the several locations. Also it was anticipated that competent black mechanics, discharged from the mechanical schools to be set up in the reserves, would flock to the towns for employment, and would naturally prefer their own sphere of society to living indiscriminately in white towns. Such an establishment would furthermore counteract the demoralizing influences attendant upon Africans residing in the European centers. Finally, while improving their pecuniary circumstances and advancing in their appreciation of civilized life, residents of these "native towns" would learn about personal property in land, the idea most important to their efficient government.[9]

Gibb's "Memoranda" acknowledged the desirability of allotting a piece of ground in the immediate vicinity of the above-named towns for the settlement of Africans in the service of inhabitants "who [could] not be accommodated on the *erven* [grounds or premises] of their masters," and who were in other ways connected with the urban centers. The recommendations were that one thousand acres be selected within two or three miles of the center of town, fifty acres of which would be laid out in lots of one acre each for "the most intelligent and sufficiently advanced natives." When these "advanced natives" proved themselves competent, the lots would then be privately made over to them, under the condition they not be alienated to white colonists, or to other Africans, below a minimum fixed price. These "reclaimed natives" would ostensibly serve as role models to the others, who, though still "in their own ignorant state," were required in the towns either as servants or in other occupations. The remaining nine hundred and fifty acres would be set apart for this latter class, who would be admitted as residents to the "native towns" under the regulations detailed below.

Residents would be required to wear clothing. They would be allowed to have one wife reside with them in a hut built on an assigned site with limited garden grounds. Furthermore, a common cattle kraal—with the rights to pasture their herds (the number of cattle to be fixed by municipal regulations)—would be made available on the town land, each occupant paying a small sum to government. Management of the settlement would be the responsibility of the diplomatic agent or an officer appointed by government under him. The more "intelligent natives," however, would be selected to manage their own affairs under the officer's superintendence. Spiritual guidance of these communities would be entrusted to a minister of religion and a site would be made available for a chapel and school.

The urgency for such an arrangement was now formally recognized, particularly at Port Natal. Indeed, the fundamental conclusion of the report was that the newly established locations were at too great a distance to enable Africans to live on them and, at the same time, employ themselves in the occupations connected with shipping and so on.[10]

Astonishingly, after all this, no such "native town" was erected in connection with Durban. Squatter licenses were occasionally granted, enabling a few Africans to occupy town lands, but the more general feature of the urban scene was that of "illegal African squatter settlements" against which eviction orders were periodically issued. Such procedures frequently interfered with trade, as in 1853, when five Europeans interested in building works at Durban complained that the Council's removal orders had compelled them to break up their establishments, an act that resulted in a rise in the price of bricks.[11]

Upon reflection, it seems evident what had happened. "Want of funds," the very same plea of poverty that had resulted in government's failure to follow through on Shepstone's initial proposal for the internal management of the rural locations, may possibly have contributed to the stillbirth of the "native town." Yet in the long run, it was recognized that the resolution of this problem lay with the municipalities; and a number of suggestions were forwarded by townspeople and civic officials designed to group African servants and laborers in one locality. These proposals, however, were thwarted by individuals who believed such arrangements "would lead to the formation of places of refuge for indolent vagrants,"[12] a sentiment that fast crystallized into more concrete objections, as revealed in testimony given before the Kafir Commission. In the commission's findings, opponents of the concept of a "native village" pointed out that high urban wages diverted labor from the farms, and that African producers living in the neighborhood represented unfair competition for the small white Durban county farmer. Others merely reiterated Cloete's dictum that "constant intercourse with the whites had a natural and inevitable tendency to bring about a contempt for the power and institutions of civilization."[13]

In addition, the public was haunted by fears of "native risings," fears that were fanned by the realities of the Cape frontier wars and Mpande's incursions into Natal. Thus, while in 1852 Shepstone still favored the idea of "a native village being established in the vicinity of towns on some such plan as that recommended by the commissioners for locating the natives in 1847," he also believed that it was both desirable and proper to remove Africans from the unsupervised areas near the urban centers, in order to secure the safety of the white inhabitants in case of an outbreak. To reduce the size of these African communities, a scale of taxation was suggested—an increased rate for those living near the towns—to encourage their relocation to a greater distance.[14] While anxieties stemming from anticipation of eminent "native revolts" diminished with time, in the coming years new complications would be added to the general debate on "native housing." By the time of Union in 1910, this issue was still unresolved in Durban.

The foregoing discussion serves as a backdrop to the urban *togt* problem. The consequences of Cloete's sweeping pronouncement, which caused the mass forced removals of Africans from lands around the chief town and the port, seriously upset established local trade, greatly interfered with labor arrangements, and profoundly disrupted housing patterns that had been in existence for workers at Durban since the founding of the European commercial community in 1824. Formerly, Africans had entered the towns in the early morning hours, engaged their services, and towards sunset returned to their family homesteads, situated on the outskirts of the European settlements. From 1846 on, for a growing number of Africans seeking town wages, this return (*tocht* or *togt*) journey was no longer feasible. The pattern that materialized in the ensuing decades must be linked to the bleak record of municipal defaults centered particularly on the question of accommodations for urban workers.

Two issues—those of food and lodging—were tied to the much broader question of municipal control of the day laboring population. But the chronic failure of town officials to deal with these questions energetically resulted in a growing residential problem characterized by overcrowded dwellings and substandard housing. My intention here, however, is not to recount what is basically a prosaic tale of civic neglect. Rather I have set for myself a far more interesting task, that of exploring the ways in which Africans not only evaluated the above situation but struggled and organized at the workplace around the questions of housing and food.

Other cultural values in northern Nguni society show that these people had a perception of moral truth by which they sought to structure their universe. A strongly held set of beliefs about common human decency, right and wrong, correct conduct, and upright behavior toward one's fellow human beings was acquired from the ancestors and transmitted to the young as part of the common cultural heritage. Altruism and kindness were exalted. Individuals were obliged by custom as well as conscience to be compassionate, courteous, and thoughtful of others. And for good reason: traditionally, communities clung to this "safety line of principles" to carry them forward in times of crisis, as was shown in Chapter 1. African workmen likewise drew heavily upon this cultural arsenal in offering potential solutions for the various contemporary problems encountered and in planning and organizing around day-to-day concerns.

This chapter attempts to demonstrate that fundamental notions, which were embodied in the concept of *ubuntu* (hospitality), were at the marrow of a militant, self-conscious working-class ethic. A central motif related to this proposition, and one for which the evidence is extraordinarily conclusive, is this: alien though these expressions might have seemed to the colonists, the entire body of African workers in Durban and Pietermaritzburg nevertheless adhered firmly to an undismissable code of ethical conduct. What is more, they brought sanctions to bear against anyone who infringed upon the moral norm. In other words, through direct and collective use of their power, these nineteenth-century black workmen extracted hospitality from the European inhabitants of the towns.

African Expectations of Hospitality

"Abantu bakona bang'abantu, bayamazisa umuntu ehambile": The people of that place are the right sort of people; they are kind to a person that has been journeying.[15]

It has already been shown how northern Nguni-speaking people imprinted their work culture on the labor organization at Durban, where workers were formed into an unequal body and ranked in an age hierarchy.[16] I believe, moreover, that the urban work force, particularly in the earlier years, consisted mainly of two classes — the more mature men, who hired out by the day, and boys and young men, who primarily engaged by the month.[17] From a legal standpoint, this distinction was critical. Only monthly engagements came under the Masters and Servants Ordinance, the statute regulating the rights and duties of employers and employees. Of special relevance is the section of Law No. 2 of 1850, which held that masters were responsible for providing suitable lodging and sufficient food of good, wholesome quality during the continuance of their contract.

Most employers were guilty of dereliction of duty in this area.[18] But for those town masters who abided by the law, the fashion was to lodge their monthly domestics in cookhouses or huts (commonly called "Kafir kitchens") that were built away from the dwelling house on account of the danger of igniting the thatched roofs. Here a fire was kept burning and all cooking operations were performed; and as these outbuildings doubled as the servant's living quarters, it was naturally here that the "kitchen boy" slept and subsisted on the regulation quart of boiled Kafir mealies or Indian corn (cooked in a black, three-legged cast-iron "Kafir pot"). Here too was spent a large portion of the servant's leisure time, entertaining visitors, family members, and friends.[19] Other employers of monthly labor such as town merchants allowed their employees to sleep in back rooms on the store's premises. Accommodations for the permanent nucleus of dockhands consisted of clusters of huts or shanties ("Kafir houses") erected by the laborers themselves on the private property of landing and shipping agents.

Differentiating the "jobber" from the monthly worker, then, was the absence of a defined legal status. Since Law No. 2 of 1850 failed to make provisions for daily laborers, this latter class of workmen could expect no consideration for their everyday sustenance and upkeep, beyond the wage earned for their day's exertion. The rough fact was that masters were not legally committed either to supply rations or to provide shelter. Matters were made worse in that the towns were essentially closed to "jobbers" at the end of the working day. Municipal corporations shouldered absolutely no ethical responsibility for the day laborer's basic needs, nor were they attentive to the fundamental requirements of African visitors traveling to the European centers for the most legitimate purposes. Private enterprise also took little initiative in this area in the early years.[20] Except for the modest efforts of town church missions, there were no eating facilities to speak of, no public resthouses or other arrangements where, for a small sum, Africans could refresh themselves and find a hot meal. Such a state of affairs — that is, the downright stinginess and mean-spirited nature of the inhabitants in the corporations — was so contrary to African standards of human decency that truly the behavior of these whites must have seemed extraordinarily unnatural to anyone accustomed to the notion of *ubuntu*.

With regard to the status of strangers and the social and cultural meaning of food and feeding, we have seen in a previous chapter that in every Zulu homestead the responsibility for the proper treatment of travelers fell to the senior wife. She had to give sustenance, drink, and shelter, and was obliged to do so cheerfully or risk being ejected from her high office.[21] This courtesy was extended to all strangers, be they black or white. Descriptions of local people by shipwrecked mariners in 1689 bear testimony to the longevity of the custom.

> Neither need one be under apprehension about meat and drink, as they have in every village or kraal a house of entertainment for travellers, where these are not only lodged but fed also; care must only be taken, towards nightfall, when one cannot get any further, to stop there, and not to go on before morning.[22]

Around 1827 Shaka affirmed the operation of this law in its application to Europeans. Nathaniel Isaacs records that when the people at Ngomane's kraal refused him refreshments, his followers went into the hut of the head wife and took two calabashes of thick milk. In explaining the incident Isaacs wrote,

> This is usual, and according to the custom of the Zoolas who compel sustenance to be offered to the traveller. Towards white people Chaka issued an especial order, that at all times they should be amply supplied with food, as it could not be expected they knew how to obtain it, therefore in any case when refused, they were to have permission to plunder, and to use force to obtain it. . . . [23]

Meat, drink, and lodging were to be given as a social right and duty that, at some future date, the wayfarer was expected to reciprocate. Considering the many times they had proffered hospitality and entertained white people calling at their kraals, Africans must have been taken aback—literally stunned—by the insulting reception they met with in the towns. In such instances, they did not hesitate to make their wounded feelings known.

A classic incident occurring in 1865 will serve as an example. It involved the wife of the mayor of Durban, who apparently was badly shaken by Africans coming onto her premises demanding food of hospitality. For those black men unfamiliar with the urban culture, the logical place to repair with the expectation of being civilly received would have been to the "mayor's compound." His wife, after all, was the chief *inkosikazi* of the town! Obviously, though, neither she nor the ordinary white householder understood the nature of that charge. Even had they understood the Africans' expectations, it is unlikely they would have been willing to comply. Most often, the white person's response was to read into the actions of these men the most contemptible and brutish motives.

As she had refused their requests for food, the mayor's wife was ridiculed, subjected to abusive language, which naturally caused a public outcry.[24] These men, who were generally characterized as "vagrants," displayed, it was said, "a manner subversive to domestic order." Predictably, whenever such incidents were reported, the editorial columns launched into long-winded tirades about how it was unsafe for households to be left without sufficient white male authority on the premises to protect "white womanhood," and they demanded rigorous social controls to put an immediate halt to these "Kafir outrages." One must take the hysteria that emerged around the issue of board and lodging to be a helpful clue in elucidating the origins of the "black peril scare." For as Randle Bennett, Durban's superintendent of police (1861–68), recognized, the "so-called Kafir outrages or attempts . . . merit more possibly only to be attributed to impertinence."[25]

Unifying Influences of the "Kitchen Associations"

Beware of that fellow; don't listen to what he says. Keep you away from him. He is a liar, a slanderer; he wants to mislead you. Don't trust in his words, he is a rogue. Don't make such a noise, keep quiet. After the supper is over, go and lie down. Don't let other fellows come to you.[26]

Linked inseparably to their notions of hospitality are the nineteenth-century commentaries that speak of Africans as emphatically social beings, preferring the company of their fellows, sharing their food in common, and so on. Being strongly group-oriented, we are told, accounts for their preference for gang work on sugar plantations.[27] Still, while the common bonds of food may have been seen in some quarters as an admirable social trait, from the practical view of, say, an estate manager, this code of etiquette had its destructive side as well. The ritual of commensuality posed enormous problems for managers' efforts to coordinate job schedules around a large labor force. Early gangs of workers stubbornly resisted attempts to rotate mealtimes, refusing to eat until all their workmates had assembled to "share in the pot."[28]

It is important not to overlook the series of obligations implied in the act of eating in common. One critical idea was that these interpersonal relations united the different parties in the duties of friendship, brotherhood, and matters of social import.[29] Masters who held this custom in little account, or who attempted to deprive African workers of the deep emotional satisfaction as well as the social support it provided, encountered spirited resistance.

Once we understand this aspect of their social character, we begin to see very clearly how the psychologically unsustaining environment of domestic work might have been a totally miserable experience for the vast number of Africans. For not only did house servants have to contend with long hours, short pay, and exacting mistresses and masters, they also faced the possibility of extended periods of isolation from their "home circle" of acquaintances. This fact explains why, when opportunities arose to affirm the moral order, it was with an overwhelming rush of relief and elation that the homesick "kitchen boy" eagerly embraced visits from family members and friends.

Bearing this in mind, let us now move to reconstruct the strategy employed by urban day laborers who found themselves among an alien people strangely bereft of that singular virtue called *ubuntu*, the primary trait that defined civilized humanity and raised man (*umuntu*) above the savage beasts.

As he was a practical individual, always on the lookout for family members and friends, the day laborer most probably tried to locate someone in monthly employ who shared his clan name, for in that person he was certain to find a brother. If there was no one in the town with whom he shared a blood link, perhaps he investigated other ties, such as those of his wife's clan. Even though his spouse belonged to a different clan, all of the members of it were in a sense betrothed to him on the day he contracted to marry. As it developed, time and again, kin connections and other mutual attachments unfailingly stood black town visitors and laborers in good stead.[30] Wrote Mrs. Shooter in 1859, "All those belonging to the same tribe, or clan, are called brothers, a circumstance which puzzled me immensely at first. I thought our domestic must be one of an uncommonly numerous family, when visitor after visitor was introduced as his 'brother.'" When a "brother" (i.e., a clansman) of a servant came to his master's house, the servant was sure to divide his food and comforts with him. [31]

Thus in backyard after backyard scattered over the boroughs of Pietermaritzburg and Durban, and in a manner similar to that described by Mrs. Shooter, "kitchen associations" sprang spontaneously into existence, providing aid, support, and structural affiliations for African workers. Men without town affiliations who might for one reason or another have eschewed these associations, or been excluded from them, were sometimes allowed to "squat" in the backyards of poor white householders in consideration of rent payments or in exchange for doing odd jobs round the premises. Later, too, a class of European, Arab, and Indian slumlords leased run-down, unsanitary hovels to Africans at criminally high rates.

Though this section will focus primarily on laborers and the activities of the "kitchen associations," it is pertinent to note the coping solutions adopted by non–work seekers (those apparently without kin ties to fall back on in the towns) on short trips to the urban centers. What is significant about this information is that it enables us to trace more exactly the provenance of some of the charges relating to breaches of master-servant contracts.

One course of action that African travelers adopted, and which attracted public notice, was this: it became quite common when on visits to the cities for black people to procure a night's board and lodging under false pretense of seeking work. On entering the city in the afternoon, for example, a group would separate into small parties of one, two, or three and apply for work, which was easily obtained, as there was a chronic scarcity of labor. The ploy ensured both food and shelter for the night. The next day, having completed their business, the men departed for their homes. Or in a slightly different pattern, two or three of a party would engage in service so as to procure food for the rest until the object of their visit had been accomplished.[32] During protracted stays in the towns, experienced workers relied less on slick expedients and social artifices, however, and more on a system of broad networks and institutions with recognizable rules and codes.

Typically, in the latter case, at the end of the work day, groups of laborers congregated in the countless "Kafir kitchens" dispersed throughout the townships, where they shared accommodations and availed themselves of a "generous repast" prepared mostly from rations allotted to domestic servants. Mason described the scene particularly well.

> Another misfortune, especially at the sea-port, is that employers do not or cannot, provide accommodation for their Caffre workpeople, so as to keep them under due control after working hours. At sundown many of the merchants ride off to their suburban villas, the stores are closed, and the Caffre attendants left to themselves till business hours next morning. Away go the Caffres; some to the shambles for meat, others to have a washdown in the

nearest stream; some to collect friends, and others to pilfer or purchase viands for the evening banquet. The largest caffre hut in one of the back yards, or a dilapidated kitchen behind one of the stores, is generally the place of rendezvous; and thither groups of ten or twelve wend their way, shouting and brandishing their knobkerries at some imaginary foe concealed in the evening's dusk.

As soon as the place is full, then begins the cookery; with uproarious singing and merriment, relieved by occasional lulls, while the jolly fellows are smoking themselves into a state of stupidity with the poisonous root of the wild hemp; and discussing the "Indaba," or news of the day. . . . [33]

European householders scarcely tolerated these men imposing themselves uninvited on their property. The practice was denounced as a "sponging system"; it was widely deprecated as encouraging petty thievery in the "kitchen boys." Yet upon closer inspection, the charge of petty thievery can be identified as a restructuring of attitudes and behavior towards the institution of *ubuntu*. Current circumstances were transforming custom; the practice was adjusting to the commercial ethos encountered in the European centers. Incorporating the spirit of profit, this natural ethical code began to assume for some workers the appearance of a mutually beneficial monetary transaction.

Exposure to severe community censure came with allowing their servants free access to their own food, or leaving the mealies so carelessly that opportunities were presented for the servants to obtain it surreptitiously. Under such circumstances, it was not unusual for the servant to offer to feed a "brother" for a shilling a month out of the resources at his command. The "brother," who might earn seven shillings a month with rations would propose to his boss that he feed himself for the additional payment of three shillings. The proposition agreed to, one shilling out of the three was paid to the "kitchen Kafir," who controlled the larder, while the "brother" pocketed the difference. Payment was also received in tobacco, game meat, or beef, for accommodations afforded to friends.[34]

Colonists' preoccupation with the alleged "sponging and pilfering" activities of their workers actually masked a more profound grievance. Whites knew quite well that these nocturnal gatherings were something more than eating associations— places where people came simply for refreshments and entertainment, or to share in good fellowship. Masters were all too aware that the "Kafir kitchens" could not be disdainfully dismissed as backyard haunts where laborers idly loitered, "smoking themselves into a state of stupidity with the poisonous root of the wild hemp." In addition to serving as vehicles for fostering homeboy networks—for workers did spend a significant portion of their leisure in these quarters, interacting with the "brothers" recently arrived from their kraals in the rural districts, which helped to reinforce old customs and kept migrants abreast of home affairs—these back kitchens represented fertile environments for social experimentation. In the out-of-the-way areas at the rear of the master's house, fresh alignments developed along novel lines, and were nurtured and sustained. These were the testing grounds for new ideas; arenas in which to debate the efficacy of a particular custom that might be temporarily discarded or renegotiated to meet urban circumstances. Here in scores of these backyard hovels, black men similarly exposed to a new set of experiences found a venue to discuss the day's events. Such places provided the space both to innovate and to accommodate ancient institutions in order to address more effectively the issues that affected their immediate lives.[35]

And, surely, some connection must exist between the above activities and the long-standing complaint that these "unwelcome visitors" "rendered the nights hideous" with their songs. Were these communities of fellows singing for power? Were the "kitchen bards" utilizing the *izibongo* (praise poems), in the manner that Gunner has described for the modern South African trade union poets, in an aggressive, rallying way?[36] That is, were these nightly performances inspired solely by remembrances of past victories on ancient battlefields, or did the poems reflect struggles more recently fought in the labor centers—over competing definitions of the workday, for example? Were satires being composed around the "mysterious sounds named 'six o'clock' or 'nine o'clock bell,' " and so forth?[37] Facts certainly point to an affirmative answer. My findings support this. We have seen in a previous chapter that such compositions were created to spread praise or heap ridicule on employers. Renditions of urban work experiences were designed to disseminate information about the general conditions of labor. All the necessary factors, as this study will continue to show, were there to promote a culture of solidarity and to give concrete definition to a common worker identity. Furthermore, we may be sure that no town dwellers who regularly employed African labor long remained unaware of this fact, unless they chose deliberately to shut their eyes to the evidence that was everywhere around them.

Such observations lead to yet another significant conclusion. The "kitchen associations" were governed bodies possessing an internal structural logic conditioned by an African-centered vision of the world. Those traditionally at the top of the social hierarchy in northern Nguni society appear to have been the same individuals occupying leadership roles in the working community. The amaWasha (Zulu washermen, and very likely other individuals of recognized rank) held executive power over many of these groups.[38]

Without straining our interpretation of the data, the analogy can be made that these "brotherhoods" operated much like modern labor unions, which is to say, black workmen joined together for mutual support and protection and were solicitous of the rights and welfare of their fellow members. Like labor bureaus, the associations were an intelligence-gathering network regarding the availability of jobs and the unsuitability of certain mistresses and masters. Europeans could only express dismay at the effectiveness of these institutions in obtaining and circulating news of this nature. One mistress, Eliza Feilden, wrote: "Curiously enough, Louisa's back was hardly turned [referring to a servant girl from a nearby mission station], when a Caffre lad came to offer himself, telling me he could do everything. . . . "[39]

Seasoned workers, men of long experience, keen observation, and a developed network of contacts, collected facts, ascertained market trends, and guided new recruits into appropriate positions of employment, while steering the unwary away from masters and mistresses of bad reputations. On this latter subject, we are told that African workmen were "extremely sensitive to any intelligence of ill-treatment received by their brethren," and were restrained from working for any employer "whose reputation was so tarnished."[40] Yet on the same question, another of our sources indicates that Africans sometimes reconciled this problem by exacting a higher wage rate from employers who had a bad name among them.[41]

Just as the traditional bards (who were discussed in Chapter 3) served as the "people's conscience," as informal mechanisms to regulate behavior in the society, so, too, the worker's ability to "punish through words" caused extreme anxiety among many European employers, like Mrs. Shooter, who understood perfectly the tremendous value of "character" in attracting labor and keeping down wages. "Nearly three months have passed since my last entry," she anxiously recorded in her diary, "but still no Kaffir has offered himself for work." Luckily, shortly afterwards,

> A queer, shabby-looking Kaffir, without a blanket or mat, offered himself this afternoon to come and work. We were only too pleased to engage him, as we are told where one is at work more will follow. . . .

And a month later, she reported:

> It is very satisfactory that another Kaffir has engaged himself, for we began to be afraid that we were not in good repute among them, in which case no one would have taken service with us. [42]

Another employer, "Honesty," was "simply horrified at the light and airy way Kafirs [had] of taking away the character of respectable [white] people. That you do not pay wages when due, and are 'cheeky,' was mild compared with the other lies disseminated by the heathen Kafir." Legal action was suggested to prevent "Kafir Libellers" from repeating in future "such scandal" and "cruel slander."[43]

If these "workmen's protective associations" could prove so capable in organizing and controlling the flow of labor, and were able through the power of the word to ensure that their "brothers" would avoid the worst forms of abuse, then the idea of Africans influencing the market in the crucial matter of fixing a price code for their services does not seem far-fetched. Indeed, there exists dramatic confirmation of this at both Durban and Pietermaritzburg, the two leading work centers, which frequently reported on their "sharp practices." The procedure prevailing among experienced city workers, for instance, was to meet "green boys" on the outskirts of town as they came seeking work and insist upon their demanding a certain monthly wage; the result was that new "boys" refused to work for less than the stipulated sum, believing that it was the current rate.[44]

Even more aggressive, confrontational tactics were employed to remedy discrepancies in pay rates. At the port town of Durban we are privileged to see more distinctly how workers took the institutions of the *izimbongi* (bards or praise poets) of Zululand and adapted them to the modern labor strategy, the protest picket.

For the benefit of the reader, I include Bryant's recollection that when he first arrived in Zululand, the official *imbongi* of John Dunn (the famous white chief under Mpande and Cetshwayo) strode up and down before the verandah of the house, shouting out "all our virtues real and imaginary."[45] Also, it is well to be reminded by Cope (and Bryant and others before him) that the object of these informal associations was to function as "agents of conformity to the approved patterns," and that social control was maintained traditionally in Nguni society by apportioning praise as well as blame, by flattery as well as censure. Thus, if individuals kept with the tenets of the society and did not stray from community standards, they were favorably recognized; but when they broke the laws of the community or opposed its values, they were verbally castigated in public forum, a degree of poetic license permitting the use of insulting epithets.[46] A. C. Jordan early drew our attention, as more recent writers have done, to the adaptability of the *izibongo* (praise poems) to modern themes.[47]

Though newspaper coverage was sporadic, I nevertheless managed to cull from the sources several references to an aggrieved laborer, or groups of disgruntled workmen or domestic servants, who, perhaps affecting some of the less extravagant mannerisms of the *izimbongi*, congregated (or paraded up and down) in front of an offending employer's home, shouting out protests and abuses. Generally, continuous harassment was kept up until the householder or master either surrendered to their demand—in many instances, the dispute involved the question of bringing a servant's salary into line with the prevailing wage in the neighborhood—or until the local constables put a halt to their activities by hauling the protesters off to jail.

Umlungo's story is a case in point. He and "other Kafirs" were brought before Durban's magistrate, charged with being "an annoyance" to Mrs. Martin living in Victoria Street—that is, they were "saying insulting things to her when her husband was away." Because of the imprecise wording of the charge, the full significance of their actions might well have eluded us but for the following brief remarks by Durban's superintendent of police, who, in a court appearance on behalf of Mrs. Martin, made the illuminating observation that,

> There was *a regular trade union* [emphasis added] amongst the Kafir boys in that and other neighbourhoods of the town, and if it was learnt that a master was paying his boy a shilling or so a month less than others, the other lads carried on a system of abuse and annoyance.[48]

Reports such as the above show rather dramatically that nineteenth-century migrant workers were already familiar with organized action. Quite clearly, they were united, self-regulated, and disciplined; moreover, they had recognized rules and approved patterns of behavior to which they expected both the employer and their fellow workers to conform. Individuals who transgressed the work code, such as by "accept[ing] a lower rate of wages than [was] fixed by 'the trade,' " or otherwise violated propriety, were fined or sternly chastised by the leadership; we hear of this as recently as 1856.[49]

The special efficacy of these groups probably lay, however, in their ability to extract charitable hospitality from town employers. About these "unbidden guests," one ratepayer derisively commented,

> Hospitality we know is a normal law of the savage, and it may be that he sees no reason why the same law should not govern the European. At any rate he assumes that it is so and vigorously acts upon the assumption.[50]

Emboldened by ties to the labor networks, monthly servants demanded the *right* to entertain visitors in their living quarters—a right they clearly took for granted as inviolable. Any master denying such permission found himself without servants. What is more, word of the incident was broadcast around the working community, discouraging others from engaging with him.

"Their mode of procedure is indeed one of the neatest examples of cool impudence that we know of," editorialized the *Mercury* in 1865. "Any attempt to eject them is regarded as a personal injury."[51] Another local journal in 1873 denounced the practice as a "species of blackmail." Six years later Durban's superintendent of police, Richard C. Alexander, stated: "A togt kaffir now on being called upon to work will first demand double the amount allowed by law; in addition to this *he demands his food and requires you to cook it for him, both of which the employer foolishly agrees to*" [emphasis added].[52] And in 1901 Alexander reported, "the practice [i.e., 'sponging'] [had] become so universal that native servants look[ed] upon it as a right and would leave the service if it were not permitted, and further do his best to boycott the man who would not permit it, from obtaining another."[53]

Efforts to keep "Kafir houses" free of outsiders during the plague scare at the turn of the century met similar opposition. J. J. Dunne, for one, attempted to explain the sanitary hazards to African workmen in his employ, warning that anyone wishing to pay a visit would have to get leave from the master. Furthermore, all *togt* boys were to be rigidly excluded. Not long after issuing these injunctions, Dunne observed a worker taking a quantity of loaves from the bakery to his room. Following, he saw five or six women seated on the floor, a loaf and a half beside them. The visitors were immediately ejected, at which point one of the workers began to incite the eight others to join him and "desert." The group reportedly vowed that "they would not work if their sisters could not visit them."[54] In another episode occurring around the same time, W. E. Higgs, a European employer charged before the borough's court with overcrowding his premises, remarked to the magistrate that "he had to do almost anything to humour the boys so as to keep them."[55]

Board, lodging, wages, and control over their leisure time were ongoing concerns, and a great deal of material has been painstakingly amassed to show that these were the weighty issues around which nineteenth-century town laborers coalesced. Their brilliant use of pressure tactics (strikes, picket lines, boycotts, and so forth) as well as their collective bargaining skills elicit our admiration and must, once and for all, silence any lingering doubts regarding the early migrant workers' alleged inability to unite around common causes. From first to last, Natal's African laboring population exhibited solidarity. Reports respecting the existence of "widespread concerts" and "conspiracies" alert us to the fact that these men were already well organized by 1852. Indeed in the year 1850 one hears the earliest verbal expressions of African worker consciousness. And as a "Working Contractor" wrote thirteen years later, those unacquainted with "Kafir affairs" would be astounded by the level of organization among them regarding work, masters, and so forth.[56] These nineteenth-century workmen were fully aware that by combining, they would obtain better wages; acting in concert and using sustained pressure ensured food and housing for fellow laborers, particularly day "jobbers" who did not have legitimate access to such amenities.

One single cohesive idea seemed to underlie much of their actions: the concept of *ubuntu* defined their "moral culture" and provided inviolate rules about the proper treatment of fellow human beings. These workers honored mutual obligations, and I think it was their deeply offended moral conscience that first brought these people together to demand in one voice the right to extend basic civilities to friends and relations who had come to town on official business, to shop, or to visit loved ones working there. Out of these initial struggles, there emerged a recognition of their collective experience *as workers*, an awareness that they were part of a community of fellows sharing a unique set of problems, interests, and objectives. The ability of these workmen to link tradition with present realities in order to deal with contemporary problems imparted a sense of strength, continuity, and direction to their lives. Judged by any standards this was an era of African worker power!

To use a common expression, the Caffre servants have the whip-hand of all small employers; and consequently of town masters more than others, because the scarcity of hands compels the master to submit to anything rather than be left Caffreless. *The fellows know this, and continually are showing their power on any employer who give offense* [emphasis added]. . . . [57]

Municipal Attempts to Control the amaWasha

To town authorities, "the evils of togt" were personified in the amaWasha. Their activities made concrete and perceptible all that was amiss with the labor policy. Indeed, no group better signified the municipal failure to control African labor and coerce the floating population into stable employment than did the Zulu washermen. For this reason, when urban officials began to institute measures to restrain the "togtmen," the guild was the preeminent target for attack.

Singling out the washermen, local news journals frequently held forth on the impositions town folks were forced to endure, and emphasized the urgent need to check their machinations.

The numerous corps of "wash Kafirs" that find profitable employment in this neighbourhood, are in the habit of sponging for their food upon Kafirs in service near the places where they resort to wash. In such cases the most insolent demand is made for food, and unless the demand is complied with . . . personal violence or threats of injury are commonly resorted to. . . . The extent to which every Kafir kitchen is made a place of resort by other Kafirs is a matter of general complaint . . . and there is certainly wanted a law or regulation by which employers should be allowed to administer chastisement on the spot, after a "notice to quit" has been once given and defied.[58]

Shortly after the appearance of the above article, the resident magistrate for Durban issued a firm warning through Otuta, the chief African constable, "particularly appli[cable] to washing Kafirs, who had a lazy life, . . . that such practices could not be allowed . . . [and] that any master would be perfectly justified in giving a sound beating to any Kafir whom he should find so intruding."[59]

In England, as in Scotland and the American slave south, municipal supervision of casual laborers developed into organized systems, with sweeping provisions and formal restrictions requiring "jobbers" to pay fees, wear badges or tallies, and report to centrally located hiring stands. The latter outlets served as centers for the redistribution of labor resources throughout the cities.[60] "[L]et such a system be introduced in Durban," urged one civic-minded resident in 1855, "my plan would be to give every Kafir who wants to wash, carry firewood, and any other sort of work that may offer, a numbered badge, he giving his name, place of residence, and agreeing regularly to wait at some place appointed by the Town Council and submit to such a rate of charges as might be considered reasonable."[61] But not till the 1860s did public officials begin to take definitive steps toward erecting a web of restraints. In a report dated March 1, 1862, Durban's superintendent of police predicted that

the time is not far distant when not only in the towns but through the whole country stringent measures must be adopted in regard to those who find it convenient to take service either for stated periods or as day labourers. The latter class are exceedingly numerous, comprising "washing Kafirs," collectors of firewood, etc. charging most exorbitantly for the work performed. . . . I must however give them their just due, linen or other articles positively entrusted to them are respected. . . . [62]

Pietermaritzburg took the initiative the following year when its Town Council "authorized to have a number of arm badges made and numbered, and also marked 'W.' " Every washerman not in permanent employ was to be registered and charged a monthly fee; individuals found washing without permission were to be prosecuted.[63] This initial confrontation between expediency and custom, on the one side, and town law, on the other, ended in a humiliating loss of face. For in that year, apparently, the laundrymen successfully resisted the badge-tariff system by abandoning Pietermaritzburg's washing sites and returning to their kraals. Householders, reluctant to take on the temporary burden of doing their own washing, did little to aid the corporation in seeing that the measures were complied with.[64]

Meanwhile, what town authorities in Durban and Pietermaritzburg were unable to achieve, private endeavors sought to bring about. "It's not creditable to the good taste of the white population," reproved the editor of the *Mercury*, "that male Kafirs are almost exclusively employed to perform the washing of household linen and clothing." The article counseled social reform, proposing that women involved in the Benevolent Society, a charitable institution catering primarily to indigent whites, might organize a washing establishment and license destitute females who would act under the supervision of a committee.[65] The trouble with this proposition was that few white women and young girls were willing to perform jobs considered "Kafir work." The fact was, as one columnist noted, young Natal girls became so accustomed to ordering "servants to carry out their slightest wish that when they grow up they have no inclination to do more than they are actually compelled by nature to do for themselves; setting aside altogether the question of doing anything for others. . . . The girls," he exclaimed, "they do menial work, *never*—perish such a thought!"[66]

A private venture, the Umgeni Washing Company, was organized in 1867 under the management of Lawrence H. Greene; its announced objective was to break the amaWasha monopoly in the town and in Durban's suburbs.[67] After less than a month in existence, the future of the new enterprise seemed assured. With so much public support thrown behind the endeavor, the promoters were encouraged to make a reduction in laundry prices and to extend operations to the Berea, Addington, and Point suburban districts.[68] Then, at this optimistic juncture, the documents fall silent. Gazetted eight months later came the notice announcing "the insolvent estate of Lawrence Henry Greene."[69]

In reviewing its brief history, the significant thing to note is that the Umgeni Washing Company did not employ modern steam laundering techniques but relied instead on a staff of workers who had been "specially selected . . . from the whole number of erratic washing Kafirs. . . . "[70] Of equal significance was the promoter's plan to obtain "exclusive use of the river frontage for the purpose of a drying ground and erecting a shed" for the storage of supplies. While permission was granted "to use the land with others on sufferance," the company's manager was informed by the Town Council that it could not legally give the washing company exclusive use of any piece of ground without putting it up to public auction.[71]

The success of this commercial effort obviously hinged on the disaffected loyalties of some amaWasha members, who, one may assume from what is known of their propensity to use violence, were aggressively persuaded by loyal guildsmen either to rejoin the association or to seek alternative employment.[72] We may also look for an explanation of the company's abrupt demise in management's failure to gain sole control of the Mgeni washing site; a stratagem that, had it succeeded, would have usurped the Zulu trade by depriving the washermen of access to the key resource in their mode of livelihood.

In the two years preceding the above developments, the mayor and Durban Town Council sent a memorandum to the Executive Office on "the evils . . . arising from the resort to the town of numbers of idly disposed natives . . . looking for day labor as workmen, washermen, woodcutters, hawkers of small articles, who came on the premises of householders. . ., and etc." The document catalogued the all-too-familiar charges that these men created a feeling of insecurity among the white inhabitants and encouraged habits of thievery in their servants. It acknowledged that the main culprits were the householders who either provided substandard housing or failed to make any description of apartments available for their monthly servants. Equally notorious was the fact that no board or lodging arrangements existed of "a public sort." The situation had dragged on far too long. Now the petitioners were anxious for a more "creditable arrangement." They were looking to government for a bill that would erect in the town a public lodging house or houses where all Africans would be compelled to register their arrival and departure, a place, furthermore, where they would be assured of getting food. The magistrate and mayor, the petitioners proposed, would manage the said accommodations, which would be subject to specified regulations as to charges and conduct. Suggestions were also forwarded for an evening school in connection with the lodging establishments, which, as they saw it, would contribute to "native progress."[73]

The reply from the Executive Office was prompt yet dampening. Writing on behalf of the governor, Shepstone was inclined to think legislative action on the subject of the memorandum was unnecessary; the power to accomplish the objects suggested was already in the hand of the corporation and the people of Durban in the form of the Masters and Servants Ordinance. As government saw it, the question was simple and brooked only one possible response. No enactment, Shepstone wrote, would hinder day laborers from sleeping on the premises of residents who themselves did nothing to prevent it. As regards the matter of public accommodations, the attorney general's sentiments were equally discouraging. He could not advise government to become "public lodging housekeepers." That, in his considered judgment, should "be left to private enterprise."[74]

Matters worsened from this time on, as the overburdened local enforcement agencies struggled to control the swelling number of Africans entering the towns. Another factor came into play about this time that shifted the focus of white agitation from the topic of "Kafir spongers" to hysterical charges of alleged "Kafir outrages" perpetrated upon European women.[75] This volatile issue set the debate off all over again. Needless to say, the nature of the new allegations was sufficient to guarantee a swift legislative response.

In September 1869, the "Law for the Punishment of Idle and Disorderly Persons and Vagrants within the Colony of Natal" was enacted. Under its provisions any person wandering over private property, or loitering near or lodging in any house without the owner's leave was subject to arrest. The corporations were also empowered to fix a curfew and erect a building for the nightly reception of "nonresident natives." Once again Pietermaritzburg took the lead, introducing a 10:00 p.m. to 5:00 a.m. curfew in 1871; the city also provided a room largely availed of by day laborers.[76] Yet in the ardent view of one Durban "Burgess," the situation called for sterner sanctions.

> [We should] [o]nly allow a certain number of Kafirs in the town, . . . make them pay a license monthly fee to the corporation, and each wear a badge numbered, and when one leaves the town the badge to be returned to the police station. . . . Then there is the washing Kafir; let him also pay his license and wear his badge; he is better paid than any Kafir in town; why should he not add to the revenue of the town. . . . [77]

Toward that end an informal investigation was undertaken by the Durban Town Council, the object of which was twofold: to determine the effectiveness of the vagrant law in Pietermaritzburg, and to ascertain whether a system for "registering day working natives" was enforced in the city.[78] Meanwhile, related economic developments in the southern African region brought matters to a head.

Durban was the entrepôt center for the colony. With the discovery of diamonds, the port gained in importance and increased in prosperity, largely because it offered the shortest supply route to the inland mine fields. In fact, throughout Durban county every branch of commerce experienced a tremendous burst of activity that led to spiraling demands for labor. Competition for that limited commodity was intensely bitter among the various industries and trades.

Quite possibly there was no other period analogous to the years 1869–1873 in the economic history of nineteenth-century Natal in which the labor market was as open and as free of legislative encumbrances. It was a time in which increasing numbers of Africans were able to exercise a wider range of choices than ever before regarding where and for whom they would work. It is impossible to read the local news journals without noticing that the *togt* work force was thriving in this environment. One daily observed in dramatic tones that "the streets of Durban are overrun with 'toch' Kafirs. You have but to whisper the word 'toch' in West Street, and like a swarm of bees the devotees of 'toch' will respond to the summons."[79]

In this context, 1873 must be seen as a turning point in Natal's labor history. For colonists, that year represented the nadir of conditions within the colonial labor market and in the quality of master-servant relations. Since 1868 Indian immigration had been disrupted pending an investigation into charges of ill-treatment of the indentured workers. A smallpox epidemic reported at Delagoa Bay in July of 1873, as well as the uncertain political scene in Zululand on Mpande's death, combined to create such unrest among the Tsonga that it resulted in the drying up of that foreign labor source. Then, the rumors and fears engendered by government military operations against Langalibalele had the immediate effect of driving Natal workers back to their kraals. Hundreds of others were absorbed by the diamond fields. And finally, as described before, the great popularity of "stopping only by the day" among rural and town workers posed an enormous hardship on white employers. Varying reports speak at this time of crops of sugar, coffee, and cotton lying in the fields, because hands were unavailable to harvest them.

1873 was a watershed year in terms of "native policy" as well. The destruction of the Hlubi, one of the most progressive African communities in nineteenth-century Natal, unequivocally demonstrated government's willingness to adopt a hardline with respect to "native affairs." It was no coincidence that women and "ringed men" of this defeated group were bound out to the colonists for three years, "a great gain to [the whites], [because of the] dreadful scarcity of labor in the colony."[80] That year also augured the beginning of the loss of the African worker's autonomy: in October Durban passed its first vagrancy bylaw, establishing a 9:00 p.m. to 5:00 a.m. curfew[81] aimed at curtailing the mobility of the entire body of casuals locally known as "togt-men"; and the well-known "Togt Minute" of Theophilus Shepstone, secretary for native affairs, culminated the following year (1874) in the framing of the "Togt Rules and Regulation"[82] —a signal document marking the transition in the status of Africans laboring in the towns from that of free to that of licensed worker.

The *togt* laws were designed to prevent the formation of worker "combinations" and to generally discourage the enormously popular jobbing types of engagements. The Rules levied a monthly 2s. 6d. fee, enjoined the jobber to wear a badge "in some conspicuous part of his person," and fixed a tariff of wages. Under the regulations, no African would be allowed to live in the boroughs of Pietermaritzburg or Durban, including the suburbs, unless he was the proprietor or renter of a house or land within the borough; or was in the monthly or yearly employ of a proprietor or renter; or had accepted the position, wore the badge indicating it, and paid the monthly license of a day laborer. Africans entering the townships to work for wages had five days in which to find employment as a monthly servant or take up the calling of a *togt* man. Contravention of the regulations would be punished by fine, imprisonment, or both. Magistrates were further empowered to prohibit such Africans from being allowed to follow the calling of a licensed laborer, and to banish him from the town.[83]

At the prompting of ratepayers, washermen were recognized as a special class to be "furnished with badges different to those supplied to others."[84] Rule six of the new law had failed to distinguish between the various *togt* trades. Thus when called upon, a *togt* man, whatever his profession, was obliged to perform the task regardless of its nature. Some modification in the law seemed advisable. For instance, as "Hand-worker" sensibly pointed out,

> suppose a member of that useful class called wash Kafirs, in search of defiled toggery, were offered the rate of wages as fixed by the magistrate under the rule, but to do other kinds of work, by various householders, it may possibly cause family inconveniences that may be avoided, perhaps by giving a different badge for that particular class, the officer appointed to give each license taking care to grant no number excessively beyond the requirements of the borough for such purpose.[85]

From the docket of "native cases" involving contravention of the regulations, one finds that the amaWasha were in fact exempted from performing jobs outside their craft.[86] In Shepstone's opinion, vendors of firewood did not fall within the purview of the *togt* laws.[87]

How did these African workmen respond to the new regulations? On the eve of the *togt* laws' coming into force at Durban, Police Superintendent Alexander made known to an assembled group of day laborers the intent and meaning of the measures. The *togt* men, it was reported, stated no general objections to the new order of things save for the fact they were agitated by the idea of a license or badge, and seemed to think that when the "letter," as they called it, was put upon them, the authorities would hold over them some secret power not previously in existence.[88]

At sunrise the next morning, when the rules came into effect, few *togt* men could be found in town. There were scarcely any at the port; most had cleared out. Several employers were forced to suspend operations, the building trades being especially hard hit by the walkouts.[89] The dominant sentiment prevailing among the *togt* men was that the new regulations would "make them a sort of slave."[90] Even those who trickled back into town and gradually fell in with the rules, and who seemed not at all averse to paying the half-crown fee (2s. 6d.), still found unsettling the experience of having their height and description taken.[91]

The above news accounts were related in a tone consistently flippant and snide and were obviously meant to entertain the reading public. In fact, general coverage of the event tended to caricature the day laborers and smirk at their anxieties, as if to say, Ah, yes, another example of the ignorant superstitious Kafirs; how amusing their unreasoning dread of the white man's "special powers." But such images could not have been further from the mark. These workers quickly fathomed the general intent of the new measures. And from what can be discovered, it seems the matter contributing most to their sense of unease may partly be explained by glancing at Togt Rule No. 3, requiring that the jobber's name and other particulars be registered in a book for purposes of identification. There were unfortunate associations attached to such registration procedures. For one thing, they were a patent reminder of the hated system of forced labor, *isibhalo*. (The word *isibhalo* derives from the verb *ukubhala*, to write down or to register.[92])

It was not long before they realized how matters stood. Generally speaking, apprehensions were dispelled the moment day workers began to perceive loopholes in the regulations, ways in which the laws could be exploited to advantage. We know, for instance, that the system was used by Africans as a tax shelter. Ownership of a badge actually exempted one from recruitment into *isibhalo* labor gangs.[93]

Not surprisingly, within a remarkably short time (less than a month after the laws' enforcement), old complaints were again being ventilated. " 'Togt' labor is now as expensive as ever it was, or, perhaps more so," wrote one columnist. "The 'togt' men are scarcer than they used to be, and they take advantage of that in every way."[94] Another aggravated Durbanite complained:

> The "togt" Kafirs in town now demand exorbitant pay for any little job they may be required to do. When the Florence arrived at the port last Friday, we wanted a person to carry our parcel of extras up to town. We could not get a Kafir to do it for less than a "scotchman," 2s. Having been in the habit of paying 1s., we refused the dark Shylock's service, when forth came a European and offered to do the job for 1s. We thought to ourselves that times have indeed changed when a whiteman can be found to do an odd job of this kind for half the sum demanded by a Kafir.[95]

And in 1876 one reads of eight hundred *togt* workers in Durban charging as high wages as ever. "There is no doubt," continued the source, "that they have formed a combination to keep the wages up. . . . "[96] The situation obviously reflected the status quo ante.

Neither was the question of board and lodging resolved. The vagrant house erected in Durban in 1873 was capable of housing only twenty-five to thirty persons, while during that year there were on monthly average four hundred day laborers in the port town.[97] Revenues from *togt* licenses were to be expended exclusively in carrying out the regulations and securing the effective working of the system. Accordingly, out of the "togt funds" the first *togt* barracks were built in 1878 with a capacity for two hundred workers. Those facilities were also inadequate. In October alone, one thousand Africans had taken up badges in Durban.[98] Additional barracks constructed toward the end of the century were boycotted. For a host of reasons the *togt* men continued to utilized the arrangements provided by the network of kitchen associations.

The feeling throughout, from almost the moment of their promulgation, was that the *togt* laws had failed. As the years elapsed and the economy expanded, so too did the *togt* population. From the litany of complaints that continued to be heard over this period and into the opening decade of the new century, there emerged two overwhelming themes: the need for wage control and for housing of the *togt* labor force. Furthermore, the *togt* system endured—despite the tensions and frustrations it produced, and despite the fact that it was widely deplored by municipal authorities and colonial officials. The fact that it endured was as much a testament of its popularity among African workmen, as it was a measure of its practicality for the fluctuating needs of shipping, the seasonality of the building trades, and, equally important, its utility for the poorer class of white ratepayers.

Continued Efforts to Displace the amaWasha

Thus notwithstanding the *togt* regulations, housewives steadily complained of the cost of laundering. One of them, Lady Barker, wrote:

> The price of washing as this spoiling process is called is enormous, and I exhaust my faculties in devising more economical arrangements. We can't wash at home as most people do, for the simple reasons that we've no water, no proper appliances of any sort, and to build and buy such would cost a small fortune. *But a tall, white aproned Kafir, with a badge upon his arm* [emphasis added], comes now at daylight every Monday morning and takes away a huge sack of linen . . . for which he received 3s. 6d.[99]

Efforts to enforce new tariff scales in 1879[100] resulted in large numbers of *togt* men withdrawing from Durban. In one incident, a hundred "very dissatisfied and independent" workers made their departure; it was further related that when "one [had] been fined for refusing to work at the price laid down . . . numbers [had] at once thrown up their badges."[101]

There is no question but that the amaWasha had effectively resisted the move to reduce their average 3s. 6d. service fee by one shilling. So for Pietermaritzburg town dwellers, it was a buoyant announcement that appeared in the newspaper on January 7, 1880: "[O]ne of the greatest wants in this city will shortly be supplied . . . the means of obtaining good washing," a want that would shortly be met by the opening of a steam laundry.[102] As another city resident commented happily,

> To have the linen of the household taken away as cast off, and returned in a thoroughly dressed and repaired condition, . . . and all at a reasonable cost, is certainly a convenience which cannot be too highly commended, particu-

larly in these times, when the old-fashioned wash Kafirs have become so scarce that most families have often been at their wits end to get their washing done.[103]

Inundated with large and small customer accounts, the proprietor of the new establishment immediately advertised for "more hands" to supplement the original staff of twenty-one—comprising eight white women, five white men, and eight Chinese laundrymen. Though the staff doubled within the first month of operation, the company continued to run short of the needed labor.[104] Encouraged by the tremendous patronage given to the fledgling venture, the local journal penned these self-congratulatory words on the apparent coup achieved over the amaWasha community.

> The Kafirs who used, in a manner, to wash for us, are considerably perplexed at the scarcity of bags entrusted to them, since the Steam Laundry has fairly started operation; and are displaying an amount of zeal which rather reflects to their discredit, as it shows what they could but would not do, until forced by serious competition. . . . [105]

A similar premature smugness was evinced by another daily:

> Our "togt" washing Kafirs are sadly exercised in their minds anent this competition, but they must feel that they brought it upon themselves, and that in this case necessity was the mother of the invention, and let us hope it will impress them that if they will not render the simple service asked of them for fair remuneration, we can find the hands and money to do for ourselves.[106]

Despite overwhelming support for the Steam Laundry, the speculative venture was ill fated. "I found I had to employ too much hand labor," explained the owner, and "wages ran away with the profits."[107] Expensive machinery was needed to salvage the operation and secure its economical working. To that end, the public was approached with a scheme to take over the institution under the Limited Liability Companies Act. In the prospectus drawn up by a committee consisting of some of Pietermaritzburg's finest citizens, the directors were sanguine that with suitable machinery and indentured labor, the Steam Laundry Co., Ltd., could reduce the cost of service to the benefit of the city while paying fair dividends to investors.[108] "It is for the public to consider," proclaimed the lead article in the *Natal Witness*, "can this profit be made of the washing of a whole city."

> Mr. Superintendent Alexander told us the other day publicly, that togt takes money away from our towns, money that never returns. He estimated that in Durban alone, no less that £30,000 is thus wasted annually. In Pietermaritzburg matters have been even worse. It is calculated that the City's washing has cost 26s. per head for the white inhabitants, or no less a sum annually than £5,980 stg., an amount of which a large proportion must fall to the washing company.[109]

Public backing fell short of the new company's projected needs, however. The Steam Laundry was soon insolvent.[110]

Rise of the Indian *Dhoby* and the Public Health Movement

After this ignominious failure of white town dwellers to release themselves from dependence on the "wash Kafir," there occurs a hiatus in the documents between 1881 and 1888. As things turned out, during this intervening period civic officials had worked out a solution that eliminated the necessity for the "old-fashioned wash Kafir." Out of their efforts came a scheme for a tremendously improved water supply, which was introduced in the two leading townships in 1887. This development meant that those Durban town dwellers who could afford the initial £2 application fee and the additional monthly water rates could enjoy a constant supply of water laid on direct to their private premises for domestic, trade, or manufacturing purposes.[111] The possibility of a water tap for every household had far-reaching social and economic consequences. For the Zulu washermen, whose eminence hinged on control over the Mgeni and the river front, the new water supply obviated the need to send the town's linen four miles away to the old washing site; thus their services were rendered obsolete. Furthermore, piped-in water made it possible to restore a substantial portion of laundering chores to the realm of household labor while it simultaneously stimulated a new urban industry—commercial laundries.[112]

Some time would pass, however, before that innovation became generally diffused among urban dwellers; and because of their costliness, neither commercial laundries nor modern home labor-saving devices, such as washing machines, would suddenly displace the nineteenth-century Zulu washerman.[113] His challenger and first effective rival, coming after some forty years of dominating the washing industry, was the Indian *dhoby*, a member of the Hindu washermen's caste, whose hand laundries in the towns operated at cheap and therefore highly competitive rates.

After serving out their indentureship on sugar estates or as specialized house servants, some of these Indians migrated to the towns, where they engaged in sundry trades, including that of ironing clothes.[114] The Hindu tradesmen were among the first consumers to take advantage of the new water system, which enabled them to capture a substantial portion of the washing industry. But the proliferation of *dhoby* "dens" created consternation among certain elements of the European population. Many Indian "wash houses" and laundries were situated in squalid, overcrowded slum areas of the city and operated under unsanitary conditions. After the alarm in 1890 caused by an outbreak of cholera among Indian immigrants just arrived from Calcutta, fear of epidemics triggered a white backlash against the Asian laundrymen and amusingly stirred in a few individuals nostalgic regrets for the fading era of the Zulu "wash Kafir." A crusade launched by the inspector of nuisances, whose nightly raids on *dhoby* premises led to a series of grim disclosures, inspired passage of a new bylaw in 1898, the effect of which was to establish a modicum of control over *dhoby* businesses. The appearance of bubonic plague in South Africa at the turn of the century renewed and intensified the sanitary campaign.

As it was, a mood had already begun to crystallize in the colony against all skilled indentured servants, who, it was charged, displaced white labor and introduced undue competition. The disease factor was merely the point at which the tinder was lit. Passionate anti-Indian protest ultimately persuaded the colonial government to halt the importation of Indian artisans, including carpenters and mechanics, as well as cooks, waiters, and *dhobies*.[115] These restrictions, however, did not prevent *dhobies* presently established from continuing in their line of business. That task was left to municipal officials, European laundrymen, and other anti-Indian forces committed to a policy of eliminating the Asiatic trading communities in Natal.[116]

In this hostile climate, Durban's medical health officer opined in 1909 that it was only necessary to bring effective bylaws into operation to force fully 90 percent of the Indian laundry establishments out of business.[117] Anticipating just such a possibility, over one hundred *dhoby* petitioners came together under the Durban Laundry Association (D.L.A.) to protest the impact the proposed laundry bylaws, then under Town Council consideration, would have on its members. Their principal concern was with the mandatory regulations requiring alterations and improvements on the premises in which they conducted their business. The petitioners pointed out that the great majority of Indian laundrymen lived in rented houses where landlords would not agree to the expense of remodeling; nor did the laundrymen have the wherewithal to comply with the law. Furthermore, the D.L.A. observed that if the proposed regulations were strictly enforced, it would cause many to go out of business; this would result in "a few syndicates of companies" being formed that would "have an undue and unfair monopoly," which was "unfair to a respectable and deserving class of workers."[118] Of course, this was precisely the aim of the new public health bylaws. Despite their impassioned protests, the regulations were passed the following month at a special meeting of the Town Council.[119]

amaWasha on the Trek

Looking back, and in the absence of direct information, we can only surmise how it must have been for the African washermen during their declining years in the Natal laundry business. While they had weathered previous challenges, their current predicament offered no possibility of recovery. Recognition of this must have come swiftly. Although white families residing near the Mgeni may have continued their services for some time, the veteran guildsmen no doubt were losing their edge on the suburban market as well. Perhaps in town a few loyal customers, and those individuals who entertained exaggerated fears of the "unsanitary *dhoby*," lingered on. But as more and more water taps were connected to private premises, it became apparent the amaWasha could not restore their fading position by selectively boycotting their clientele or resorting to strikes, as they had done in the craft guild's heyday. Indeed, their reduced importance is seen in the recurring complaint, previously unheard of, that white householders were refusing to pay guild members upon completion of the job.[120]

Apart from the incursions made by the aggressive *dhobies* and to a lesser extent the commercial laundries, a significant portion of the craft guild's business fell to the "wash *umfazi*," many of whom came from Edendale and other outlying mission stations where they had been trained in the industrial arts.[121] Later at Inanda Mission, African women were taught and afterwards employed to operate a commercial laundry commenced in 1889. Clothes were collected by *togt* boys in Durban on Saturday and taken by wagon to Inanda. Sorting was done on Monday, washing on Tuesday, ironing on Thursday, then the clothes were ticketed, packed, and sent into town by wagon on Friday, and distributed by *togt* boys on the following Saturday morning.[122]

Mission-trained women were in great demand, especially as live-in servants. In a letter dated May 23, 1888, Ellen Mcleod declared, "we mean to have a native girl from Indaleni Station. . . . Those girls are very industrious; they wash and iron well. . . . " But as she had so often done, Ellen concluded this topic of thirty-eight years on a resigned note: "The great difficulty with us is we have so little money."[123]

Since working independently in the towns brought better wages, many *amakholwa* (Christian) women, such as Mrs. Lettie Mcunu, traveled several times a month to the city, where they worked as laundresses in private homes.[124] From 1907, *togt* statistics for Durban reveal that badges were being issued to both washermen and washerwomen.[125]

Against the strength of this rivalry, the Zulu craft guild had to contend with broadside assaults from the state. For 1892–93, the first year for which there are figures, three hundred Zulu washermen were reported occupying eighty-five huts at the Mgeni; and for the first time since they established tenancy on the banks of that river, the amaWasha were forced to pay a monthly two shillings per hut "for the right to squat on town lands . . . [and] by way of asserting authority over them."[126] Nor were the African laundrymen exempted from the washhouse bylaws ostensibly passed to regulate "*dhoby* dens."[127] Furthermore, an amendment to the 1901 identification pass law encompassed Africans engaged in the major prestige town occupations.[128] In 1904 new Durban bylaws raised the monthly *togt* fee to five shillings and provided compulsory compounds for the use of *togt* workers.[129]

In the end, modernization and white ethnocentrism overmastered the washermen's guild in Natal. So long as the boroughs lacked adequate water conveniences, labor employed in laundry work was suitably divided: washing was done primarily by Zulu guildsmen; starching, mangling, or ironing, and mending were generally performed by women laundresses, both African and European.[130] Later on, Indians also took up professional ironing.[131] However, unlike the *dhoby* who had gained an advantage in the town laundry business by renting space from Arab and Indian property owners, or the community encouragement held out to enterprising whites, the aspiring African entrepreneur experienced all manner of frustrations in trying to establish town-based operations. Van Onselen overlooks a crucial fact when he writes of the gold reef amaWasha that

> despite the fact that many of the guild's members did manage to make considerable cash savings, none of them *chose* [emphasis added] to convert their businesses to employ the mechanized processing techniques of modern laundrymen. Looking back. . ., rather than ahead [!!!]. . ., the washermen *chose* [emphasis added] to invest their savings in land and cattle [rather] than in plant and equipment. . . . [132]

During this period whites were as adverse to African competition in the trades as they were to the pronounced Asian presence in commercial activities. Racism precluded any choice in the matter of the amaWasha's future as entrepreneurs in the developing industrialized laundry business in South Africa.[133]

So it was this combination of factors, with the concurrent crises of drought and diseases, that led some veteran guildsmen, together with many of their countrymen, to migrate to the gold-mining towns on the Rand. By 1890 there were several hundred amaWasha at work in the Braamfontein Spruit. Three years later their numbers had risen to seven hundred; and an all-time record of over twelve hundred washermen were located at Johannesburg washing sites in 1896.[134]

Among other considerations, this focus on the amaWasha has allowed us to trace the economic development of one branch of European housework. Laundering chores evolved from the home industry stage to the craft stage, represented by the Zulu guild; then to industrial operations performed in commercial laundries. Eventually, however, the task returned to the home, where clothes washing was industrialized by the electric washing machine.[135] This process was succinctly summarized by the Native Economic Commission, which met at Durban in 1931:

A number of native women undertake the washing of clothes and household linen on the premises of Europeans. The practice of taking the linen away to recognized washing centers such as the Umbilo and Umgeni rivers has died out. . . . The improved methods of domestic washing by electricity and the improvements in steam laundrying have accounted for the loss of occupations to natives in this line.[136]

Conclusion: "The Most Curious Aspect of the Labour Question Natal Has Yet Been Troubled With"

One never-to-be-forgotten scene etched in the minds of newcomers landing at Port Natal was of the universal presence of Africans engaged in jobs that the new arrivals had been accustomed to seeing white working men and women perform at home. Black laborers, mainly of the "Zulu and Kafir races," were employed by white settlers in the colonial towns exclusively to do menial work—running messages, scavenging, portering, repairing roads, grooming horses, washing clothes, and the like. What caught the recent immigrants' attention so sharply and rendered this social fact most memorable was not so much that working people of various descriptions and origins flocked into Durban and Pietermaritzburg by the scores; rather, they were seized by the deeply felt conviction that included in this diverse population were races said to represent the extreme poles of civilization. Behind that idea were a host of related images and complicated issues that were bound to stir emotions.

Newly arrived strangers, for instance, were flooded with feelings of revulsion, or experienced acute self-conscious distress, or found themselves staring in amazement at the "not-quite-naked tribesmen" whom they were constantly encountering. In evidence everywhere were Africans lavishly decked out in a profusion of ornaments, their hair coiffed extravagantly in bizarre and fantastic arrangements. Hairstyles in northern Nguni societies, as shown in previous chapters, both symbolized social status and reflected the changing tastes that governed their fashion-conscious world. But aside from these embellishments, white observers were acutely aware, "the natives" made little attempt otherwise at bodily concealment.

It took a long time, therefore, before foreign visitors and colonial residents could rid themselves of their aversion to the sight of these men making their way along the city thoroughfares, wearing nothing more than the *umutsha*, consisting of a cord of goat skin round the hips from which hung in front tails of the genet cat, and a flap of the skin of some other small animal behind. Enhancing this meager outfit were such accessories as bead necklaces and arm bands, brass bangles and finger rings, head-dresses of porcupine quills and long tail feathers, wooden pendants, and horn ear plugs. Each male, in addition, was armed with an ox-hide shield and a full comple-ment of weapons—sticks, assegais, and knobkerries. One such imposing band of work seekers, consisting of a dozen young men, hired out in George Mason's employ: "None of these fellows had ever been to service before," he wrote in 1855, "in fact, they had only just escaped from Panda. . . ."[1] Many colonists never got used to the "natives' impudicity" (or shameless nakedness), which ultimately was made an offense against the municipal bylaws.

Those African town workers who "bore traces of civilization" did not escape the notice of early European travelers. There was the spectacle of brawny Zulus working on the beachfront, clothed in meal sacks or an old flannel shirt and nothing else! And there was the strange sight of laborers incongruously attired in cast-off garments and other articles of clothing that had been imported into the colony from used army stores and factory warehouses in the West. Whether they were busily engaged at their work or in attitudes of repose, black men "arbitrarily" arrayed—in tattered trousers, top hats, or red woolen nightcaps; or knee breeches, or old gray soldier's coats loaded down with shiny trinkets and other cheap gewgaws—presented odd appearances indeed, exhibitions strikingly out of the ordinary. When to these visual experiences (and they were plentiful) one adds the Africans' other "objectionable traits," it at once becomes clear how it might have been difficult for whites to extricate themselves from their negative preconceptions, particularly when those sentiments were apparently being reinforced on a regular basis.

Stark images of Africans, from the "primitive" and menacing to the absurd, helped to substantiate the accepted wisdom that asserted a connection between a people's outward circumstance and their level of cultural, moral, and intellectual development. Europeans, of course, made boastful claims about their own culture, which they imagined represented the epitome of civilization. This inflated notion of themselves ran so deep that it made it dangerously easy to cultivate a blanket con-tempt for black people, to feel smugly comfortable holding them up to mockery or dismissing them peremptorily as an example of arrested growth. The thing is, so long as the whites were rigidly anchored to their Eurocentric biases, they would never have to take the black man seriously.

Thus, where most of these whites were concerned, it would have strained the limits of credulity to suggest that these ill-clad creatures, sometimes "comically done up," possessed any but the crudest ideas about the mechanics of the labor market. It would have contradicted their expectations still further to see anything other than coincidence (surely not the workings of ingenious minds; surely not men guided by a fraternal bonding expressed in practical ways) in the apparent successes that these "inferior beings" might have had in manipulating the wage economy to their advan-tage.

Yet, every now and again, a voice within the settler community—one fully cog-nizant that the current realities differed significantly from the prevailing myths—spoke out boldly about that which by common consent and convention had been deliberately ignored or perhaps subconsciously suppressed: namely, that although these men had just recently escaped from (to borrow an idiom of the missionaries) the "degradation of heathenism," they had quickly adapted to the demands of the labor economy and were exhibiting a solidarity that was manifested in a variety of ways. Above all, those bonds came to be expressed in the formation of clubs or small-scale rural- and urban-based trade unions, "worthy of workmen in a manufacturing town in the old country."[2]

The only logical conclusion to be drawn from statements such as the above was that *obviously* Africans, incontestably equipped with the same intellectual resources as white people, were responding to the demands of the new capitalist economy in ways typical of wage earners elsewhere. But instead of opening their minds to these ideas and developments, most whites were distressed and agitated by the information. The very thought of Africans unionizing was totally incompatible with their most deeply ingrained prejudices. Certainly the above image did not correspond to the stereotype of the "slow-witted Kafir," who was supposedly incapable of intelligent acts or rational decisions. Thus not only did the majority of the colonial population stubbornly resist these facts, they went a step further: they reacted by inventing a wholly different truth.

The pattern of events that followed, then, was hardly a coincidence. For just as these nineteenth-century workmen were demonstrating effective discipline and apparently coordinating their activities, they were also gaining notoriety as "spongers," "slanderers," and "indolent scoundrels," who were growing ever more costly and less manageable. It comes as no surprise that these accusations ("campaigns of disinformation") corresponded to those periods when workers' organizational efforts in Durban and Pietermaritzburg were apparently the most pronounced.

Such reflections raise certain other difficult questions, to which there are no definite answers. For example, it seems worth asking how things might have turned out differently for the settler community, and for colonial labor relations in particular, had the issues of organized workers and labor-generated unrest been openly acknowledged and addressed in a fair and balanced way. Change might have been effected in at least one area. The "keystone of Kafir policy," the argument that Africans could not achieve "civilized progress" without the beneficent but firm guidance of their "more sophisticated white neighbors," might have fallen to the ground—though, one cynically hastens to add, probably not without first being replaced, given the economic pressures, by an equally vile rationalization for exploiting the black man's labor. Nevertheless, the question still holds a certain fascination. In what ways and with what results might the socioeconomic history of the region been altered, if that "most curious aspect of the labour question" had been given some degree of formal recognition and permitted to advance, as, for example, along the lines of the labor movement "in the old country"?

> The character for cleanliness of the seaport town is . . . dependent on a host of young Kafirs, who like other great social elements, have some organization among themselves. The other day, a rumour got wind amongst them that their monopoly was to be interfered with; that their rights were to be restricted, and their profession fettered. As usual in such cases, they struck. They evacuated en masse, and Durban was without clean clothes for a week. A magisterial announcement appeased their anxieties, and brought them to their senses and their sacks. *This is the most curious aspect of the labour question Natal has yet been troubled with* [emphasis added].[3]

Here we meet with what seems to me the crowning passage of this book. It states the situation clearly and succinctly and confirms the nagging "sense of wrongness" I felt all along with the conventional version of Natal's labor woes. From the very beginning, not only did the story not ring true to this listener, the argument was filled with so many internal inconsistencies and such ridiculous imagery that it had a surreal quality. And in effect, this is what the author of the above passage seems to imply when, in writing about collective action among the washermen, he declares: "This is the most curious aspect of the labour question Natal has yet been troubled with."

My research has led me to understand, and the evidence exists for anyone who cares to pursue it, that at the heart of the prolonged labor crisis was an invented fallacy, an idea concocted out of the imagination of the European mind to fit its mode of perceiving things. That is to say, whites created the "lazy Kafirs" by believing them real. After all, this was how they had been taught by their culture to view and explain the world. Then, after saddling the African with a string of negative misattributions and having thoroughly vilified his actual nature, they set out to refashion— profoundly—*that which never objectively existed in the first place* into what they thought the black man ought to be. Their mental model of the most congenial reality, the colonialists' ideal at the end of this long and arduous transformative process, was a continual stream of robotized black folk who would perform functions efficiently and faithfully.

Throughout this era, as the reader has learned, Natalians talked, argued, and debated "the labor question" *ad nauseam*. But social conditioning and presuppositions greatly hampered their programs and policies. In part, we have come to understand this problem as relating to their negative stereotypes of black people. At best, whites were equipped only to see a race of "primitives" with exaggerated qualities, not the least being that of unmitigated stupidity. At worst, they saw hordes of "lazy niggers," who possessed the instincts of brutes and, in consequence, required stiff social controls. Racial chauvinism, I have argued, was one leading cause of the countless failures of Natal's colonial labor schemes.

Another thing this book has attempted to show is the range of ways African laborers effectively fought against the alien ideologies and pernicious labeling introduced by the European immigrants. The portrait I have endeavored to reconstruct is that of a people whose cultural arsenal was firmly intact. If not for the resilience of their values and institutional structures, these workers would not have been able to ward off those potentially psychologically damaging ideas. Natal's African working population did not allow the colonialists' negative opinions of them as a people to become their reality. Indeed, throughout the nineteenth century and into the twentieth century, they pressed insistently for the basic considerations due all human beings; in addition, they persisted in demanding their rights as workers.

To restate some of the most salient points pertaining to their activities: it is important to keep in mind that Natal Africans were not only motivated by a series of social and economic misfortunes; their entrance into the colonial economy was also guided by an inner compulsion or ethos embodied and presented in certain social attitudes about prestige, precedence, and hierarchy. These traditional notions, including the emotional concepts and values that fostered a corporate spirit, formed an inseparable matrix in their minds. Their responses to the wage economy, as well as their work choices and their on-the-job behavior, were shaped by these ancient considerations. Or to put this a little differently, the ideas, values, and emotions that formed their cultural matrix constituted what we have now come to clearly recognize as an African work ethic.

Nor can it be overemphasized that these shared terms of reference were molded to fit a different situation (the market culture) and a different style of life (that of the wage earner). It may be true that in the urban setting and on European farms and plantations, laborers seem to have banded together in the first instance out of a cultural sense of common or moral obligation, meaningfully expressed in the concept of *ubuntu*. Yet a further, crucially important point in this connection must be kept in mind. It is this: a remarkably short period passed from the time these "unsophisticated rustics" first began to enter the labor market until the time they were transformed by hard, sobering experience into individuals possessing a practical as well as shrewd and materialistic understanding of human affairs. This brief period marked one beginning of the African workers' conscious appearance on the labor scene. For these black men clearly believed that through a creative adaptation of indigenous institutions to modern concerns their common grievances as *workers* and the general conditions of labor could be improved or effectively resolved.

Signs of this are evident only three short years after the establishment of Natal as a British colony. At that time, African workmen at Durban had begun to develop sufficient ideas about the wage market to inspire public commentaries about the noticeable increase in self-confidence on the part of workers, which apparently infused them with "an unwholesome kind of independence."[3] The upshot of these complaints was the passage in 1850 of the Masters and Servants Ordinance. But the strongest testimony to this effect has been obtained from information coming out of Esidumbini mission station in 1854. This source makes it graphically clear that not only were these men *fully conscious* of the colony's dependence upon their labor, they were keenly aware that this dependence could be used to their own advantage. The Reverend Josiah Tyler was in a position to inform us firsthand that

> [s]ometimes a company of natives, like operatives in a factory, will rise *en masse* and strike for higher wages, which if denied, influences them to leave us entirely helpless. . . . They show that they are not unconscious of the fact that we in our isolated homes, are in a great measure dependent upon them: "For who but natives," say they, "could drive our wagons, herd our cattle, bring our wood and water, and carry our mails over this hilly country."[4]

Thus the documentation fully authorizes us to speak of these men as possessing a well-defined and disciplined consciousness. Indeed, as has been argued, all the necessary ingredients were in place to promote a culture of solidarity. We know they had a unifying ideology as well as networks for gathering intelligence. In addition to being a rallying tool, the main function of such institutions as the *izimbongi* (bards or praise poets) in the labor market culture was to transmit orally information pertaining to wages, masters, and general work conditions. So, clearly, these nineteenth-century workmen had effective organizational structures. Their successful efforts at price fixing and controlling the direction and general flow of labor were, among other things, what necessitated the 1874 enactment of the colony's first explicit piece of anticombination legislation. The reader should remember that the ostensive pur-

pose of the *togt* laws was to curtail the workers' autonomy and discourage their associations by establishing a tariff of wages.

This must be viewed in context. A long series of background events and cumulative actions are what finally led to the passage of this legislation. That is, the "Togt
Rules and Regulations" were enacted precisely because the Masters and Servants
Ordinance, which had come into existence over a generation earlier, and which had
made illegal and punishable by imprisonment such worker activities as "molesting
servants for not joining a club or not submitting to rules for regulating his wages or
work," had proven utterly ineffective in dealing with the problem of organized
labor.[5]

While there are people who will continue to entertain old habits of thinking that
would see a "foreign hand" directing the activities of these black workers, such sentiments must be resisted. Natal's African wage-earning population did not wait
around for the example of white workers to radicalize their consciousness, any more
than they needed to be inspired by the presence of the East Indian immigrant before
the idea of washing clothes as a profession would have occurred to them. Just as we
are empirically sure the Indian *dhobies* were nowhere on the scene when the "brothers" first took up the craft of laundering, we must disabuse our minds of any notion
that white men were on the sidelines choreographing their strategies. Europeans
must not be given ultimate credit for the accomplishments of these nineteenth-
century African workers.

And their accomplishments were impressive, to say the least. Adapting the *izimbongi* to that modern labor strategy, the protest picket, and manipulating the power
of the word to force employers to abide by the standards or moral norms of the working community are but two of the numerous examples that attest to the ability of
these people to adjust their culture and to innovate in order to meet new challenges.
This they did in very imaginative and culturally coded ways.

By no means were all of their actions "hidden" or "disguised," however. The
most conclusive evidence on this score are the vivid accounts that survive in the
archival record of African workmen marching in a body, "like operatives in a factory," to the employer's premises, announcing loudly, "The moon is dead! Give us
our money!" and striking until they received satisfaction. "Although not in name, in
practice, [they] perfectly under[stood] what [wa]s meant by a 'dock-yard str[i]ke,'
and illustrate[d] it daily.... "[6] Such a picture requires no further explanation or
debate. These men were workers.

NOTES

1. Anthony Trollope, *South Africa* (Cape Town: A. A. Balkema, 1973), 205.
2. "Mr. Greenstock's Notes of Travel," *Mission Fields* (1875), 371.
3. Wyn Rees, ed., *Colenso Letters From Natal* (Pietermaritzburg: Shuter and Shooter, 1958), 273.
4. For example, while the recently published *Natal and Zululand: From Earliest Times to 1910, A New History* (Pietermaritzburg: University of Natal and Shuter and Shooter, 1989), edited by Andrew Duminy and Bill Guest, places great emphasis on "the economic forces that were at work" in the region, there is a conspicuous absence of any discussion of the role and contributions of Natal's African population to the colonial wage labor market.
5. Natal Africans who entered the colonial wage economy computed time by the phases of the moon. Each *inyanga*, or lunar month, lasted from new moon to new moon, making each "month" twenty-eight days. As African workers were not being paid according to the "moons," but rather according to the Western calendar, they often thought they were being cheated out of two or three days work every month.

CHAPTER 1

The "Forbidden Journey": Natal's Refugee Problem

1. James Stuart, ed., *The Diary of Henry Francis Fynn* (Pietermaritzburg: Shuter and Shooter, 1950), 91–100, 197.
2. A. T. Bryant, *A History of the Zulu and Neighbouring Tribes* (Cape Town: C. Struik, 1964). Bryant maintains that the first campaign undertaken by Shaka in Natal occurred in 1817 against the emaCubeni, 49.
3. Stuart, *Fynn's Diary*, 91–100, 197; Nathaniel Isaacs, *Travels and Adventures in Eastern Africa* (Cape Town: C. Struik, 1970), 17–18. Two South African historians, Julian Cobbing and John Wright, have recently challenged the validity of the notion of the *mfecane*. Both writers argue that the Zulu state was not the only agency of change in the region and that the depopulation or "devastation theory" was a colonial-made myth. See Julian Cobbing, "The *Mfecane* as Alibi: Thoughts on Dithakong and Mbolompo," *Journal of African History* 29 (1988), 487–519, and John Wright, "The Dynamics of Power and Conflict in the Thukela–Mzimkhulu Region in the Late 18th and Early 19th Centuries: A Critical Reconstruction," Ph. D. thesis, Univesity of Witwatersrand, Johannesburg, 1989.
4. Stuart, *Fynn's Diary*, 211–12.
5. Evidence of Henry Francis Fynn before the Proceedings of the Commission Appointed to Inquire into the Past and Present State of the Kafirs in the District of Natal [hereafter Evidence before the Kafir Commission], (Pietermaritzburg: J. Archbell and Son, 1852–53), Part V, 45. The testimony of Mpatshana kaSodondo provides relevant insight into the custom

of giving protection: "suppose an *isikulu* a big man, a little chief finds a man doing wrong and reports the matter to the king, who directs the *isikulu* to kill him, and the man, hearing he is about to be killed, escapes and takes refuge with another *isikulu*, the latter does not hesitate beyond the second day to proceed to the king to report the arrival of one who alleges he is to be killed by the other *isikulu*, and to ask the king for instructions. The king might ask him if he wishes to take the man under his patronage, and he might say he would like to do so, reserving to himself the right of turning him out should his conduct in the future prove unsatisfactory. Or the king might say, 'Won't the *isikulu* who has driven him out want him?' I have seen this myself. I have known of cases where people have fled from the Zulu country to Somkele, and after these have been reported to the king he has referred to their first *isikulu*, who has pressed for the man being killed. . . . Cetshwayo then said, 'I am defeated. Follow him and take him away.'" In C. Webb and J. Wright, eds., *The James Stuart Archive of Recorded Oral Evidence Relating to the History of the Zulu and Neighbouring Peoples* [hereafter *Stuart Archive*], III (Pietermaritzburg: University of Natal Press and Killie Campbell Africana Library, 1982), 308–9.

6. Rosalind Mael, "The Problem of Political Integration in the Zulu Empire" (Ph.D. thesis, University of California, Los Angeles, 1974), Ch. 2, 59–81.

7. Stuart, *Fynn's Diary*, 211–12.

8. Felix Okoye, "Tshaka and the British Traders, 1824–1828," *Transafrican Journal of History* (January 1972), 2, 16–20. Apart from his desire to acquire powerful firearms and other European trade goods, Shaka believed the white man's medicines would restore his manly vigor. By 1828, we are told, his longing had become such an obsession that he no longer exchanged ivory for cloth and beads; all he desired was the white man's medicine. See also *Fynn's Diary*, 142–43.

9. Allen Gardiner, *Narrative of a Journey to the Zoolu Country* (Cape Town: C. Struik, 1966), 140–41, 145–46; *Fynn's Diary*, 232.

10. Cape of Good Hope Government Commission on Native Laws and Customs (Cape Town: W. A. Richards and Sons, 1883). Minute of Evidence of Theophilus Shepstone, Part I, Vol. 2, 55.

11. Testimony of Dinya kaZokozwayo in *Stuart Archive*, I, 106.

12. Gardiner, *Narrative*, 162.

13. Stuart, *Fynn's Diary*, 220–25.

14. Gardiner, *Narrative*, 108, 126–27, 192–215.

15. See Lazarus Mxaba under testimony of John Kumalo, in *Stuart Archive*, I, 243.

16. Mael, "Political Integration," Ch. 3, 115–67.

17. John Bird, ed., *The Annals of Natal*, II (Pietermaritzburg: P. Davis and Son, 1888). Mr. H. Cloete to the Hon. J. Montagu, Secretary to Government, 10 November 1843, 311.

18. Mael, "Political Integration," 116.

19. Bird, *Annals*. Major Smith to Sir George Napier, 10 July 1843, II, 198–99.

20. Under the 1835 treaty Gardiner was constrained to return several refugees to Zululand where they were immediately tried before a male assembly and executed. Gardiner, *Narrative*, 145–84; Major Smith to the Hon. J. Montagu, Secretary to Government, Cape Town, 14 November 1843, in *Annals*, II, 316–17; South African Archival Records II [hereafter SAAR] (Cape Town: Union Archives in collaboration with the Archives Commission, Government Printers, 1960), Minute of the Import of Panda's Message, 11 February 1846, 71.

21. Bird, *Annals*. Major Smith to Sir George Napier, 10 July 1843, II, 212.

22. In July 1843 Smith had consented to "use his influence to induce them [the refugees] to return, on the condition that they were not to be molested; and, finally, that such cattle as they claim belong to the chief should be taken by his messengers." *Annals*, II, 212. But "upon mature consideration of the question," he thought it wrong to accede to the king's demand. Smith therefore opposed the plan adopted by Cloete (see note 23). *Annals*. Major Smith, Natal to the Hon. J. Montagu, 14 November 1843, II, 316; SAAR. Minute of the

Import of Panda's Message, II, 70.

23. Bird, *Annals.* The Hon. H. Cloete to the Hon. J. Montagu, 28 October 1843, II, 293.

24. SAAR. Reply of His Honor the Lt. Governor to Panda, 6 August 1846, II, 104.

25. SAAR. Message from Lt. Governor to Mpanda, 8 June 1848, II, 305. In Shepstone's opinion the policy of restoring the king's cattle upheld Zulu power and he was convinced "that the moment this order is suspended the Zulu power [would] fall." See evidence before the Kafir Commission, Part II, 27.

26. In the magistracy of Ladysmith, for instance, African police recovered 103 head of cattle, 78 of which were sent to Pietermaritzburg; the remaining 25 were disposed of as follows:10 head were given as a reward to the police, 3 head were slaughtered as food for the refugees (40 men, women, and children), 6 head were given them for food on the road to Maritzburg, 1 head slaughtered for Panda's captains, 1 slaughtered for Panda's captains on their way home, 2 slaughtered for food on the road to Maritzburg for the second party consisting of 18 women and children, 1 head for the police escorting them, 1 died. SNA, No. 9l, RM Ladysmith, 7 July 1855.

27. SAAR. Minute of the Import of Panda's Message, 11 February 1846, II, 70–72.

28. CSO, file 44, pt. 2. Statement of Zatshuke Messenger sent by the Lt. Governor of Natal to Panda king of the Zulus. No. 45, 5 July 1848.

29. Ibid., Statement of Zatshuke.

30. Ibid.

31. SAAR. T. Shepstone, Diplomatic Agent to Honorable the Secretary to Government, Natal, 22 February 1848, II, 293.

32. Evidence of Rev. C. L. Dohne before the Kafir Commission, Part IV, 18–19.

33. Even Chiefs Soqweba and Umvula, who had been sent to patrol the border, ran away to Natal. SNA 1/3/4. RM Greytown, 15 June 1855.

34. SAAR. Extracts from instructions issued to Mr. J. Shepstone, dated 11 August 1852, IV, 116.

35. J. R. Sullivan, *The Native Policy of Sir Theophilus Shepstone* (Johannesburg: Walker and Snashall, 1928), 17–78; John Agar-Hamilton, *The Native Policy of the Voortrekkers* (Cape Town: M. Miller, 1928), 35–36.

36. Agar-Hamilton, *Policy of the Voortrekkers,* 170–75; W. Kistner, "The Anti-Slavery Agitation Against the Transvaal Republic 1852–1868," *Archives Year Book for South African History* (Cape Town: Cape Times, Ltd., 1952), II, 226–27.

37. Sullivan, *Policy of T. Shepstone,* 20.

38. Agar-Hamilton, *Policy of the Voortrekkers,* 171–72.

39. Kistner, "Anti-Slavery Agitation," 226–43; Peter Delius and Stanley Trapido, "Inboekselings and Oorlams: The Creation and Transformation of a Servile Class," *Journal of Southern African Studies* 1 (1981), 226–31.

40. Delius and Trapido, "Inboekselings," 231.

41. Proclamation. Sir George Napier, 12 May 1843, in *Annals,* II, 166–67.

42. Agar-Hamilton, *Policy of the Voortrekkers,* 175.

43. Evidence of T. Shepstone before the Kafir Commission, Part II, 30–31; and Part VI, 61.

44. Evidence of George Robinson before the Kafir Commission, Part IV, 20.

45. Evidence of Benjamin Blaine before the Kafir Commission, Part III, 35–36; Evidence of Pieter A. Otto, Part III, 42; Evidence of Walter Macfarlane, Part III, 43.

46. SNA1/1/5, No. 88. Circular to Magistrates enclosing revised regulations relative to refugees (no date; c. May 1854).

47. *Natal Government Gazette* (hereafter *NGG*), 23 December 1856.

48. SNA 1/1/7, No. 89. Circular to Magistrates; Inanda, Tugela, and Durban, 3 February 1857.

49. SNA 1/1/7, No. 7. Meeting of Planters and Merchants and others held at Durban, 5 January 1857; SNA 1/1/7, No. 69. SNA's reply to W. R. Thompson, Junior, Esquire, 13 January 1857. CO 179/111 (Natal, No. 3281). Returns of Corporal Punishment Under the Master and Servant Ordinance 2, 1850.

50. SNA 1/3/3, No. 162. Meller to SNA, 15 November 1854; SNA 1/1/5, No. 87. SNA's draft reply to Meller to the effect that badges would not be an effective deterrent in discouraging refugees from running away (no date, c. November 1854).

51. SNA 1/3/6, No. 49. Meller to SNA, 2 February 1857; SNA 1/1/7, No. 91. SNA's reply approving Meller's proposal offering a reward of 2s. 6d. for the apprehension of runaways, 4 February 1857.

52. The circular dated 23 December 1856 that accompanied the regulations stated (par. 11) that the conditions under which refugees were to be registered were not to be taken to include married women and young children. SNA 1/3/29, Mr. M. H. Gallowey, Acting SNA, 14 September 1877; see also circular minute from the SNA for the information and guidance of resident magistrates and administrators of native law respecting "regulations with regard to refugees entering the colony, in addition to those in force," wherein instruction No. 2 stipulated "when refugees are indentured or apprenticed to farmers, their families dependent on them should always accompany them," SNA 1/1/64; and SNA's reply to request from planters at Little Umhlanga for child labor, 11 May 1859, that it was not in the Lt. Governor's power "to require the apprenticeship of the children of natives who are residing in the colony. This is a matter which must be voluntary on the part of parents," SNA 1/1/9, No. 262.

53. SNA 1/3/4, No. 110. RM Tugela Division, 27 July 1855.

54. SNA 1/3/8, No. 206. RM Ladysmith, 11 February 1859; and No. 156, 14 April 1859.

55. SNA 1/3/8, No. 156. RM Ladysmith, 14 April 1859.

56. Extracts from the Bishop's Journal of his Second Visitation of the Diocese, *The Mission Field* (London: United Society for the Propagation of the Gospel, March 1857), 55–59.

57. Ibid., 57.

58. Ibid., 58.

59. Ibid., 58–59. This event was discussed in a letter from Colenso to the noted philologist Wilhelm Bleek. See O. H. Spohr, ed., *The Natal Diaries of Dr. W.H.I. Bleek, 1855–56* (Cape Town: A. A. Balkema, 1965), 58.

60. SNA 1/1/7, No. 10. Colenso to Lt. Governor Scott, 20 February 1857; SNA 1/1/7, No. 47. Colonial Office to RM Durban, 21 February 1857; SNA 1/3/6, No. 82. Reply RM Durban to SNA, 24 February 1857.

61. The most recent injunctions were reissued in 1883.

62. SNA 1/3/29, No. 9. Case of Ushoi, 14 September 1877; and SNA 1/1/70, Petition of Usikunyana with reference to certain relatives of his apprenticed as refugees, 23 January 1884; SNA 1/1/65, Extracts from the *Natal Witness*, 4 October 1883.

63. SNA 1/3/29, No. 9. Case of Ushoi; and SNA 1/1/70, Petition of Usikunyana.

64. Ibid.

65. For example, according to the definition given in the *Report of the Natal Native Commission, 1881–82* (Pietermaritzburg: Vause, Slatter and Co., 1882), "a 'Refugee' is not one fleeing into Natal merely for the preservation of life. Some of our 'refugees' may be included in such an appellation, but it means generally those blacks who have come into the colony, since the cession to England by the Dutch Boers, for diverse reasons—chiefly, as an authoritative witness acknowledged, to increase more safely their cattle and wives," 19.

66. "Mr. Greenstock's Notes of Travel," *The Mission Field* (1 March 1876), 92.

67. CO 179/112, No. 63. Complaint of Mr. Ridley respecting Administration of Native Affairs and Praying for an Inquiry by Commission, 19 April 1873.

68. "What is a Refugee?" *Natal Mercantile Advertiser* [hereafter NMA], 8 August 1885.

69. CSO, VII, No. 44. Ralph Clarence to Donald Moodie, 29 May 1847.

70. Sullivan, *Policy of Shepstone*, 20.

71. SNA 1/3/8, No. 60. RM Weenen, 19 September 1859; SNA 1/3/9, No. 441. RM Weenen, 16 July 1860. The magistrate for Durban was disposed to admit that "in some instances one might be naturally led to conclude they were not properly treated, as considerable arrears

of wages were abandoned" by the absconding refugees. See SNA 1/3/9. "Annual Report of the State of the Native Coloured Population in the Town and County of Durban for the year 1858."

72. SNA 1/3/15, No. 12. RM Newcastle, 16 July 1865.
73. SNA 1/3/4, No. 19. RM Kahlamba, 14 February 1855.
74. "The Zulu Refugees," *Natal Mercury* [hereafter *NM*], 5 October 1855.
75. "Questions by Lieutenant Governor Scott on the Conditions of the Natives in Natal; and Answers by the Secretary for Native Affairs," (Pietermaritzburg: ?, 16 Octoer 1864), 6–7.
76. "Legislative Council," *Natal Witness* [hereafter *NW*),28 October 1859.
77. ABC: 15.4, Vol. 5, Lewis Grout, 10 April 1852.
78. SNA 1/3/4, No. 19. RM Kahlamba, 14 February 1855; SNA 1/3/4, No. 165. RM Greytown, 29 October 1855; *NM,* 4 April 1855.
79. SNA 1/3/4, No. 19. RM Kahlamba, 14 February 1855.
80. Major T. C. Smith, for instance, clearly understood this dynamic in 1843. Smith reported that he had summoned several chiefs in the vicinity to appear before him and "pointed out the ruin they would inevitably bring on themselves by the encouragement thus given" to refugees. Major T. C. Smith to Sir George Napier, 10 July 1843, in *Annals,* II, 212–13; SNA 1/3/8, No. 119, 23 May 1859.
81. See Ndukwana under the testimony of John Kumalo in *Stuart Archive,* I, 236–37.
82. Rees, *Colenso Letters From Natal,* 252–55; see also noes 56–66, above.
83. "Questions by the Lieutenant Governor," 7.
84. Ibid.
85. *Report of the Natal Native Commission, 1881–2.* Appendix G, Statistics furnished by John C. Walton, 32.
86. Ibid., 33.

Chapter 2
Crisis of Reconstruction and the Mobilization of Labor

1. Henry Slater, "The Changing Pattern of Economic Relationships in Rural Natal: 1838–1914," in Shula Marks and Anthony Atmore, eds., *Economy and Society in Preindustrial South Africa* (London; New York: Longman, 1980), 154.
2. Igor Kopytoff, "The Internal African Frontier: The Making of African Political Culture," in Igor Kopytoff, ed., *The African Frontier: The Reproduction of Traditional Societies* (Bloomington; Indianapolis: Indiana University Press, 1987), 21–22.
3. Adam Kuper, *Wives for Cattle: Bridewealth and Marriage in Southern Africa* (London; Boston: Routledge and Kegan Paul, 1982), 10–25; Mrs. Shooter, "Off to Natal. By a Clergyman's Wife," *Golden Hours: A Weekly Journal of Good Literature for Young Folks* 1, 1869, 609.
4. Shooter, "Off to Natal," 606–10.
5. Ibid.
6. SNA 1/3/14, No. 163. J. Shepstone, Administrator of Native Law to Secretary of Native Affairs, 15 September 1864.
7. SNA 1/3/14, No. 142. Statements of Ukondo and Umkuba before Henry F. Fynn, Esq., Assistant Resident Magistrate, Durban, 8 October 1855.
8. Ibid.
9. SNA 1/3/2, No. 45. Extract from Resident Magistrate's notes on certain cases adjudicated by him. Ladysmith, 26 July 1853.
10. SNA 1/3/14, No. 163. J. Shepstone, Administrator of Native Law to Secretary of Native Affairs, 15 September 1864.
11. SNA 1/3/2, No. 45. Extract from Resident Magistrate's notes on certain cases adjudicated by him. Ladysmith, 26 July 1853.
12. William Charles Baldwin, *African Hunting and Adventures* (Cape Town: C. Struik, 1967), 22.

13. SNA 1/3/23. Resident Magistrate of Newcastle to Secretary of Native Affairs, 12 December 1873.
14. Ibid.
15. SNA 1/3/27. RM Newcastle, 15 February 1876.
16. SNA 1/1/7. Circular to Magistrate 17 January 1857. In Zululand, "The lobola was only one beast to begin with and afterwards a second beast, no more, for all the cattle belonged to the king. It was very hard indeed to get cattle, and if you should accumulate many you would be accused of making a chief of yourself, whereupon someone would report this to headquarters, and some pretext for killing you would be found. This was one reason then why the lobola was so low." Testimony of Lunguza kaMpukane, *Stuart Archive*, I, 317.
17. ABC: 15.4, 4 (204), No. 297. Daniel Lindley to Rev. R. Anderson, D. D. Inanda, Port Natal, South Africa, 16 November 1855.
18. *Natal Witness* [hereafter NW], 21 September 1855; "Natal," extracts from the Bishop of Natal's journal of his second visitation, June 1856, in *The Mission Field*, January and February 1857, 7, 28–29 respectively. Rev. J. W. Colenso, *First Steps of the Zulu Mission* (London: ?, 1860), 71. See also 53, 57, and 79.
19. "Natal," *The Mission Field*, January 7, and February, 1857, 28–29.
20. SNA 1/3/8, No. 214. Annual Report. Resident Magistrate for Inanda, 29 January 1859.
21. "Taxation by a Native Chief," *Natal Mercury* [hereafter NM], 25 January 1856.
22. Jeff Guy, "Ecological Factors in the Rise of Shaka and the Zulu Kingdom," in Shula Marks and Anthony Atmore, eds., *Economy and Society in Pre-Industrial South Africa*, 102–19. For another writer who makes a strikingly similar argument that the age class system was a powerful mechanism of population control, see Asmarom Legesse, *Gada—Three Approaches to the Study of African Society* (New York: Free Press, 1973), Ch. 5. Legesse states, in his study of the Gada system of the Oromo of Boran, that the marriage rules that put off marriage and the right to have first male and then female children, can be traced to the sixteenth century. These restrictions were desired by the Oromo, he argues, to slow down rapid population growth that had been occurring for various historical and ecological reasons in that period.
23. A. T. Bryant reckoned that, "Owing to the great and constant war-losses and to the fact that, throughout the whole period from 1824 to 1840, fighting-men up to 40 years of age were not permitted to marry, we think that the total increase of population during that period could not have exceeded one-quarter of the normal Bantu peace figure (roughly, 35,000, or, say, 9000 souls), if indeed there was any increase at all." See his *Olden Times in Zululand and Natal* (London; New York: Longmans, Green and Company, 1929), 81.
24. Stuart, *Fynn's Diary*, 162, 164–65.
25. Ibid.
26. Senzangakhona was Shaka's father.
27. Testimony of Ndukwana kaMbengwana, *Stuart Archive*, IV, 337–39.
28. Testimonies of Mtshapi kaNoradu and Ndukwana kaMbengwana, *Stuart Archive*, IV, 97, 311, 338.
29. Testimony of Mtshayankomo kaMagolwana, *Stuart Archive*, IV, 121.
30. Testimony of Ndukwana kaMbengwana, *Stuart Archive*, IV, 338–39.
31. Testimony of Ndabankulu kaQubabanye, *Stuart Archive*, IV, 180.
32. Bernardo Bernardi, *Age Class Systems: Social Institutions and Politics based on Age* (Cambridge: Cambridge University Press, 1985), 27–37.
33. Bryant, *Olden Times*, 127.
34. Ibid.
35. ABC: 15.4, 6, No. 45. Report of Ukulobolisa. Amanzimtote, 25 November 1867. By Messrs. D. Rood and H. A. Wilder; Lewis Grout, *Zululand: Or Life Among the Zulu Kafirs* (Philadelphia: Presbyterian Publication Committee, 1864), 166.
36. Mael, "The Problems of Political Integration," Chs. 3–4.

37. Ibid. , 157–58.

38. Grout, *Zululand*, 164.

39. See, for example, the testimonies of Msthapi kaNoradu, Mtshayankomo kaMagolwana, and Ndukwana kaMbengwana, *Stuart Archive*, IV, 78–80, 132–35, 337–39.

40. SNA 1/3/17. Annual Report. Resident Magistrate for Inanda, 18 January 1867; SNA 1/7/7. Memorandum by Theophilus Shepstone, Secretary of Native Affairs for the Colony of Natal, on the Law No. 1, 1869; ABC: 15.4, 6, Report on Ukulobolisa; Shooter, "Off to Natal," 532–33; Rev. Joseph Shooter, *The Kafirs of Natal and Zulu Country* (London: E. Stanford, 1857), 53.

41. Ibid.

42. Grout, *Zululand*, 164.

43. Ibid. , 170–71.

44. Shooter, "Off to Natal," 532–33.

45. For another instance of elders manipulating brideprices to retain control of women, see Patrick Harries, "Kinship, Ideology and the Nature of Pre-Colonial Labour Migration," in Shula Marks and Richard Rathbone, eds., *Industrialisation and Social Change in South Africa* (London; New York: Longman, 1982),) 142–66.

46. See under "Alfred County," *Natal Herald*, 3 November 1870.

47. See, for instance, H. P. Braatvedt, "Zulu Marriage Customs and Ceremonies," *South African Journal of Science*, XXIV (December 1927), 553–65.

48. See under "Legislative Council," *NW*, 3 July 1863.

49. Stuart, *Fynn's Diary*, 243; Grout, *Zululand*, 166.

50. Her Majesty's Commissioner in Natal (Mr. H. Cloete) to the Hon. J. Montagu, Secretary to the Government, 10 November 1843, in Bird, *Annals*, II, 314.

51. "The Zulu Border," *NM*, 13 September 1854.

52. "Murder of a British Subject in the Zulu Country," *NM*, 25 October 1854; "Natal," *The Mission Field*, February 1857, 34–35.

53. SNA 1/1/5, No. 71. Circular to Magistrate, 17 August 1854; *Natal Government Gazette* [hereafter *NGG*], 21 November 1854.

54. Grout, *Zululand*, 166.

55. Quoted in Mael, "Political Integration," 148. There is a strong possibility that Mpande's move to repopulate the area may also have been related to the fact that some portions of the uninhabited districts of Zulu country were becoming infested with tsetse. By 1860 fifty square miles of country between the Black and White Mfolozi had been completely swept of cattle and the pest was making its appearance in the Mhlatuze bush. See *Port Elizabeth Telegraph*, 28 June 1860, and *Eastern Province Herald*, 23 December 1862.

56. Colenso, *First Steps*, 99, 129.

57. Mrs. Wilkinson, *A Lady's Life and Travels in Zululand and the Transvaal During Cetewayo's Reign* (London: J. T. Hayes, 1882), 162.

58. Testimonies of Mtshapi kaNoradu and Ndukwana kaMbengwana, *Stuart Archive*, IV, 97, 311, 338.

59. Captain Henry Hallam Parr, *A Sketch of the Kafirs and Zulu Wars* (Pretoria: State Library Reprint #56, 1970), 121–22.

60. See, for example, the testimonies of Mtshapi kaNoradu, Mtshayankomo kaMagolwana, and Ndukwana kaMbengwana, *Stuart Archive*, IV, 78–80, 132–35, and 337–39.

61. For example, see the testimony of Dabula kaMgingqiyizana in which he describes the Chief of the Dunge, Kotsini, as "an insizwa and has one daughter who has married. He is of the age of the Mavalana regiment. He is going to *tunga* (to sew on the headring) during 1917. He has three wives; one died," in *Stuart Archive*, I, 89.

62. Augustus Lindley, *After Ophir: Or a Search for the South African Gold Fields* (London: Cassell, Petter, and Galpin, 1870), 222.

63. A. T. Bryant, *The Zulu People as They Were Before the White Man Came* (Pietermaritzburg: Shuter and Shooter, 1949), 599.

64. G. H. Mason, *Zululand: A Mission Tour* (London: J. Nisbet, 1862), 94–95; ABC: 15.4, 5, No. 7. Lewis Grout to Rufus Anderson, Umvoti, 16 April 1847. Grout, *Zululand*, 164.

65. S. M. Seymour, *Bantu Law in South Africa* (Cape Town: Juta, 1970), 71, 108.

66. Ibid., 91.

67. ABC: 15.4, 5, No. 7. Lewis Grout to Rufus Ander son, Umvoti, 16 April 1847.

68. *Proceedings and Report of the Commission Appointed to Inquire into the Past and Present State of the Kafirs in the District of Natal* (Pietermaritzburg: J. Archbell, 1852–53). Hereafter cited as the *Kafir Commission*. Evidence of George Peppercorne, Part III, 63.

69. Bryant, *The Zulu People*, 233.

70. "Years may elapse before such a female meets with her real relations, under such circumstances her guardian refunds the cattle received by him on her being married, retaining or claiming from her parents one head termed "isonhlo," for nurture, and all such other cattle as were slaughtered at her marriage festival or have been sacrificed on her behalf." Evidence of Henry F. Fynn befor the Kafir Commission, Part V, 65–66.

71. Rev. Shooter, *The Kafirs of Natal*, 49; Mason, *Zululand*, 93; Seymour, *Bantu Law*, 104.

72. Seymour, *Bantu Law*, 71.

73. C. R. M. Dlamini, *The New Legal Status of Zulu Women* (KwaDlangezwa: University of Zululand, 1983), 11–12.

74. Henry J. Barrett, *Fifteen Years Among the Zulu and the Boers* (Hull: M. C. Peck and Son, 1879), 43.

75. *NA*, under "Echoes of the Week," 9 September 1893.

76. Johannes August Winter, "The Mental and Moral Capabilities of the Natives, Especially of Sekukuniland (Eastern Transvaal)," *South African Journal of Science* (1914), 371–83.

77. Kuper, *Wives for C attle*, 28; Seymour, *Bantu Law*, 66–71.

78. Seymour, *Bantu Law*, 71–72, 128–29.

79. When Rev. Shooter asked a husband who wished to take a second wife how he procured property from his first wife for the purpose, the man said, "by flattery, and coaxing, or if that did not succeed, by bothering her until she yielded and told him not to do so 'tomorrow.' Sometimes she becomes angry and tells him to take all, for that they are not hers but his. If she comply with her husband's polygamous desires and furnish cattle to purchase and endow a new wife, she will be entitled to her services; and will call her 'my wife.' She will also be entitled to the cattle received for a new wife's eldest daughter." Rev Shooter, *The Kafirs of Natal*, 84–85.

80. Mason, *Zululand*, 93–95.

81. Communication with Chief M. G. Buthelezi, cited in David Welsh, *The Roots of Segregation: Native Policy in Colonial Natal, 1845–1910* (Cape Town; New York: Oxford University Press, 1971), 169; Rev. Shooter, *The Kafirs of Natal*, 84–85; Seymour, *Bantu Law*, 128–29; Kuper, *Wives for Cattle*, 27.

82. Percival R. Kirby, ed., *Andrew Smith and Natal* (CapeTown: Van Riebeeck Society, 1955), 42.

83. Thomas B. Jenkinson, *The Amazulu: The Zulus, Their Past History, Manners, Customs, and Language* (New York: Negro University Press, 1969), 47–49.

84. See, for example, Audrey Richards, *Hunger and Work in a Savage Tribe* (Glencoe, Illinois: Free Press, 1948), 56–57, 78; Rev. T. Cullen, ed., "Habits and Customs of the Olden Days Among the Tumbuka-Kamanga People," *Africa* (1936), 315–19, 323–25, 353.

85. Barrett, *Fifteen Years*, 43.

86. Stuart, *Fynn's Diary*, 289.

87. Delegorgue, "Voyage dans l'Afrique-australe," in Bird, *Annals*, I, 477.

88. Godfrey Callaway, *Sketches of Kafir Life* (London: A. R. Mowbray and Company, 1905), 27–28. For a broader discussion of this dynamic see Louise Lamphere, "Strategies, Cooperation, and Conflict Among Women in Domestic Groups," in Michele Zimbalist Rosaldo and

Louise Lamphere, eds., *Woman, Culture and Society* (Stanford: Stanford University Press, 1974), 97–112.

89. Callaway, *Sketches*, 27–28; Callaway, *Building for God in Africa* (London: Society for Promoting Christian Knowledge, 1936), 14–16.

90. A. T. Bryant, *Olden Times in Zululand and Natal*, Part I, 19–20. Mankulumana kaSomapunga states that Nozidiya "had a quantity of *amabele*. People used to come and buy from her. She got a *dark-brown* beast in exchange for the *amabele*, and this beast gave birth to a number of white or whitish beasts. Either the *dark-brown* beast was given by Nozidiya to her younger son Zulu, or some of its progeny. Qwabe, seeing Zulu favoured, accordingly separated; hence the separation between the Qwabe and Zulu tribes." In *Stuart Archive*, II, 226.

91. ABC: 15.4, 6, No. 127. Katie Lloyd, June 1868.

92. For another discussion of the plight of women in crisis see Marcia Wright, "Women in Peril: A Commentary on the Life Stories of Captives in Nineteenth Century East-Central Africa," *Africa Social Research*, 20, December 1975.

93. Evidence of Henry F. Fynn before the Kafir Commission, Part V, 66.

94. See Chapter 5, below.

95. For an instance of this see John Wright, "Control of Women's Labour in the Zulu Kingdom," in J. B. Peires, ed., *Before and After Shaka* (Grahamstown: Rhodes University, 1981), 82–97.

96. S. Bourquin, ed., *Paulina Dalamini: Servant of Two Kings* (Durban: University of Natal, 1986). "Girls of the *isigodlo* who belonged to the age-groups making up the Amadlundlu, Amaqwaki, and Amaduku regiments were instructed in the use of firearms. The guns with which the king armed these women were supplied by John Dunn. The idea was that, while the army was in the field, these young women would defend the royal residence, if attacked by an enemy," 54; see also the testimony of Mpatshana kaSodondo in the *Stuart Archive*, V. 3, 328.

97. Slater, "Changing Economic Relationships," 148–70.

98. T. Rowell, *Natal and the Boers* (London: J. Dent, 1902), 160–67; Agar-Hamilton, *Voortrekkers' Native Policy*, 36–40.

99. Agar-Hamilton, *Voortrekkers' Native Policy*, 41.

100. Sullivan, *Shepstone's Native Policy*, 33–34.

101. Evidence of Henry Cloete before the Kafir Commission, Part I, 42; also evidence of Theophilus Shepstone, Part II, 30.

102. Evidence of T. Shepstone before the Kafir Commission, Part I, 60; SNA 1/1/11, No. 116. Surveyor General to Secretary of Native Affairs, 16 September 1861; T. J. D. Fair, *The Distribution of Population in Natal* (Cape Town; New York: Oxford University Press, 1955), III, 10.

103. Evidence of Evert F. Potgieter before the Kafir Commission, Part I, 18–19; Evidence of T. Shepstone, Part II, 37; Evidence of G. Peppercorne, Part III, 67.

104. Evidence of Lewis Grout before the Kafir Commission, Part IV, 50; ABC: 15.4, 4 (204), No. 297. Daniel Lindley to Rev. R. Anderson, D. D., Inanda, 16 November 1855.

105. Evidence of T. Shepstone before the Kafir Commission, Part IV, 59.

106. Slater, "Changing Economic Relationships," 148–70.

107. T. R. Davenport, and K. S. Hunt, eds., *The Right to the Land* (Cape Town: D. Phillip, 1974), 33.

108. ABC: 15.4, 4 (204), No. 297. Daniel Lindley to Rev. R. Anderson, D. D., Inanda, 16 November 1855.

109. SNA 1/3/18. Resident Magistrate for Richmond, 20 October 1868.

110. SNA 1/3/10, No. 64. Annual Report for 1860. Resident Magistrate Tugela Division to Secretary for Native Affairs, 25 March 1861.

111. SNA 1/1/10, No. 163. Memorandum for His Excellency the Lieutenant Governor, 15 May 1860.

112. "Taxation by a Native Chief," *NM*, 25 January 1856.

113. SNA 1/1/11, No. 276. Memorandum for His Excellency the Lieutenant Governor, 7 September 1861.
114. Resident Magistrate Pietermaritzburg Letter Book, 1859–1865. John Bird to Secretary for Native Affairs, 3 May 1864.
115. SNA 1/3/19. Resident Magistrate Newcastle to Secretary for Native Affairs, 2 June 1869.
116. Ibid.
117. SNA 1/3/19. Resident Magistrate to Secretary for Native Affairs, 26 May 1869. I suspect the following news item is in reference to Sotondozi's purchase. Although it contains an apparent inaccuracy, it is nonetheless worth noting: "a tribe in the Klip River district have bought a farm, paying a large sum of cash for the same. The property is to be transferred to the chief in trust, whilst various members of the tribe will have what may be termed squatting rights. No individual members of the tribe will have any portion of land transferred to him, so that by no means can the purchase be alienated from the tribe. We also hear that a native teacher will take up his residence with them." See "Progress," *Natal Herald*, 21 January 1869.
118. Testimony of Dinya kaZokozwayo, *Stuart Archive*, I, 99.
119. For a fuller discussion of "dependents," see Rev. Shooter, *The Kafirs of Natal*, 92–96.
120. Pietermaritzburg Letter Book. Report of John Bird to Secretary for Native Affairs, 12 November 1864.
121. Kopytoff, *African Frontier*, 22.
122. CSO V. II, Part I, No. 21. Ralph Clarence to J. Shepstone, Esq., Port Natal, 17 May 1847; *NW*, 28 May 1847.
123. *NW*, 28 May 1847.
124. Mason, *Zululand*, 48.
125. Sophr, *The Natal Diaries of Dr. W. H. I. Bleek*, 27.
126. Bryant, *The Zulu People*, 441–42; SNA 1/3/4, No. 19. Resident Magistrate Kahlamba, 14 February 1855.
127. Mason, *Zululand*, 49, 94.
128. Bryant, *The Zulu People*, 497, 509–10; James Stuart, *History of the Zulu Rebellion, 1906* (London: Macmillan and Company, 1913), 76.
129. Evidence of Rev. Aldin Grout before the Kafir Commission, Part V, 31–32.
130. SNA 1/3/8, No. 50. Resident Magistrate, Weenen to Secretary for Native Affairs, 4 October 1859.
131. Mason, *Zululand*, 94.
132. *NW*, 14 April 1848.
133. Lead article, *NM*, 14 August 1863.
134. SNA 1/3/8, No. 96. Resident Magistrate, Lower Umkomas, Umzinto, to Secretary for Native Affairs, 4 July 1859.
135. Ibid.
136. SNA 1/3/8, No. 126. Resident Magistrate, Inanda to Secretary for Native Affairs, 13 May 1859; SNA 1/3/9, No. 60. Annual Report, 21 March 1860.
137. SNA 1/3/8, No. 213. Resident Magistrate, Inanda to Secretary for Native Affairs, 31 January 1859.
138. SNA 1/3 /8, No. 126. Resident Magistrate, Inanda to Secretary for Native Affairs, 13 May 1859.
139. For another case of the role of chiefs in encouraging labor migrancy, see Judy Kimble, "Labour Migrations in Basutoland, c. 1870–1885," in Marks and Rathbone, *Industrialisation and Social Change*, 119–41.
140. "Native Panic at the Rand: Natal Natives Returning. Summoned Back by Chiefs," *NM*, 1 December 1896.
141. Papers Relating to the Supply, by Native Chiefs, of Native Labour, in Connection with the Public Works of the Colony (Pietermaritzburg: Vause, Slatter and Company, 1880).

142. Ibid. I suspect, though I have no direct data to support this, that the rush of young men to marry may also have been a strategy to avoid government work parties.

143. John W. Colenso, *Zulu-English Dictionary* (Pietermaritzburg: P. Davis, 1861), 497.

144. Charles van Onselen, "AmaWasha: The Zulu Washermen's Guild of the Witwatersrand, 1890-1914," in his *Studies in the Social and Economic History of the Witwatersrand, 1886-1914* (London; New York: Longman, 1984), II, 76.

145. An example of this is Slater's statement that by the mid-1850s "primitive accumulation" had not advanced sufficiently among Natal's African population to the extent that they would voluntarily enter labor relationships. In "Changing Patterns of Economic Relationships," 154.

CHAPTER 3
Traditions of Labor Organization, Prestige Occupations, and White Masters

1. Here I diverge radically from such writers as Bryant on the critical point relating to the degree of power inherent in the role of senior wife.

2. Bryant, *Zulu People*, 184-85, 426.

3. Ibid., 459, 461.

4. Ibid., 413, 463; Eileen Krige, *The Social System of the Zulus* (Pietermaritzburg: Shuter and Shooter, 1957), 212.

5. Bryant, *Zulu People*, 463; Testimony of Mandhlakazi kaNgini in *Stuart Archive*, II, 178-79.

6. Mandhlakazi, *Stuart Archive*, II, 178-81.

7. Bryant, *Olden Times*, Part I, 113.

8. Testimony of Lunguza kaMpukane in *Stuart Archive*, I, 324-25.

9. Ibid., 44.

10. David Leslie, *Among the Zulus and Amatongas* (New York: Negro University Press, 1969), 50.

11. Testimony of Baleni kaSilwana in *Stuart Archive*, I, 36.

12. Testimony of Magidigidi kaNobebe in *Stuart Archive*, II, 93-97.

13. See, for example, the evidence of G. R. Peppercorne before the Kafir Commission, Part III, 64; and Evidence of H. F. Fynn, ibid., Part V, 64.

14. J. L. Dohne, *A Zulu-Kafir Dictionary* (Cape Town: G. J. Pike, 1857), 253-54.

15. Bryant, *Zulu People*, 376-77.

16. For a broader discussion of this, see Bernardi, *Age Class Systems*. I should point out that certain aspects of the age grade system described in this section are applicable only to the pre-conquest Zulu state. Their place here is to show the varying ways in which northern Nguni cultural institutions found expression in nineteenth-century colonial Natal.

17. R. C. Samuelson, *Long, Long Ago* (Durban: Knox Printing & Publishing Company, 1929), 354.

18. Bryant, *Zulu People*, 186; Krige, *Social System*, 76; Testimony of Ndukwana kaMbengwana in *Stuart Archive*, IV, 378-79; R. C. Samuelson, *Long, Long Ago*, 354-56.

19. Krige, *Social System*, 81-87. A purely military function is often ascribed to the *izindibi*, but Dohne significantly defines the *udibi* as "Commonly a boy who carries the effects of equipage of an older man in going to war (or in travelling)" (*Zulu-Kafir Dictionary*, 61). Note, too, for example, the business of the young assistant (*impakatha*) of the Zulu medicine man in A. T. Bryant, *Zulu Medicine and Medicine Men* (Cape Town: C. Struik, 1970), 10; and Bryant, *Zulu People*, 187.

20. Krige, *Social System*, 107-15; Bryant, *Zulu People*, 187-89; Stuart, *Zulu Rebellion*, 76.

21. Bryant, *Zulu People*, 141-42; Krige, *Social System*, 118-19; Shooter, "Off to Natal," 162.

22. Evidence of H. F. Fynn before the Kafir Commission, Part V, 55-57; Dohne, *Zulu-Kafir Dictionary*, 253-54; Bryant, *Zulu People*, 178; Krige, *Social System*, 211-12.

23. Krige, *Social System*, 212.

24. Bernardi, *Age Class Systems*.

25. See, for example, the lead article in *NM*, 22 March 1864; and "To the Editor," *NM*, 8 April 1864.

26. Ibid.

27. William Holden, *A Brief History of Methodism and Methodist Missions in South Africa* (London: Wesleyan Conference Office, 1877), 431–32. Holden's observations were made between the years 1847 and 1852.

28. A fuller account of their origins can be found in Keletso Atkins, "Origins of the AmaWasha: The Zulu Washerman's Guild in Natal, 1850–1910," *Journal of African History* 1 (1986), 41–57.

29. "Kafir Dodges," *NM*, 24 October 1856.

30. "Day Laborers," *Natal Star* [hereafter *NS*], 10 December 1856.

31. Theophilus Shepstone, "Togt Memorandum," *NGG*, 31 March 1874.

32. Bryant, *Zulu People*, 376–77; idem, *Zulu Medicine*, 10–11; Krige, *Social System*, 209, 297–305.

33. "Kafir Dodges," *NM*, 24 October 1856; T. Eastwood to Mayor Durban, 17 November 1874, Durban Corporation Letters [hereafter DCL], File 352; "Wash Boys' Parade," *Standard and Digger News*, 2 July 1895; Durban Corporation Superintendent of Police Report Book [hereafter DCSPRB], File 3310: reports dated 2 June 1905 and 3 July 1905.

34. Testimony of Bikwayo kaNoziwawa, in *Stuart Archive*, I, 63–73.

35. DCL File 429: Umgeni Magistrate to Mayor of Durban, 31 March 1892; and DCL File 435: Umgeni Police Station to Superintendent of Police, 31 January 1893. Charles van Onselen, "AmaWasha: The Zulu Washermen's Guild on the Witwatersrand, 1890–1910," *Studies in the Social and Economic History of the Witwatersrand, 1886–1914*, II, 76.

36. "Echoes of the Week," *Natal Advertiser* [hereafter *NA*] 15 January 1910.

37. Eliza Whigham Feilden, *My African Home* (London: Sampson Low, Marston, Searle and Rivington, 1887), 226. Emphasis in the original.

38. See, for example, Thomas S. Weisner and Ronald Gallimore, "My Brother's Keeper: Child and Sibling Caretaking," *Current Anthropology*, 18, 2 (June 1977), 169–90.

39. Testimony of Majuba kaSibukula (of Tongaland), in *Stuart Archive*, II, 157.

40. Testimony of Ndukwana kaMbengwana, in *Stuart Archive*, IV, 263, 300, 357–58; Bryant, *Olden Times*, 134.

41. Testimony of Melapi kaMagaye, in *Stuart Archive*, III, 81–82.

42. Testimony of Lunguza kaMpakane, in *Stuart Archive*, I, 337.

43. Charles van Onselen, "The Witches of Suburbia: Domestic Service on the Witwatersrand, 1890–1910," in *Studies in the Social History*, II, 28–29.

44. Testimony of Mkando kaDhlovu, in *Stuart Archive*, III, 145.

45. Lunguza, in *Stuart Archive*, I, 325; Ndukwana, *ibid.*, IV, 379.

46. Ndukwana, in *Stuart Archive*, IV, 379.

47. Stuart, *The Zulu Rebellion*, 76.

48. Bryant, *The Zulu People*, 509; O. F. Raum, *The Social Functions of Avoidances and Taboos among the Zulu* (Berlin; New York: Walter De Gruyter, 1973), 102.

49. Testimony of Mandhlakazi kaNgini, in *Stuart Archive*, II, 180. Mandhlakazi tells the story of Zulu kaNogandaya from the Qwabe country, who came to *khonza* (pay respects to) Shaka, whereupon he was "moved up to Tshaka's place where he became an *inceku* (servant) responsible for smearing Tshaka's hut floor with cowdung. He thenceforward remained an *inceku.*"

50. A. I. Berglund, "Heaven-Herds: A study of Zulu Symbolism," in Michael Whisson and Martin West, eds., *Religion and Social Change in Southern Africa* (Cape Town: D. Phillip, 1975), 35.

51. In 1857 the Reverend Shooter wrote, "The Zulu army ... consists of two classes, namely 'men' and 'boys'—the former being those entitled to wear the head-ring, and the latter all others. Both classes are divided into regiments. . . . The regiments bear the same name as the kraals where they assemble. Two or three years ago, Pande's army embraced the fol-

lowing. (1) Of old 'men,' he had four regiments, namely *Tuguza, Isiklepini, Imbelibeli, Nobambe* (the last being particularly ancient people). (2) OF YOUNGER 'MEN' [sic] (*amakehla*) he had six regiments, namely *Bulawalo, Nodwenge, Dumazulu, Lambongwenya, Swongindaba, Indbaka-aumbi.* (3) The 'BOYS' were distributed into four regiments, *Tuluawa, Isangu, Ingulubi, Hlambehlu.* (Some of the Hlambehlu 'boys' were thirty-five years of age)." Shooter, *Kafirs of Natal*, 338.

52. Holden, *History of Methodism*, 431.

53. Again, in no way do I mean to imply that all colonists had the traditional usage in mind when they adopted the expression "boy" as a form of address. From the beginning, many whites used the term condescendingly and applied it with pejorative intent to all African males, irrespective of age or marital status. On the other hand, I suspect strongly that when the settlers complained that Zulu "men" would not work, it was largely to the class of *amakhehla* that they referred.

54. There were undoubtedly degrees of dependency. How quickly one recovered from a servile state was contingent upon the conditions of one's kinship network. Families that survived the bad times and remained economically viable fared much better than aged dependents who were less economically productive, and who lacked social ties to fall back on. Furthermore, a master would do all in his power to attract and retain dependents with large families, for their numbers would make his kraal appear full and would enhance the patron's wealth through their labor. For this see Shooter, *Kafirs of Natal*, 119–34.

55. Ibid., 93.

56. Fynn, *The Diary of Henry F. Fynn*, 3. Testimony of Madikane kaMlomowetole, in *Stuart Archive*, II, 50.

57. Testimony of Mbulo kaMlahla, in *Stuart Archive*, III, 51.

58. Testimony of Kambi kaMatshobana, in *Stuart Archive*, I, 209.

59. Robert Levine, "Patterns of Personality in Africa," in George De Vos, ed., *Responses to Change: Society, Culture and Personality* (New York: Van Nostrand, 1976), 1976), 120.

60. SNA 1/1/14, No. 24. A. Behrens to Shepstone, Pietermaritzburg, 27 June 1851.

61. CSO IV9, Part I, Grievance of Mooy River Farmers, 28 February to 11 March 1849.

62. Evidence of Rev. Aldin Grout before the Kafir Commission, Part V, 30. More often than not, women led the fight against conversion to Christianity, i.e., the onslaught against polygamy. See Norman Etherington, *Preachers, Peasants and Politics in Southeast Africa, 1835–1880* (London: Royal Historical Society, 1978), 61–63.

63. Evidence of T. L. Dohne before the Kafir Commission, Part VI, 40.

64. Augustus Lindley, *After Ophir*, 222–23.

65. MMS: 317 (1860–61). Extracts from the Journal of Joseph Jackson, 20 May 1861.

66. John William Colenso, *Ten Weeks in Natal* (Cambridge: Macmillan, 1855), 52.

67. Stuart, *Fynn's Diary*, 81.

68. Bryant, *Zulu People*, 485; Leslie, *Among the Zulus*, 79.

69. Shooter, "Off to Natal," 162.

70. Spohr, *Diaries of Dr. Bleek*, 69.

71. Ibid.

72. Testimony of Mahaya kaNongqabana, in *Stuart Archive*, II, 130.

73. Bryant, *Olden Times*, Part I, 60–61.

74. See Chapter 2, above, for further examples of how this process worked; see also the testimony of Mayinga kaMbekuzana, in *Stuart Archive*, II, 258.

75. Dohne, *Zulu-Kafir Dictionary*, 171.

76. Ibid. "I have concluded that it will be best to make the Kafirs around us feel as much as possible the value of time, labor and skill," wrote Rev. Henry Callaway in 1859, "and I have therefore determined to give them as little as possible. Among other things, they are to pay a small sum for medicines, enough to prevent my being a loser. I was explaining this to one of them, who asked for medicine for his child, and he said, 'But you are our Chief; I am one

of your people; and will you not cure your child?' " "There are many Kafirs willing enough to acknowledge the white man as their chief," Callaway went on to state, "so long as his government consists in giving them everything they ask. But such a system is most mischievous, and tends to keep them, not only in idleness, but in childish dependence; when what is really required is, to rouse in them the sense of manliness and self-reliance." Rev. Dr. Henry Callaway's Journal, *Mission Field* (1 October 1859), 36–37.

77. Shooter, *Kafirs of Natal*, 92–96.

78. See above, note 70.

79. The career of John Dunn, the white "Zulu chief," was perhaps as interesting as those of the early hunter/traders.

80. Etherington, *Preachers, Peasants and Politics*, 90–91.

81. "Ploughed Land for Natives," *NM*, 4 November 1858.

82. See Chapter 2 on the refugee communities.

83. See Chapter 2 for a discussion of *isibhalo*.

84. Robert J. Mann, ed., *The Colony of Natal* (London: Jarrold and Sons, 1859), 189.

85. *Natal Herald* [hereafter *NH*], 16 August 1866.

86. Archie Mafeje, "The Role of the Bard In a Contemporary African Community," *Journal of African Languages*, 6, Part 3 (1967), 193–223.

87. Trevor Cope, *Izibongo: Zulu Praise-Poems* (Oxford: Clarendon Press, 1968), 28.

88. Krige, *The Social System of the Zulu*, fn. 1, 113; Bryant, *The Zulu People*, 485–89; A. C. Jordan, *Towards An African Literature: The Emergence of Literary Form In Xhosa* (Berkeley: University of California Press, 1973), 21; Samuelson, *Long, Long Ago*, 354.

89. See Elizabeth Gunner, "Orality and Literacy: Dialogue and Silence," in Karin Barber and P. F. deMoraes Farias, eds., *Discourse and Its Disguises: Interpretation of African Oral Texts* (Birmingham: Birmingham University African Studies No. 1, 1989), 49–56, for an insightful discussion of the *izibongo* (praise poems) and the trade union poets (*izimbongi*) of FOSATU and COSATU, as a function in the growth of worker consciousness. Gunner's materials are based on interviews with the leading worker-poet, A. T. Qabula.

90. "Speech of Mr. Leyland Fielden before the Blackburn Commercial Association," *NW*, 11 July 1851; "To the Editor," *NW*, 11 December 1846; Mann, *The Colony of Natal*, 189.

91. For example see, Robin Cohen, "Hidden Forms of Labor Protest in Africa," paper presented to a conference organized by the Joint Committee on African Studies, Social Science Research Council, on "Inequality in Africa." Mt. Kisco, New York, 6–9 October 1976.

92. Shooter, *Kafirs of Natal*, 119.

93. United Society for the Propagation of the Gospel [hereafter USPG]: 1860. Journal of Henry Callaway, 1 October–31 December 1860.

94. Feilden, *My African Home*, 120–21.

95. *Ibid.* The matter of how African workmen related to a female as their superior, is an important one, which is dealt with more fully by Mrs. Wilkinson, who wrote that, "I have no difficulty in managing, for I am held in great respect by all the men. The know that the word of the 'Inkosikazi' 'Chieftainess' is like the word of the 'Inkosi' 'Chief,' and I always hold the food, which is a great point with the Zulus." Mrs. Wilkinson's remarks merely confirm what we already know about the prestige of the principal wife in all aspects of Zulu affairs. See Mrs. Wilkinson's *A Lady's Life and Travels*, 125.

96. Ibid., 113.

97. Ibid., 56.

98. Ibid., 253. Emphasis in the original.

99. Mann, *Colony of Natal*, 210.

100. Colenso, *Ten Weeks*, 52.

101. Baldwin, *African Hunting and Adventure*, 5.

102. Feilden, *My African Home*, 53–54.

CHAPTER 4
"Kafir Time," Wage Claims, and Other Sociocultural Antecedents of *Togt*, or Day Labor

1. E. P. Thompson, "Time, Work-Discipline, and Industrial Capitalism," *Past and Present*, XXXVII (1967), 56–97.

2. "Labor," *NW*, 11 December 1846.

3. C. W. Posselt, *The Zulu Companion Offered to the Natal Colonist to Facilitate Intercourse with the Natives* (Pietermaritzburg: D. D. Buchanan, 1850), 8.

4. Henry Callaway, *The Religious System of the AmaZulu* (Cape Town: C. Struik, 1970), 397; Bryant, *The Zulu People*, 251–52.

5. Leslie, *Among the Zulus and the Amatongas*, 394–96; Bryant, *The Zulu People*, 254–56; Krige, *The Social System of the Zulus*, 412.

6. Bryant, *The Zulu People*, 254–56; Samuelson, *Long, Long Ago*, 304. Both Zulu *izinyanga* (professional men and women, i.e., doctors, philosophers, etc.) and ordinary people observed the sun, moon, and stars, contemplated the origins of the heaven and the cosmic bodies, and developed a system of theories about their cyclic movement. See also Callaway, *Religious System*, 393–99. The idiom *-file*, Colenso noted, was used by Africans in all sorts of ways to indicate a diminishing of something, or to express failure of one kind or other. "When the moon is changing and disappears it is *file*; if a necklace is broken, it is *file*, spoiled; if a dish, cup or chair is shattered. . . , it is reported as *file*. One day a messenger, who had travelled all night on my account in wet and cold, came to me with a piteous air to ask for scoff (food), because, he said, 'his stomach was file.'" Colenso, *Ten Weeks in Natal*, 200. See also Dohne, *A Zulu-Kafir Dictionary*, 75.

7. Frances Ellen Colenso, *The Ruin of Zululand: An Account of British Doings in Zululand Since the Invasion of 1879* (London: W. Ridgway, 1884–85), I, 169; Testimony of Mpatshana kaSodondo, in *Stuart Archive*, III, 301.

8. "Contracts with Native Laborers," *NW*, 6 November 1846.

9. Alfred Rivett, *Ten Years' Work in Natal* (London: Jarrold and Sons, 1890), 22.

10. "Strike among the Kafir Mail Carriers," *NM*, 14 January 1858.

11. "Monthly Native Servants," *NM*, 25 April 1896.

12. Posselt, *Zulu Companion*, 3.

13. Charles Barter, *The Dorp and the Veld* (London: W. S. Orr, 1852), 223–24.

14. D. T. Cole, "Fanagalo and the Bantu Languages in South Africa," *African Studies* 12, 1 (March 1953), 1–9. Fanagalo, a hybrid of Zulu, English, and Afrikaans, developed primarily out of the interaction of English and Zulu. Cole explains that "In the name Fanagalo we have it retaining its demonstrative significance—*fana* (be like, resemble), *ga* (with, of), *lo* (this), hence *fanagalo* (thus, like this). Since *Enza fanagalo!* (Do like this! Make like this!) is one of the most commonly used expressions in the language–certainly the new and inexperienced "boy" has it dinned into his ears from morning till night—it is hardly surprising that the language has come to be known as Fanagalo," 2, 6.

15. Faye, *Zulu References*, 52.

16. Bryant, *The Zulu People*, 249–51.

17. ABC: 15.4, 10. Charles Kilbon to Judson Smith, 21 July 1884.

18. Extracts from the Journal of Rev. Dr. Henry Callaway, *Mission Field* (1 October 1859), 37.

19. Posselt, *Zulu Companion*, 8. Dohne translates "umuNyaka" as "Literally:—a space of a year; = civil year, a period of a year." (*Zulu-Kafir Dictionary*, 251). In the third edition of J. Cullingsworth, *Zulu Vocabulary and Phrasebook for the use of Immigrants and Settlers in the Colony of Natal* (Pietermaritzburg: J. Cullingsworth, 1865), we find the phrase "Ungathanda kuhlala kumina umnyaka na?" ("Will you stop with me a year?"), 26. Zulu phrase books comprised a large body of popular colonial literature. Cullingsworth's volume alone saw thirteen editions between 1850 and 1918. These publications must have found their way into practically every European household. However, the mistranslations of critical words in

order to inculcate industry, "that vital part of religion," had unintended consequences. The great popularity of these volumes with their very obvious flaws ironically helped perpetuate the fundamental problem plaguing master-servant relations: failure of communication.

20. SNA 1/3/18. Annual Report for the County of Alexandra, 14 January 1868; George Russell, *The History of Old Durban, and Reminiscences of an Emigrant of 1850* (Durban: P. Davis and Sons, 1899), 104.

21. SNA 1/3/5. H. F. Fynn to T. Shepstone, 19 January 1856; Colenso, *Ten Weeks in Natal*, 26; Mann, *The Colony of Natal*, 188–89.

22. Bryant, *The Zulu People*, 256–57.

23. Edward Hall, *The Dance of Life: The Other Dimension of Time* (New York: Anchor Press/Doubleday, 1984), 3–4.

24. C. L. S. Nyembezi, *Zulu Proverbs* (Johannesburg: Witwatersrand University Press, 1963), 113.

25. ABC: 15.4, 5, Josiah Tyler to Rugus Anderson, 14 February 1853; Jenkinson, *AmaZulu: The Zulus, Their Past History*, 30; Axel-Ivar Berglund, *Zulu Thought-Patterns and Symbolism* (London: C. Hurst, 1976), 276–78, 286, 364.

26. SNA 1/3/18. Resident Magistrate Newcastle to Secretary for Native Affairs, 9 October 1868; Captain Walter R. Ludlow, *Zululand and Cetewayo* (London: Simkin, Marshall, and Company, 1882), 99.

27. Peter Richardson, "The Natal Sugar Industry in the Nineteenth Century," in W. Beinart et al., *Putting a Plough to the Ground* (Johannesburg: Ravan Press, 1986), 136–37.

28. "A Description of the Farm Compensation," by Edmund Morewood (Durban, 1853). In Alan Hattersley, *The Natalians* (Pietermaritzburg: Shuter and Shooter, 1940), 89–91.

29. "Labor," *NM*, 13 June 1856.

30. "Mr. Babbs' Letter," *NM*, 5 October 1855.

31. "Labor," *NM*, 13 June 1856.

32. Ibid.; Hugh Tinker, *A New System of Slavery: The Export of Indian Labor Overseas, 1830–1920* (London; New York: Oxford University Press, 1974), 27.

33. "Labor," *NM*, 13 June 1855.

34. "A Visit to Springfield," *NM*, 27 June 1855.

35. Lead Article, *NM*, 21 September 1855.

36. "The Labor Question," *NM*, 5 October 1855.

37. "Sugar Planting in Natal," *Natal Times and Mercantile and Agricultural Gazette*, 5 November 1852; Resident Magistrate Report Inanda Division, 1880, in *Blue Book for the Colony of Natal* (Pietermaritzburg: 1880), Section JJ, 101.

38. "Eclipse," *NM*, 18 April 1874.

39. Russell, *The History of Old Durban*, 128–29.

40. Jacques Le Goff, *Time, Work and Culture in the Middle Ages* (Chicago: University of Chicago Press, 1980), 48.

41. Russell, *The History of Old Durban*, 130. But Lunguza kaMpukane informs us that mealtimes varied during those periods when the army was being mobilized for war. "I may say here that food in the old days was taken first thing in the morning even before daybreak. . . . This became the practice owing to warriors having to be in a state of constant readiness to proceed to headquarters for military service when called, for these summonses came usually at night," in *Stuart Archive*, I, 335.

42. H. Callaway, *The Religious System of the Amazulu*, 397.

43. The noun *umngcelu* could refer generally to any very early bird. See John Colenso, *Zulu-English Dictionary*, 4th Edition (Farborough: Gregg Press, 1967), 385.

44. Samuelson, *Long, Long Ago*, 45–46, 413–19; Lunguza kaMpukane, in *Stuart Archive*, I, 322; Nyembezi, *Zulu Proverbs*, 60.

45. Russell, *The History of Old Durban*, 495.

46. On the prevalent use of the bell as a time signal in South Africa, see Chapter XVII in O. F. Mentzel, *Life at the Cape in Mid-Eighteenth Century (1784)* (Cape Town: Darter Brothers, 1920). "In all the Company's East Indian possessions, as well as at the Cape," he wrote, "the whole work of the day is planned out in the same fashion, and everywhere the passage of time is marked in the same way, that is, by striking the hours by hand upon a bell. It is this fact that has given rise to the adage so frequently heard in the East and even in Holland: Hütet euch für das land, wo man die glocke schlägt mit der hand: Beware of the land, where the clocks are struck by hand," 162. For their use elsewhere, see David Landes, *Revolution in Time: Clocks and the Making of the Modern World* (Cambridge: Harvard University Press, 1983), 72–78.

47. "Time," *NM*, 7 February 1854; see also "Uniformity of Time," *NM*, 17 March 1853; Russell, *The History of Old Durban*, 436.

48. Bertram Mitford, *Through the Zulu Country: Its Battlefields and Its People* (London: K. Paul, Trench, 1883), 148.

49. Russell, *The History of Old Durban*, 130.

50. For a wider discussion of the "week," see Eviatar Zerubavel, *The Seven Day Circle: The History and Meaning of the Week* (New York: Free Press, 1985).

51. Rees, *Colenso Letters From Natal*, 322.

52. Bryant, *The Zulu People*, 256.

53. Testimony of Ndukwana kaMbengwana, in *Stuart Archive*, IV, 334. Emphasis in the original.

54. "Coolie Masters and Kafir Servants," *Natal Colonist* [hereafter *NC*], 7 January 1873.

55. Methodist Missionary Society [hereafter MMS]: File 317. Extracts from the Journal of Reverend Joseph Jackson, 7 January 1861. According to Lunguza kaMpukane, "There was no such thing as Sunday or a day of rest in Zululand. We worked any and every day. We knew nothing of Sunday, Monday, Tuesday, etc. We heard of all this in Natal. It was incumbent on every man to work every day. Should he not work he would be asked who told him not to work." *Stuart Archive*, I, 339.

56. See for example, "Togt Kafirs Again," *NM*, 11 June 1881.

57. United Society for the Propagation of the Gospel [hereafter USPG]: Walter Baugh to E. Hawkins, 8 May 1859.

58. Shooter, "Off to Natal," 233; USPG: Report of D. E. Robinson, Missionary at Durban, 30 June 1873.

59. Apart from a small electrical plant laid down in the Market Square in 1886, oil continued to be the universal method of lighting until the late 1890s. See, for example, John McIntyre, "From Settlement to City," in Allister Macmillan, ed., *Durban Past and Present* (Durban: William Brown and Davis, 1936), 51.

60. USPG: Walter Baugh to E. Hawkins, 10 October 1860.

61. Russell, *The History of Old Durban*, 128–29.

62. J. Forsyth Ingram, *The Colony of Natal* (London: J. Causton and Sons, 1895), 91; McIntyre, "From Settlement to City," 51.

63. Russell, *The History of Old Durban*, 286.

64. *Life at Natal a Hundred Years Ago. By a Lady.* (Cape Town: C. Struik, 1972), 78, 127.

65. *Natal Advertiser* [hereafter *NA*], 9 May 1893.

66. "Labor Demands," *NW*, 26 November 1895.

67. "Native Work on Saturday: Lower Court Decision Quashed," *NA*, 15 April 1899.

68. "Native Labor: Employers Taking Action," *NM*, 11 July 1902.

69. Etherington, *Preachers, Peasants and Politics*, 54.

70. Chief Native Commissioner [hereafter CNC], Vol. 12. Chief Constable, Durban to Arthur J. Shepstone, the Acting Chief Native Commissioner, 5 July 1911.

71. Russell, *The History of Old Durban*, 495.

72. See Chapter 6, below.

73. Philip Mayer, *Townsmen or Tribesmen: Conservatism and the Process of Urbanization in a South African City* (Cape Town; New York: Oxford University Press, 1971), 160, 163–64.

74. Sture Lagercrantz, "African Tally-Strings," *Anthropos* 63 (1968), 115–28; *idem*, "Tallying By Means of Lines, Stones, and Sticks," *Paideuma* 16 (1970), 52–62; *idem*, "Counting by Means of Tally Sticks or Cuts on the Body in Africa," *Anthropos* 68 (1973), 569–88. While it has been suggested that these elements of their material culture were borrowed from either European or Oriental sources, evidence from Ishango, Zaire, dated c. 9000 B.C. to 6500 B.C., tell a very different story. See Lagercrantz, "Counting by Means of Tally Sticks," 582–83; William Burchell, *Travels in the Interior of Southern Africa* (London: Batchworth Press, 1953), II, 245–46; Jean de Heinzelin, "Ishango," *Scientific American* 206 (June 1962), 105–16.

75. Dohne, *Zulu-Kafir Dictionary*, 14.

76. Lagercrantz, "Counting by Means of Tally Sticks," 575, 579, 581; O. F. Raum, "The Rolling Target (Hoop-and-Pole) Game in Africa," *African Studies* 12 (1953), 105, 108.

77. Percival R. Kirby, ed., *Andrew Smith and Natal* (Cape Town: Van Riebeeck, 1955), 80–81; Stuart, *Fynn's Diary*, 127.

78. Testimony of Mauinga kaMbekuzana, in *Stuart Archive*, II, 252. In this manner, too, African messengers in service to the colonial government kept records of cattle, groups of prisoners, and parties of refugees entrusted to them for safe transport and escort. On arriving at their destination a "receipt stick" was presented to the magistrate against which the delivery could be checked. SNA 1/3/8, No. 144. Ladysmith, 29 April 1859.

79. Lagercrantz, "African Tally-Strings," 121; Bryant, *The Zulu People*, 202. Bryant maintains that tying knots was the prerogative of women, but there is evidence that men also used string tallies. For example, the old Zulu messenger, Mfunzi, tied 70 knots in a string to show the number of his cattle. For this see F. E. Colenso, *The Ruin of Zululand*, 85.

80. Lagercrantz, "African Tally Strings," 119.

81. Ludlow, *Zululand and Cetewayo*, 145–46.

82. Barrett, *Fifteen Years Among the Zulus*, 45.

83. ABC: 15.4, 2. Extracts from Mr. Champion's Journal, 30 August 1836 to 1837; "A Native Claim," *NA*, 19 October 1909; Lagercrantz, "Counting by Means of Tally Sticks," 581.

84. Posselt, *Zulu Companion*, 8.

85. Burchell, *Travels*, 245–46.

86. Mentzel, *Life at the Cape*, 157.

87. Not all Khoi were as skillful as Speelman in mastering European time concepts. See Henry Lichtenstein, *Travels in Southern Africa, in the Years 1803, 1804, 1805, and 1806* (London: Henry Colbum, 1815), II, 71–72.

88. Barrett, *Fifteen Years Among the Zulus*, 44. Emphasis italics in the orignal.

89. Ibid.

90. ABC: 15.4, 5, Josiah Tyler to Rev. Anderson, 20 May 1854; "Monthly Servants," *NM*, 25 April 1896; Rivett, *Ten Year's Work*, 22.

91. "Native Labor," *NM*, 13 September 1854.

92. "Kafir Labour," *NM*, 16 April and 24 April 1863.

93. Robert Hutchins, ed., *Statues of Natal, 1845–1899* (Pietermaritzburg: P. Davis and Sons, 1901), II.

94. Under "Magistrate's Court, Durban," *NC*, 11 July 1871.

95. ABC: 15.4, 5, Josiah Tyler to Rev. Anderson, 20 May 1854; "Natives' Wages Claim," *NA*, 30 October 1906.

96. Mason, *Zululand*, 24.

97. Colenso, *Ten Weeks in Natal*, 256–57. Prominent Zulus were eager to hear the European's explanation of cosmologic phenomena as well. Colenso relates that one day Captain Struben went to see Nodada, a powerful chief who settled in the Klip River Division, and found him full of inquiries. "'Where did the new suns come from? Every day a new fiery circle rose in the East, and went down in the West.' The Captain took a mealie stalk, and

gave him a rough illustration of the rising and setting of the sun. Then he had questions about the stars and the moon—all showing a remarkable shrewdness of intellect. All night long, from 7 p.m. to 4 a.m., Capt. S. lay upon his mat, discoursing thus with this Kafir chief," 20–21.

98. Extracts from the Journal of Rev. Henry Callaway, Mission Field (1 October 1859), 37.
99. "Kaffir Almanac," *Eastern Province Herald*, 5 December 1862.
100. Hall, *Dance of Life*, 7.
101. "Kafir Reasoning," *NC*, 1 March 1879.
102. Testimony of Ndukwana kaMbengwana, *Stuart Archive*, IV, 266.
103. Testimony of Mcotoyi kaMnini, in *Stuart Archive*, III , 63. See Eugenia W. Herbert, *Red Gold of Africa* (Madison: University of Wisconsin Press, 1984), for a discussion of the role of iron in traditional African value systems.
104. *NW*, 17 July 1846; "Labor," *NW*, 11 December 1846.
105. *NW*, 27 April 1849.
106. "Indirect Benefit of the Lungsickness," *NM*, 30 November 1855.
107. See for example, "Taxation by a Native Chief," *NM*, 25 January 1856.
108. Colenso, *First Steps of the Zulu Mission*, 91–92.
109. "Labor," *NW*, 11 December 1846; "The Work of Civilization," *NW*, 4 October 1850; also Durban Civil Record Books, 1846–1865.
110. Posselt, *Zulu Companion*, 47–48.
111. "Police Report," *Natal Independent*, 20 February 1851.
112. Lindley, *After Ophir*, 78–79; Russell, *The History of Old Durban*, 104; Colenso, *Zulu-English Dictionary*, 4th edition, 544.
113. Posselt, *Zulu Companion*, 56–57.
114. "Another Stave in the Labor Question," *NH*, 1 August 1870.
115. "Kafir Labor," *NM*, 4 March 1873.
116. "Chimes from the Town Clock," *NMA*, 14 April 1885.
117. Charles van Onselen, "Worker Consciousness in Black Miners: Southern Rhodesia, 1900–1920," in I. R. Phimister and C. van Onselen, *Studies in the History of African Mine Labor in Colonial Zimbabwe* (Gwelo: Mambo Press, 1978), 9; Sharon Stichter, *Migrant Labourers* (Cambridge; New York: Cambridge University Press, 1985), 194.
118. *NH*, 24 January 1867.
119. CO 179/111 (Natal, No. 3281). Returns of Corporal Punishments under the Masters and Servants Ordinance No. 2, 1850, Musgrave to Lord Kimberley, 25 February 1873. The report stated that the impression was unavoidable that "want of labor of which the sugar planters complain may in great measure arise from a dislike on the part of the natives to encounter risk of sharp punishment for petty offences which may not be quite justly alleged against them." If this were the case, the report concluded, then "it would not be the first instance of a too stringent policy defeating the end in view—that end in the case of the planters being to obtain ready, abundant and faithful service from the native tribes.
120. "Justice in Magistrates' Court," *NW*, 9 September 1880; "Chimes from the Town Clock," *NMA*, 14 April 1885.
121. "Chimes from the Town Clock," *NMA*, 14 April 1885.
122. Ibid.
123. Ibid.

CHAPTER 5
The Evolution of the *Togt* Labor Market Within the Political
Economy of Natal, 1843–1875

1. Henry Slater, "Land, Labor and Capital in Natal: The Natal Land and Colonisation Company, 1860-1948," *Journal of African History* XVI, 2 (1975), 263-64.

2. Slater, "Changing Economic Relationships," 155–63.
3. Charles Ballard, "Migrant Labor in Natal, 1860–79: With Special Reference to Zululand and the Delagoa Bay Hinterland," *Journal of Natal and Zulu History* I (1978), 31.
4. Mrs. Wilkinson, *A Lady's Life*, 248–49.
5. John Robinson, *A Life-Time in South Africa: Being the Recollections of the First Premier of Natal* (London: Smith, Elder and Company, 1900), 188–89.
6. "The State of the Port," *NW*, 11 September 1877; Trollope, *South Africa*, 199–200.
7. Posselt, *Zulu Companion*, 44–45.
8. Gareth Stedman Jones, *Outcast London* (Oxford: Clarendon Press, 1971), 47.
9. SGO IV/5/1. Commissioner for Locating the Natives' Correspondence. Mr. Cloete's schedule of aboriginal Zulu tribes settled in the Natal territory, 10 November 1843.
10. SNA 1/1/24, No. 24. William Campbell to Lt. Governor Pine, 2 March 1874.
11. *NC*, 28 September 1878.
12. "Native Identification Act," *NM*, 24 October 1903.
13. SNA V. 306. Casual labor by women and children from the locations, 24 October 1903.
14. See Chapter 2.
15. SNA 1/3/7, No. 158. Weenen magistrate to Secretary for Native Affairs, 6 November 1858.
16. " 'Dag' or 'Toch' Labor," *NM*, 14 January 1873.
17. Ibid; SNA 1/3/8, No. 208. Resident Magistrate, Durban, 3 February 1859.
18. As for example, William Campbell, who was strongly opposed to the introduction of Indian labor into Natal, and used nothing but Natal African labor. His sons carried on the same tradition at their Muckle Neuk Sugar Estate. Robert Osborn, *Valiant Harvest: The Founding of the South African Sugar Industry, 1848–1926* (Durban: South African Sugar Association, 1964), 233. Natal Africans were also preferred by Mr. Osborn of the Umtata Estate, Mr. Shire in Umhlanga Valley, and on the Oatlands Estate of Mr. Reynolds. John Robinson, eds., *Notes on Natal: Old Colonists' Book for New Settlers* (Durban, 1872), 10, 15, 53.
19. See Chapter 4.
20. See Chapter 3.
21. SNA 1/3/8, No. 96. Henry F. Fynn, Lower Umkomas Division, Umzinto, 4 July 1859.
22. Carmel Rickard, ed., "Charles Barter Natal Diary, 14 August 1852—26 April 1853" (unpublished B.A. Honours thesis, University of Natal, Pietermaritzburg, 1975), 45.
23. "Provisional Instructions for Magistrates Relative to Native Labor," *NGG*, 14 September 1852.
24. "Wash Kafirs," *NS*, 24 December 1859.
25. Lead Article, *NM*, 24 March 1863.
26. SPG: 1862–63. Walter Baugh, Umlazi Mission Station, 30 September 1863.
27. Lead Article, *NM*, 24 March 1863.
28. See Chapter 4.
29. Samuelson, *Long, Long Ago*, 376–77.
30. "News Among the Natives," *NW*, 14 January 1853; *NM*, 9 November 1853; *NM*, 22 November 1854. Many correspondences to local news journals complaining about African labor were usually initialed by the authors of the letters or pseudonyms were affixed as a precautionary measure, rather than be identified through their signatures, for fear of retaliation from black workmen.
31. *NW*, 23 October 1846; SNA 1/3/9, No. 73, H. F. Fynn to Secretary of Native Affairs, 31 March 1860.
32. Lead Article, *NM*, 24 March 1863.
33. Russell, *History of Old Durban*, 104.
34. *NW*, 23 October 1846.
35. Ibid.
36. Gardiner, *Narrative of a Journey*, 86.
37. *NW*, 28 May 1847.

38. See Chapter 4.

39. See, for example, "First Impressions of Natal" by a Perthshire Ploughman (Thomas Duff), in *Natalia* No. 7 (December 1977), 14.

40. One task of this study was to try to ascertain the origins of the word *togt*. The earliest reference to come to my notice appeared in an article " 'Dag' or 'Toch' Labor," *NM*, 14 January 1873, which suggested that "toch" was a corruption of the Dutch "dag" or day. This explanation did not ring true. An alternative thought was that *togt* might have derived from "tagewerk." In central Europe the "tagewerk" was the common unit of area, i.e. an areal equivalent to what a man could plough in a day. But since I was on unfamiliar terrain, I referred the problem to authorities in the field. Professor Jan Vansina's insights were helpful; personal correspondence (7 May 1982) with Dr. Jean Branford and her *Dictionary of South African English* were useful; as was my correspondence with Dr. Hauptfleish, chief editor of *Die Afrikaanse Woordenboek*. According to Dr. Hauptfleish, "Togt is an obsolete form of the modern Afrikaans word *tog*, 'journey, trip; a moving from one place to another,' which is derived from Dutch *tocht* with the same meaning. The form *togt* is still used in South African English combinations such as *togt labour* and *togt labourer* = casual or day labour(er)." Personal correspondence, 25 February 1983. Thus the word *togt* seems to refer neither to a time unit nor a unit of area, rather it denotes a state of itinerancy. This has been a great source of confusion in the literature.

41. S. Daniel Neumark, *Economic Influences on the South African Frontier* (Stanford: Stanford University Press, 1956), 145–51. The term *togt* was also defined as "a trading venture by waggon"; in phrase form, e.g., "togtganger," "a transport rider or an itinerant trader." See Branford, *Dictionary of South African English*, 301–2.

42. Lead article, *NW*, 21 September 1855.

43. Russell, *History of Old Durban*, 92.

44. *NW*, 23 October 1846.

45. Posselt, *Zulu Companion*, 38.

46. Mason, *Life with the Zulus of Natal*, 195.

47. Russell, *History of Old Durban*, 434.

48. See *NGG*, 22 July 1879, for a short list of *togt* occupations.

49. Russell, *History of Old Durban*, 129, 131.

50. See, for example, "Trade," *NM*, 31 May 1854.

51. Russell, *History of Old Durban*, 100.

52. Daphne Child, ed., *A Merchant Family in Early Natal: Diaries and Letters of Joseph and Marianne Churchill, 1850–1880* (Cape Town: A. A. Balkema, 1979), 69–70.

53. "Pietermaritzburg Agricultural," *NW*, 2 November 1875; Russell, *History of Old Durban*, 216.

54. To cite some of the more recent publications: Faye E. Dudden, *Serving Women: Household Service in Nineteenth-century America* (Middleton, Connecticut: Wesleyan University Press, 1983), 106, 142–43; Pamela Horn, *The Rise and Fall of the Victorian Servant* (Dublin: Gill and Macmillan; New York: St. Martins Press, 1975), 69–70; David Katzman, *Seven Days a Week* (New York: Oxford University Press, 1978), 62, 85, 90–92, 124; Susan Strasser, *Never Done: A History of American Housework* (New York: Pantheon Books, 1982), 104–24; David Sutherland, *Americans and Their Servants from 1820–1920* (Baton Rouge: Louisana State University, 1981), 133–34. All these studies generally concede that of the myriad tasks performed by women in the home, hand laundry work, i.e. washing and ironing, was the most onerous. See also Catherine Beecher, *A Treatise on Domestic Economy* (Boston: T. H. Webb, 1842), 284–96, for the fullest account of the tremendous labor involved in laundry chores.

55. Ruth Gordon, *Dear Louisa: A History of a Pioneer Family in Natal, 1850–1888* (Cape Town: A. A. Balkema, 1970).

56. Ibid., 18, 29, 71, 101.

57. Russell, *History of Old Durban*, 216.

58. Gordon, *Dear Louisa*, 118.

59. Lady Barker, *A Year's Housekeeping in South Africa* (London: Macmillan, 1894), 68–70; Shooter, "Off to Natal," 159; Colenso, *Ten Weeks in Natal*, 14.

60. Barbara I. Buchanan, *Pioneer Days in Natal* (Pietermaritzburg: Shuter and Shooter, 1934), 15; Allan F. Hattersley, ed., *John Shedden Dobie's South African Journal, 1862–6* (Cape Town: The Van Riebeeck Society, 1945), 15.

61. Feilden, *My African Home*, 224.

62. Buchanan, *Pioneer Days*, 13–14.

63. Shooter, "Off to Natal," 159; Russell, *History of Old Durban*, 216; Thomas Eastwood to Mayor and Town Council, Durban, 17 November 1874. DCL, File 352.

64. Atkins, "Origins of the AmaWasha," 41–53.

65. Russell, *History of Old Durban*, 216–17.

66. "Kafir Dodges," *NM*, 24 October 1856.

67. See, for example, "Culprit Caught," *NM*, 10 April 1863.

68. "A Wood Grievance," *NW*, 29 July 1880.

69. Durban Mayor's Minute for year ending 31 July 1874, 3.

70. "In the town, there are some familiar cases in which Kafir labor is employed to a ridiculous extent: for in what quarter of the globe would male adults be found performing the offices of nurses to infants and children, or as laundresses of female apparel. These docile achievements are certainly not very congruous with their manly habits, nor compatible with the character given them of blood thirsty savages." Evidence of George Peppercorne before the Kafir Commission, Part IV, 6.

CHAPTER 6
Emergence of an African Work Culture, 1846–1900

1. Evidence of Henry Cloete before the Kafir Commission, Part I, 28.

2. Sullivan, *Shepstone's Native Policy*, 71–78.

3. Under "Notes of the Week," *NW*, 11 June 1847.

4. *NW*, 31 July 1846.

5. "Observer," *NW*, 14 August 1846.

6. Under "Notes of the Week," *NW*, 11 June 1847.

7. "Report of the Commissioners for Reporting upon the division of Natal territory into separate magistracies, the selection of sites for towns, and etc.," William Stanger, Surveyor General, Theophilus Shepstone, Diplomatic Agent, and C. J. Gibb, Lt. Royal Engineers. Natal Government Notices, 1848.

8. CSO. V. 44, Pt. I. "Memoranda proposing the establishment of a Native Town to be attached to the Towns of the District of Natal, particularly of Pietermaritzburg and D'Urban," 20 January 1848.

9. CSO. V. V44, Pt. I. Letter to Colonial Secretary re Gibb's "Native Town Plan," T. Shepstone, N. Adams, C. J. Gibb, and D. Lindley, 20 January 1848.

10. "Memoranda proposing the establishment of a Native Town."

11. "The Brick Trade," *NM*, 5 October 1853.

12. For example, see "Proposal for Settling Native Laborers," *NW*, 13 October 1854.

13. Evidence of Evert Fredrick Potgieter before the Kafir Commission, Part I, 18; Benjamin Blaine, Part III, 32; Walter Macfarlane, Part III, 50; H. F. Fynn, Part V, 75.

14. Evidence of Dewald Johannes Pretorius, Part I, 54; T. Shepstone, Part II, 38, and Part VI, 86; Jacobus Nicolass Boshof, Part II, 11.

15. Colenso, *Zulu-English Dictionary*, 422.

16. See Chapter 3.

17. Such prestige government occupations undertaken by older men as the job of "native messenger," "Kafir postman," and "native constables" were generally paid by the month.

18. CSO, File 218. "The Memorial of the Mayor and the Council of the Borough of Durban," to

the Lt. Governor of the Colony of Natal, 21 March 1865; Mason, *Zululand*, 9–10.

19. Ludlow, *Zululand and Cetewayo*, 5; Feilden, *My African Home*, 12; Shooter, "Off to Natal," 88, 90.

20. CSO, File 218. "The Memorial of the Mayor and the Council of the Borough of Durban."

21. See Chapter 2.

22. "Extracts from a Despatch of Commander van Der Stel and Council to the Chamber of XVII," in Bird, *Annals*, I, 46–47.

23. Isaacs, *Travels and Adventures*, 114.

24. See lead article, *NM*, 16 March 1865.

25. 3DBN: 4/1/1/2 Correspondence File No. 3, Police Matters (1861–63) Durban Police Report, 1 January 1863.

26. Posselt, *Zulu Companion*, 53–54. What is being revealed here, I am convinced, is an example of early labor-organizing activities: a demonstration perhaps of the recruitment and education of a "raw," i.e., inexperienced, worker. Certainly this was one mode by which intelligence was verbally circulated around the laboring community regarding employers, work conditions and so forth. The fact that this scenario was included in the "work script" found in the phrasebooks tells us that these practices were standard among the working population.

27. " 'Dag' or 'Toch' Labour," *NM*, 14 January 1873.

28. See, for example, Russell, *History of Old Durban*, 130.

29. Richards, *Hunger and Work*, 174–82.

30. See Godfrey Callaway's discussion of *ubuntu* in *The Fellowship of the Veld* (London: Society for Promoting Christian Knowledge, 1926), 21–31.

31. Shooter, "Off to Natal," 162; Colenso, *Ten We eks*, 53–54.

32. Lead supplement to *The Times of Natal and Southeast Africa*, 24 December 1856.

33. Mason, *Zululand*, 9–10.

34. "Kafir Dodges," *NM*, 24 October 1856.

35. See note 15, above.

36. Gunner, "Orality and L iteracy," 49–50.

37. For instance, Rubusana's anthology of Xhosa praise-poems includes the praises of a young man ("six o'clock"). After his experiences in the work centers at Rhini (Grahamstown), Qonce (Kingwilliam's Town), and Tinarha (Uitenhage), the young man wrote a satirical poem in praise of himself, a "boy" who had challenged the mysterious "six o'clock bell," the mere sound of which had rendered the "men," the supposed "gods" in the traditional community, helpless and impotent:

> A mighty bell is six o'clock!
> I went to Rhini and found the men
> Driven by six o'clock;
> I went to Qonce and found the men
> Toiling at six o'clock;
> Back at Tinarha I found the men
> Bullied by six o'clock.

Cited in Jordan, *Towards an African Literature*, 22.

38. Atkins, "Origins of the AmaWasha," 44–53.

39. Feilden, *M y African Home*, 46.

40. *NC*, 23 June 1871.

41. "The rate of wages for native labourers ranges from 3 to 5 shillings per month," reads one news article, "but I have heard of one or two parties (who, perhaps, have a bad name among them) paying as high as 7s. 6d., this, of course, exclusive of food. . . . " *NW*, 4 May 1849.

42. Shooter, " Off to Natal," 236–38.

43. "Kafir Libellers," *NA*, 18 January 1898; also *NH*, 16 August 1866; and *NW*, 11 December 1846. See Chapter 3.

44. "Sharp Practices," *NW*, 7 October 1880.

45. Bryant, *The Zulu People*, 489.

46. Ibid., 485–89; Cope, *Izibongo*, 31; Landeg White, "Poetic Licence: Oral Poetry and History," in Karin Barber, et al., eds., *Discourse and Its Disguises: The Interpretation of African Oral Texts* (Birmingham: Birmingham University African Studies No. 1, 1989), 34–38.

47. Jordan, *Towards an African Literature*, 27; Archie Mafeje, "The Role of the Bard in a Contemporary African Community," *Journal of African Languages* VI, 3 (1967), 193–223; and Gunner, "Orality and Literacy," 49–58.

48. "An Impudent Kaf ir," *NMA*, 15 September 1882. The criminal archives tell us a great deal about their methods of operation. For example, another "umfaan" ("boy") was brought before Captain Lucas, Durban's resident magistrate, charged with inducing servants to leave their mistress, Mrs. Hammond. The prisoner, who was engaged at a house near by Mrs. Hammond's, advised "boys" seeking positions not to work for the complainant because she did not pay her servants. "Mrs. Hammond said she was unable to keep servants for any length owing to the conduct of the prisoner. She had lost about half a dozen during the last two months." *NA*, 20 May 1892.

49. "Kafir Dodges," *NM*, 24 October 1856.

50. Lead article, *NM*, 16 March 1865.

51. Ibid.

52. "Vagrant House," *NM*, 15 May 1873; Superintendent of Police, Richard Alexander, 18 April 1879. DCL File 368.

53. DCSPRB File 3309: Richard Alexander, Report No. 169, 28 January 1901.

54. "No 'Sisters' without Permission," *NM*, 23 May 1901.

55. "Humouring Native Servants," *NM*, 20 June 1901.

56. "Day Labourers," *NS*, 10 Dece mber 1863.

57. Mason, *Zululand*, 11.

58. Another justification given for the need for a vigorous policy to control the AmaWasha was that, according to one report, "£800 to £1000 a year [was] thus paid to Kafirs in this neighbourhood alone; and to Kafirs, be it remembered, who are not in regular service, but form a lazy and independent class, pocketing all their earnings to purchase slave-wives, and living meanwhile on the stolen bounty of the white people." "Kafir Dodges," *NM*, 24 October 1856.

59. "Kafir Spongers," *NS*, 19 November 1856.

60. "A Lover of Order," *NS*, 10 September 1855; Walter Stern, *The Porters of London* (London: Longmans, 1960); and Richard Wade, *Slavery in the Cities: The South 1820–1860* (New York: Oxford University Press, 1964). See especially Wade's Chapter 2, "Bondsmen and Hirelings," 28–53.

61. "A Lover of Order," *NS*, 10 November 1855.

62. DTC. File 816. Superintendent of Polic e to Mayor and Town Council, 1 March 1862.

63. Pietermaritzburg Minutes of the Town Council, Minute Book [hereafter, PMB Minute Book] 1/1/2, 8 June 1863, 550–51.

64. "Since the passing of the new municipal law," read the Mayor's Minutes of 1863, "a regular system of registration has been adopted, but it is a matter of regret that from its being so little understood and believed to be unimportant, it is yet but partially in operation." PMB Minute Book, 1/1/2, 4 August 1863, 581.

    When in 1874 a more elaborate system of regulations was adopted, Shepstone in reference to those "togt laws," but speaking from hindsight, cautioned that "It is not improbable that at first the effect of these regulations will be to make labour scarce in the towns; their object may be misapprehended, perhaps suspected by those to whom they are intended to apply, so that temporary inconveniences may be felt by the householders. A great deal will depend upon the success of the explanation made to the labourers. . . . It must, however, be clearly understood that if regulations of this nature, whatever the inconvenience they produce at first may be, are not strictly carried out, it is better not to attempt to put them in force at all." *NGG*, 31 March 1874, 152.

65. "Kafir Dodges," *NM*, 24 October 1856.

66. "Echoes of the Week," *NA*, 21 June 1890. Individual white women bid for and were awarded laundry contracts, such as the one granted to Mrs. Margaret Lally for washing the clothing, bedding, etc., for the Durban Hospital (*NGG*, 27 August 1878). But apart from such women, the handful of white laundresses whose names regularly appeared in the *Natal Almanac Directory and Yearly Register* from the mid-1870s onwards, or the widows who owned or managed rooming houses and to supplement their incomes took in their boarders' laundry, few white women were willing to do this kind of rough work.

67. "Umgeni Washing Company," *NH*, 11 July 1867.

68. Ibid., 1 August and 29 August 1867.

69. *NGG*, 21 April 1868.

70. "Umgeni Washing Company," *NH*, 11 July 1867.

71. Minutes of the Durban Town Council, File 8, 13 August and 20 August 1867.

72. For an example of their use of forceful tactics, see "Kafir Dodges," *NM*, 24 October 1856; and "The Washboys' Parade," *SDN*, 2 July 1895.

73. "Memorial of the Mayor and the Council of the Borough of Durban." It is significant that what precipitated the writing of this memorial was an unpleasant incident involving the mayor's wife and a group of *togt* workers who came upon her premises demanding food of hospitality. See lead article, *NM*, 16 March 1865.

74. "Memorial of the Mayor and the Council of the Borough of Durban."

75. See for example, "Kafir Assaults on Europe ans," *NC*, 7 November 1871.

76. *NGG*, 13 June 1871.

77. "Day Kafirs," *NM*, 9 November 1871.

78. DTC, File 233. Police report No. 304, 19, 1871.

79. "The Evils of 'toch,'" *NM*, 6 February 1873.

80. SNA 1/1/24 (Doc. 14), William Campbell to Lt. Gov. B. C. C. Pine, 2 March 1874; *NM*, 14 April 1874.

81. *NGG*, 20 January 1874.

82. *NGG*, 31 March 1874, 151–53.

83. Ibid.

84. Ibid.

85. "Registration," *NM*, 19 June 1873.

86. Durban (Native) Case Book 2/3/4, Cases 17 November 1873 to 29 August 1874. In the case of the Supreme Chief vs. Umdukumban—"Richard Baynes duly sworn deposes yesterday (15 April 1874) I sent one of my boys to get a native to carry some planks to the Botanic Gardens. He brought the prisoner. The two planks, 12 feet long, 9 inches wide and 1 inch thick, were to be carried by prisoner and another boy. When prisoner refused the other boy carried them out himself." Judgement: "Cautioned and discharged (wash boy)"; and in a similar case, the Supreme Chief vs. Umgama, the superintendent of police tendered as evidence the *togt* record wherein the prisoner was entered as a "washboy" and "therefore not obligated to do other work. Cautioned and discharged."

87. *NGG*, 31 March 1874.

88. "'Togt' Regulations," *NM*, 14 April 1874.

89. Ibid., 16 April 1874 and 21 April 1874.

90. Ibid., 16 April 1874.

91. Ibid., 18 April 1874.

92. Dohne, *Zulu-Kafir Dictionary*, 14.

93. For example, the Richmond magistrate report for the year 1862 reads that "Generally the

native servants prefer seeking service in the towns, and many now go out to service for short periods to avoid being called upon to labour on the public works." Richmond Resident Magistrate Letter Book, Upper Umkomanzi (1853–1863). Forty years later, Chief Ndhlovu's grievance was that on account of the regulations compelling work on the roads, members of his "tribe" went off to European towns and there remained, being afraid to return for fear of having to serve on the roads. See t estimony of Mbovu kaMtshumayeli, in *Stuart A rchive*, III, 24.

94. " 'Togt' Regulations," *NM*, 16 May 1874.
95. "What Are We Coming T o?," *NM*, 7 May 1874.
96. "Togt Kafirs," *NC*, 15 February 1876.
97. "Shelter for Vagrants," *NM*, 15 July 1873; "Togt," *NM*, 24 June 1873.
98. "Togt," *NC*, 10 October 1878.
99. Lady Barker, *A Year's Housekeeping*, 124–25.
100. *NGG*, 22 July 1879.
101. DCSPRB File 2, No. 3305. Police Report No. 451, 7 October 1879.
102. "A Steam Laundry," *Times of Natal* [hereafter *TN*], 7 January 1880.
103. "The Steam Laundry," *TN*, 30 January 1880.
104. "The Steam Laundry," *NW*, 21 February 1880; "Our Laundry," *NW*, 11 March 1880.
105. *NW*, 25 March 1880.
106. "The Steam Laundry Company," *TN*, 7 April 1880; see also "The Wash-Kafir Question," *NW* Supplement, 20 May 1880.
107. Master of the Supreme Court, Insolvent Estates File 1/108, Case No. 254. In the Insolvent Estate of Louis George Jullien trading under the style of the Steam Laundry Company, Pietermaritzburg, Natal.
108. "Prospectus of the Steam Laundry Company," *TN*, 12 May 1880.
109. "The Steam Laundry Company," *NW*, 8 May 1880.
110. "City Letters," *NMA*, 11 May 1880.
111. *NGG*, Durban Corporation Water Service Bye-Laws, 1 May 1888 and 15 January 1889; William Henderson, *Durban: Fifty Years of Municipal History* (Durban: Robinson, 1904), 225–48.
112. See Susan Strasser, *Never Done*, for a fuller discussion of the economic process involved in this transition to commercial laundries, 112–24.
113. Susan Strasser, "An Enlarged Human Existence? Technology and Household Work in Nineteenth Century America," in Susan Fenstermaker Berk, ed., *Women and Household Labor* (California: Sage Publications, 1980), 29–51. Strasser draws attention to the fact that although "The technological potential of the nineteenth century house was fairly high; it could only be achieved, however, by wealthy people in urban areas. Indoor plumbing, electricity and gas, the innovations which ended the necessity for making fires and carrying water, were luxuries," 30.
114. See for example, Verasammy to the Mayor and Town Council, Durban, 21 March 1892. DCL File 427.
115. "Indian Immigration Board: No More Cooks and Dhobies," *NM*, 10 October 1896; "Man in the Moon," *NM*, 17 October 1896.
116. See, for example, R. Nozaic, Proprietor, Berea English Laundry, to Mayor, Durban, 29 March 1909. DCL File 582. Nozaic suggested the need to license all laundries, maintaining that under the current system, no customer of an Indian laundry had even an implied warranty that his clothes received a thorough cleansing by a method of boiling the soiled linen. A major grievance of white laundrymen, the letter pointed out, was, while according to Law 24 of 1878 Europeans were not allowed to trade or deal on Sundays, in contrast *dhobies* in an unrestricted manner made house-to-house visits to collect washing on the Sabbath, "a system that practically amounted to touting, with the result that when the

European laundry man calls on Monday he finds nothing left owing to the previous visit of his Indian competitor. . . . "

117. "Factories of the future," *NA*, 15 February 1910.

118. Petition of Durban Laundrymen to Mayor, 29 March 1910. DCL File 590; see also "The Proposed Licensing Measure," and "A Petition to Parliament," *African Chronicle*, 4 December 1909. According to the provisions of the proposed bill gazetted 19 October 1909, hawkers of colonial produce, such as vegetables and other green dealers, egg sellers, milk dealers, butchers, dhobies, fruit sellers and in fact every man who made a livelihood by petty dealing would be liable to take a license from the Corporations. The Natal Indian Congress strongly opposed the measure because of the wide discretionary powers vested in licensing officers who could "utterly refuse" a hawkers' or *dhoby* license "without rhyme or reason." The NIC felt this "class legislation" threatened the daily bread of thousands of poor Indians and would also impose an indirect penalty upon the poorer class of Europeans, who would be the next great sufferers.

119. "New public health 'Bye-laws for the Borough of Durban Relating to Laundries, Wash-House, Cleaners, Dyers' establishment, etc. . . ," *Natal Provincial Gazette*, 9 June 1910. This is not to suggest that the saga of the Indian *dhoby* ended with the passage of this piece of legislation. It is that our sources stop at this juncture in their history. A further detailed study of the Indian *dhoby* would make a valuable contribution to Natal's social history.

120. Evidence of Togt Inspector William A. Hines, in Native Affairs Commission, 1906/07, 39; see also DCSPRB File 3310; report dated 2 June 1905.

121. *Life at Natal*, 93–94. "In one respect," wrote this woman visitor, "Maritzburg differs much from Durban. Mission Kafirs swarm here. . . . The women are mostly laundresses, and are able, therefore, to starch their own muslins. . . . "

122. SNA 1/1/112. Report on Inanda Laundry, dated 19 June 1890.

123. Gordon, *Dear Louisa*, 264.

124. SNA 1/1/356. Mrs. Lettie Mcunu of Thorny Bush, 4 December 1906.

125. DCSPRB File 3310: reports dated 7 September 1907 to January 1910. See also File 3311: reports dated February 1910 to December 1914.

126. DCL File 429: Umgeni Magistrate to Mayor of Durban, 31 March 1892; and DCL File 435: Umgeni Police Station to Superintendent Police, 31 January 1893.

127. DCL File 485: W. C. Daugherty, Inspector of Nuisances to Chairman of Sanitary Committee, 30 December 1898.

128. *NGG*, "To amend Act No. 49 , 1901, entitled 'To Facilitate the Identification of Native Servants,'" 29 March 1904.

129. *NGG*, "New Bye-Laws for the Borough of Durban," 5 April 1904.

130. Lady Barker, *A Year's Housekeeping*, 125. African males used also to perform "mangling" tasks. See Russell, *History of Old Durban*, 217–18, for a description of the "Colonial Mangle."

131. For example, Verasammy to Mayor and Town Council of Durban, 21 March 1892, DCL File 427.

132. van Onselen, "Amawasha," 75.

133. *South African Native Affairs Commission, 1903-5*, V, (Cape Town: Cape Times, Government Printers), 185; *Report and Evidence of the Native Commission, 1906-7*, (Pietermaritzburg: P. Davis and Sons,1907), 822, 824–25; Sheila T. van der Horst, *Native Labour in South Africa* (London: Oxford University Press, 1942), 236–38; Shula Marks, "The Ambiguities of Dependence: John L. Dube of Natal," *Journal of Southern African Studies*, I, 2 (1975), 69.

134. van Onselen, "AmaWasha," 77.

135. This paragraph is based on Strasser, *Never Done*, 112–24.

136. *Native Economic Commission*, 1930, 16.

CONCLUSION

1. George H. Mason, *Life with the Zulus of Natal, South Africa* (London: Longmans, Brown, Green and Longsman, 1855), 194.
2. *NW,* 11 July 1876.
3. *Cape Argus,* 20 January 1860.
4. *NW,* 23 October 1846.
5. ABC: 15.4, V. 5. Josiah Tyler to Dr. Anderson, 20 May 1854.
6. Anyone who tries, by force or threats, to make a servant leave his master or his work, or tries to keep persons from hiring themselves to a master, or molests a servant for not joining a club or for submitting to rules for regulating his wages or his work is liable to imprisonment. Summarized extract, "Ordinance, For regulating the relative rights and duties of Masters, Servants, and Apprentices," No. 2, 1850, 25–26.
7. Josiah Tyler to Dr. Anderson, 20 May 1854; *NH,* 16 August 186.

BIBLIOGRAPHY

Archival Sources

Missionary Archives

American Board of Commissioners for Foreign Missions, Houghton Library, Harvard University
The Methodist Missionary Society, London
United Society for the Propagation of the Gospel, London

Official Records

Great Britain, Public Record Office. Colonial Office, Original Correspondence
Natal Colony, Pietermaritzburg Depot of the South African Archives, Pietermaritzburg, Natal
Chief Native Commissioner Series
Colonial Secretary Office Series
Secretary for Native Affairs Series
Natal Economic Commission, 1930
Municipal Files
    Durban Civil Record Books
    Durban Corporation Letters
    Durban Corporation Superintendent of Police Report Book
    Durban (Native) Case Books
    Durban Town Council
    Pietermaritzburg Letter Book
    Pietermaritzburg Minutes of the Town Council, Minute Book

Published Sources

Periodical Publications

Blue Book of the Colony of Natal
Natal Government Gazette
Natal Provincial Gazette
Natal Almanac and Yearly Register

Commissions and Miscellaneous Official Publications

Proceedings and Report of the Commission Appointed to Inquire into the Past and Present State of the Kafirs in the District of Natal, 1852–53, 77 parts (Pietermaritzburg: J. Archbell and Son, 1852–1853).
Questions by Lieutenant Governor Scott on the Conditions of the Natives in Natal and Answers by the Secretary for Native Affairs (Pietermaritzburg: ?, 1864).
Papers Relating to the Supply by Native Chiefs of Native Labour in Connection with the Public Works of the Colony (Pietermaritzburg: Vause, Slatter and Co., 1880).

Report and Evidence of the Natal Native Commission, 1881–82 (Pietermaritzburg: Vause, Slatter and Co., 1882)

Report and Evidence of the Native Commission, 1906–7 (Pietermaritzburg: P. Davis and Sons, 1907)

Report and Proceedings of the Government Commission on Native Laws and Customs (Cape Town: W. A. Richards and Sons, Government Printers, 1883)

South African Native Affairs Commission, 1903–5 (Cape Town: Government Printers, 1905)

Newspapers

African Chronicle
Cape Argus
Eastern Province Herald
Natal Advertiser
Natal Colonist
Natal Herald
Natal Mercantile Advertiser
Natal Mercury
Natal Star
Natal Times and Mercantile and Agricultural Gazette
Natal Witness
Port Elizabeth Telegraph
Times of Natal
Times of Natal and Southeast Africa
Standard and Digger's News

Missionary Periodicals

Mission Field

BOOKS AND ARTICLES

Agar-Hamilton, J. *The Native Policy of the Voortrekkers* (Cape Town: M. Miller, 1928).

Atkins, K. E. "'Kafir Time:' Preindustrial Temporal Concepts and Labour Discipline in Nineteenth Century Colonial Natal," *Journal of African History* 29 (1988).

————. "Origins of the AmaWasha: The Zulu Washermen's Guild in Natal, 1850–1910," *Journal of African History* 27 (1986).

Baldwin, W. C. *African Hunting and Adventures* (Cape Town: C. Struik, 1967).

Ballard, C. C. "Migrant Labour in Natal, 1860–79: With Special Reference to Zululand and the Delagoa Bay Hinterland," *Journal of Natal and Zulu History* I (1978).

Barker, Lady. *A Year's Housekeeping in South Africa* (London: Macmillan, 1894).

Barrett, H. J. *Fifteen Years Among the Zulu and the Boers* (Hull: M. C. Peck and Son, 1879).

Barter, C. *Dorp and Veld* (London: W. S. Orr, 1852).

Beecher, C. *A Treatise on Domestic Economy* (Boston: T. H. Webb, 1842).

Berglund, A. I. "Heaven-Herds: A Study of Zulu Symbolism," in M. Whisson and M. West, eds., *Religion and Social Change in Southern Africa* (Cape Town: D. Phillip, 1975).

Berglund, A. I. *Zulu Thought-Patterns and Symbolism* (London: C. Hurst, 1976).

Bernardi, B. *Age Class Systems: Social Institutions and Polities Based on Age* (Cambridge: Cambridge University Press, 1985).

Bird, J., ed. *The Annals of Natal* (Pietermaritzburg: P. Davis and Son, 1888).

Bourquin, S., ed. *Paulina Dlamini: Servant of Two Kings* (Pietermaritzburg: University of Natal, 1986).

Braatvedt, H. P. "Zulu Marriage Customs and Ceremonies, *South African Journal of Science* XXIV (December 1927).

Branford, J. *Dictionary of South African English* (Cape Town; New York: Oxford University Press, 1980).

Bryant, A. T. *Olden Times in Zululand and Natal* (London; New York: Longmans, Green and Company, 1929).

————. *The Zulu People as They Were Before the White Man Came* (Pietermaritzburg: Shuter and Shooter, 1949).

————. *A History of the Zulu and Neighbouring Tribes* (Cape Town: C. Struik, 1964).

————. *Zulu Medicine and Medicine Men* (Cape Town: C. Struik, 1970).

Buchanan, B. I. *Pioneer Days in Natal* (Pietermaritzburg: Shuter and Shooter, 1934).

Burchell, W. J. *Travels in the Interior of Southern Africa* (London: Batchworth Press, 1953).

Callaway, G. *Sketches of Kafir Life* (Oxford: A. R. Mowbray and Company, Limited, 1905).

————. *The Fellowship of the Veld.* (London: Society for Promoting Christian Knowledge, 1926).

————. *Building for God in Africa* (London: Society for Promoting Christian Knowledge, 1936).

Callaway, H. *The Religious System of the AmaZulu* (Cape Town: C. Struik, 1970).

Child, D., ed. *A Merchant Family in Early Natal: Diaries and Letters of Joseph and Marianne Churchill, 1850–1880* (Cape Town: A. A. Balkema, 1979).

Cobbing, J. "The Mfecane as Alibi: Thoughts on Dithakong and Mbolompo," *Journal of African History* 29 (1988), 487–519.

Cohen, R. "Hidden Forms of Labour Protest in Africa." Paper presented to a conference on Inequality in Africa, organized by the Joint Committee on African Studies, Social Science Research Council, Mt. Kisco, New York, 6–9 October 1976.

Cole, D. T. "Fanagalo and the Bantu Languages in South Africa," *African Studies* 12, 1 (March 1953).

Colenso, F. E. *The Ruin of Zululand: An Account of British Doings in Zululand Since the Invasion of 1879* (London: W. Ridgway, 1884–85).

Colenso, J. W. *Ten Weeks in Natal* (Cambridge: Macmillan, 1855).

————. *First Steps of the Zulu Mission* (London: ?, 1860).

————. *Zulu-English Dictionary* (Pietermaritzburg: P. Davis, 1861).

————. *Zulu-English Dictionary*, 4th edition (Farnborough: Gregg, 1967).

Cope, T. *Izibongo: Zulu Praise-Poems* (Oxford: Clarendon Press, 1968).

Cullen, T. "Habits and Customs of the Olden Days Among the Tumbuka-Kamanga People," *Africa* (1936).

Cullingworth, J. *Zulu Vocabulary and Phrasebook for use of Immigrants and Settlers in the Colony of Natal* (Pietermaritzburg: J. Cullingworth, 1865).

Davenport, T. R., and K. S. Hunt. *The Right to the Land* (Cape Town: D. Phillip, 1974).

Delius, P., and S. Trapido. "Inboekselings and Oorlams: The Creation and Transformation of a Servile Class," *Journal of Southern African Studies* 8 (October 1981).

Dlamini, C. R. M. *The New Legal Status of Zulu Women* (KwaDlangezwa: University of Zululand, 1983).

Dohne, J. L. *A Zulu-Kafir Dictionary* (Cape Town: G.J. Pike, 1857).

Dudden, F. E. *Serving Women: Household Service in Nineteenth Century America* (Middleton, Connecticut: Wesleyan University Press, 1983).

Duff, T. "First Impressions of Natal" by a Perthshire Ploughman, *Natalia* No. 7 (December 1977).

Duminy, A., and W. Guest, eds. *Natal and Zululand From Earliest Times to 1910: A New History* (Pietermaritzburg: University of Natal and Shuter and Shooter, 1989).

Etherington, N. *Preachers, Peasants and Politics in Southeast Africa, 1835–1880* (London: Royal Historical Society, 1978).

Fair, T. J. D. *The Distribution of Population in Natal.* Natal Regional Survey, V. 3 (Cape Town; New York: Oxford University Press, 1955).

Faye, C. *Zulu References for Interpreters and Students* (Pietermaritzburg: City Printing Works, Limited, Printers & Publishers, 1923).

Feilden, E. W. *My African Home* (London: Sampson Low, Marston, Searle and Rivington, 1887).

Gardiner, A. *Narrative of a Journey to the Zoolu Country* (Cape Town: C. Struik, 1966).

Gordon, R. E. *Dear Louisa: A History of a Pioneer Family in Natal, 1850–88* (Cape Town: A. A. Balkema, 1970).

Grout, L. *Zululand; or Life Among the Zulu Kafirs* (Philadelphia: Presbyterian Publication Committee, 1864).

Gunner, E. "Orality and Literacy: Dialogue and Silence," in K. Barber and P. F. deMoraes Farias, eds., *Discourse and Its Disguises: Interpretation of African Oral Text* (Birmingham: Birmingham University African Studies No. 1, 1989).

Guy, J. "Ecological Factors in the Rise of Shaka and the Zulu Kingdom," in S. Marks and A. Atmore, eds., *Economy and Society in Preindustrial South Africa* (London; New York: Longman, 1980).

Hall, E. *The Dance of Life: The Other Dimension of Time* (New York: Anchor Press/Doubleday, 1984).

Harries, P. "Kinship, Ideology and the Nature of Precolonial Labour Migration," in S. Marks and R. Rathbone, *Industrialisation and Social Change in South Africa* (London; New York: Longman, 1982).

Hattersley, A. F. *The Natalians* (Pietermaritzburg: Shuter and Shooter, 1940).

——— , ed. *John Shedden Dobie's South African Journal, 1862–6* (Cape Town: The Van Riebeeck Society, 1945)

de Heinzelin, J. "Ishango," *Scientific American* 206 (June 1962).

Henderson, W. P. M. *Durban: Fifty Years of Municipal History* (Durban: Robinson, 1904).

Herbert, E. *Red Gold of Africa* (Madison: University of Wisconsin, 1984).

Holden, W. C. *A Brief History of Methodism and Methodist Missions in South Africa* (London: Wesleyan Conference Office, 1877).

Horn, P. *The Rise and Fall of the Victorian Servant* (Dublin: Gill and Macmillan; New York: St. Martin's Press, 1975).

Hutchins, R. L., ed. *Statues of Natal, 1845–1899* (Pietermaritzburg: P. Davis and Sons, 1901).

Ingram, J. F. *The Colony of Natal* (London: J. Causton and Sons, 1895).

Isaacs, N. *Travels and Adventures in Eastern Africa* (Cape Town: C. Struik, 1970).

Jenkinson, T. B. *Amazulu: The Zulus, Their Past History, Manners, Customs, and Language* (New York: Negro University Press, 1969).

Jones, G. S. *Outcast London* (Oxford: Clarendon Press, 1971).

Jordan, A. C. *Towards an African Literature: The Emergence of Literary Form in Xhosa* (Berkeley: University of California Press, 1973).

Katzman, D. *Seven Days a Week* (New York: Oxford University Press, 1978).

Kimble, J. "Labour Migrations in Basutoland, c. 1870–1885" in Marks and Rathbone, eds., *Industrialization and Social Change in South Africa* (London; New York: Longman, 1982).

Kirby, P. R. , ed. *Andrew Smith and Natal* (Cape Town: The Van Riebeeck Society, 1955).

Kistner, W. "The Anti-Slavery Agitation Against the Transvaal Republic 1852–1868," *Archives Year Book for South African History* (Cape Town: Cape Times, Ltd., 1952), 2.

Kopytoff, I., ed., *The African Frontier: The Reproduction of Traditional Societies* (Bloomington; Indianapolis: Indiana University Press, 1987).

Krige, E. *The Social Systems of the Zulus* (Pietermaritzburg: Shuter and Shooter, 1957).

Kuper, A. *Wives for Cattle: Bridewealth and Marriage in Southern Africa* (London; Boston: Routledge & Kegan Paul, 1982).

Lagercrantz, S. "African Tally-Strings," *Anthropos* 63 (1968).

——— . "Tallying by Means of Lines, Stones, and Sticks," *Paideuma* 16 (1970).

——— . "Counting by Means of Tally Sticks or Cuts on the Body in Africa," *Anthropos* 68 (1973).

Lamphere, L. "Strategies, Cooperation, and Conflict Among Women in Domestic Groups," in M. Z. Rosaldo and L. Lamphere, eds., *Women, Culture and Society* (Stanford: Stanford University, 1974).

Landes, D. *Revolution in Time: Clocks and the Making of the Modern World* (Cambridge: Harvard University, 1983).

Le Cordeur, B. A., ed. *South African Archival Records*, 5 Vols. (Cape Town: Union Archives in collaboration with the Archives Commission, Government Printers, 1959-1964).

Le Goff, J. *Time, Work and Culture in the Middle Ages* (Chicago: University of Chicago Press, 1980).

Legesse, A. *Gada–Three Approaches to the Study of African Society* (New York: Free Press, 1973).

Leslie, D. *Among the Zulus and Amatongas* (New York: Negro University Press, 1969).

Levine, R. A. "Patterns of Personality in Africa," in George De Vos, ed. *Responses to Change: Society, Culture and Personality* (New York: Van Nostrand, 1976).

Lichtenstein, H. *Travels in Southern Africa, in the Years 1803, 1804, 1805, and 1806*, II (London: Henry Colbum, 1812).

Life at Natal a Hundred Years Ago. By a Lady. (Cape Town: C. Struik, 1972).

Lindley, A. *After Ophir: Or a Search for the South African Gold Fields* (London: Cassell, Petter, and Galpin, 1870).

Ludlow, W. R. *Zululand and Cetewayo* (London: Simpkin, Marshall, and Company, 1882).

Mafeje, A. "The Role of the Bard in a Contemporary African Community," *Journal of African Languages*, 6, Part 3 (1967).

Mann, R. J., ed. *The Colony of Natal* (London: Jarrold and Sons, 1859).

Marks, S. "The Ambiguities of Dependence: John L. Dube of Natal," *Journal of Southern African Studies* I, 2 (1975).

McIntyre, J. "From Settlement to City," in *Allister Macmillan*, ed., *Durban Past and Present* (Durban: William Brown and Davis 1936).

Mason, G. H. *Life with the Zulus of Natal* (London: Longmans, Brown, Green and Longmans, 1855).

——— . *Zululand: A Mission Tour* (London: J. Nisbet, 1862).

Mayer, P. *Townsmen or Tribesmen: Conservatism and the Process of Urbanization in a South African City* (Cape Town; New York: Oxford University Press, 1971).

Mentzel, O. F. *Life at the Cape in Mid-Eighteenth Century (1784)* (Cape Town: Darter Brothers, 1920).

Mitford, B. *Through the Zulu Country: Its Battlefields and Its People* (London: K. Paul, Trench, 1883).

Neumark, S. D. *Economic Influences on the South African Frontier* (Stanford: Stanford University Press, 1956).

Nyembezi, C. L. S. *Zulu Proverbs* (Johannesburg: Witwatersrand University Press, 1963).

Okoye, F. "Tshaka and the British Traders, 1824–1828," *Transafrican Journal of History* (January 1972).

Osborn, R. F. *Valiant Harvest: The Founding of the South African Sugar Industry, 1848–1926* (Durban: South African Sugar Association, 1964).

Parr, H. H. *A Sketch of the Kafirs and Zulu Wars* (Pretoria: State Library Reprint #56, 1970).

Posselt, C. W. *The Zulu Companion, Offered to the Natal Colonist to Facilitate Intercourse with the Natives* (Pietermaritzburg: D. D. Buchanan, 1850).

Raum, O. F. "The Rolling Target (Hoop-and-Pole) Game in Africa," *African Studies* 12 (1953).

——— . *The Social Functions of Avoidances and Taboos among the Zulu* (Berlin; New York: Walter De Gruyter, 1973).

Rees, W., ed. *Colenso Letters from Natal* (Pietermaritzburg: Shuter and Shooter, 1958).

Richards, A. I. *Hunger and Work in a Savage Tribe* (Glencoe, Illinois: Free Press, 1948).

Richardson, P. "The Natal Sugar Industry in the Nineteenth Century," in W. Beinart et al., *Putting a Plough to the Ground* (Johannesburg: Ravan Press, 1986).

Rivett, A. W. L. *Ten Years' Work in Natal* (London: Jarrold and Sons, 1890).

Robinson, J., ed. *Notes on Natal: An Old Colonist's Book for New Settlers* (Durban: Robinson and Vause, 1872).

——— . *A Life-Time in South Africa: Being the Recollections of the First Premier of Natal* (London: Smith, Elder and Company, 1900).

Rowell, T. *Natal and the Boers* (London: J. Dent, 1902).

Russell, G. *The History of Old Durban, and Reminiscences of an Emigrant of 1850* (Durban: P. Davis and Sons, 1899).

Samuelson, R. C. A. *Long, Long Ago* (Durban: Knox Printing & Publishing Company, 1929).

Seymour, S. M. *Bantu Law in South Africa* (Cape Town: Juta 1970).

Shooter, Mrs. J. "Off to Natal. By a Clergyman's Wife." *Golden Hours; A Weekly Journal of Good Literature for Young Folks* 1 (1869).

Shooter, J. *The Kafirs of Natal and Zulu Country* (London: E. Stanford, 1857).

Slater, H. "Land, Labour and Capital in Natal: The Natal Land and Colonisation Company, 1860–1948," *Journal of African History* 2 (1975).

————. "The Changing Pattern of Economic Relationships in Rural Natal: 1838–1914," in S. Marks and A. Atmore, eds. *Economy and Society in Preindustrial South Africa* (London; New York: Longman, 1980).

Spohr, O. H., ed. *The Natal Diaries of Dr. W. H. I. Bleek, 1855–6* (Cape Town: A. A. Balkema, 1965).

Stern, W. M. *The Porters of London* (London: Longmans, 1960).

Stichter, S. *Migrant Laborers* (Cambridge; New York: Cambridge University Press, 1985).

Strasser, S. "An Enlarged Human Existence? Technology and Household Work in Nineteenth Century America," in S. F. Berk, ed., *Women and Household Labor* (California: Sage Publications, 1980).

————. *Never Done: A History of American Housework* (New York: Pantheon Books, 1982).

Stuart, J. *History of the Zulu Rebellion, 1906* (London: Macmillan and Company, 1913).

————, ed. *The Diary of Henry Francis Fynn* (Pietermaritzburg: Shuter and Shooter, 1950).

Sullivan, J. R. *The Native Policy of Sir Theophilus Shepstone* (Johannesburg: Walker and Snashall, 1928).

Sutherland, D. *Americans and Their Servants from 1820–1920* (Baton Rouge: Louisana State University Press, 1981).

Thompson, E. P. *The Making of the English Working Class* (New York: Vintage Books, 1966).

————. "Time, Work-discipline, and Industrial Capitalism," *Past and Present*, 28 (1967).

Tinker, H. *A New System of Slavery: The Export of Indian Labour Overseas, 1830–1920* (London; New York: Oxford University Press, 1974).

Trollope, A. *South Africa* (Cape Town: A. A. Balkema, 1973).

van der Horst, S. T. *Native Labour in South Africa* (London: Oxford University Press, 1942).

van Onselen, C. "Worker Consciousness in Black Miners: Southern Rhodesia, 1900–1920," in I. R. Phimister and C. van Onselen, *Studies in the History of African Mine Labour in Colonial Zimbabwe* (Gwelo: Mambo Press, 1978).

————. *Studies in the Social and Economic History of the Witwatersrand, 1886–1914* II (London; New York: Longman, 1982).

Wade, R. *Slavery in the Cities: The South 1820–1860* (New York: Oxford University Press, 1964).

Webb, C., and J. Wright. *The James Stuart Archive of Recorded Oral Evidence Relating to the History of the Zulu and Neighbouring Peoples*, 4 Vols. to date (Pietermaritzburg: University of Natal Press and Killie Campbell Africana Library, 1976–1986).

Weisner, T. S., and C. Gallimore. "My Brother's Keeper: Child and Sibling Caretaking," *Current Anthropology* 18, 2 (June 1977).

Welsh, D. *The Roots of Segregation: Native Policy in Colonial Natal, 1845–1910* (Cape Town; New York: Oxford University Press, 1971).

White, L. "Poetic Licence: Oral Poetry and History," K. Barber et al., eds., *Discourse and Its Disguises: The Interpretation of African Oral Texts* (Birmingham: Birmingham University African Studies Series No.1, 1989).

Mrs. Wilkinson, *A Lady's Life and Travels in Zululand and the Transvaal During Cetewayo's Reign* (London: J. T. Hayes, 1882).

Winter, J. A. "The Mental and Moral Capabilities of the Natives, Especially of Sekukuniland (Eastern Transvaal)," *South African Journal of Science* (1914).

Wright, J. 'Control of Women's Labour in the Zulu Kingdom,' J. B. Peires, ed., *Before and After Shaka* (Grahamstown: Rhodes University, 1981).

Wright, M. "Women in Peril: A Commentary on the Life Stories of Captives in Nineteenth Century East-Central Africa," *Africa Social Research* 20 (December 1975).

Zerubavel, E. *The Seven Day Circle: The History and Meaning of the Week* (New York: The Free Press, 1985).

UNPUBLISHED THESES

Mael, R. "The Problem of Political Integration in the Zulu Empire" (Ph.D. thesis, University of California, Los Angeles, 1974).

Rickard, C. , ed. "Charles Barter Natal Diary, 14 August 1852 to 26 April 1853" (B. A. Honours thesis, University of Natal, 1975).

Wright, J. "The Dynamics of Power and Conflict in the Thukela–Mzimkhulu Region in the Late 18th and Early 19th Centuries: A Critical Reconstruction (Ph. D. thesis, University of the Witwatersrand, Johannesburg, 1989).

INDEX

Bridewealth. *See Lobolo*
British Natal: declared British colony, 13; labor abuse and, 16–17; land issues, 46–49; slavery and, 24. *See also* Natal
Bryant, A. T., 31, 33, 39, 56, 62, 73, 82
Buchanan, Barbara, 112
Burchell, William, 93
Bushranging, 10
Buthelezi, Chief, 41
Byrne colonization scheme, 75

Calendar, 92–95
Calendar rod, 93
Callaway, Rev. Henry, 74–75, 83, 95
Carrier-boys and -girls (*izindibi*), 65
Cattle, 28–31; as currency, 95, 96; fines for harboring, 17; homestead production complex and, 26–27; lungsickness, 30, 96; "native town" policy for, 118; purchase by indentured servants, 29; of refugees, 17, 29–30; ritual and, 28; value and uses of, 28; women's rights to, 42
Cattle confiscation order, 13–15, 28
Cattle dung (*amalongwe*), 28
Cattle rustling, 30, 36
Cele people, 11
Celibacy, rules of, 31, 32
Cetshwayo, 30, 38, 93
Chiefs: counsel by, 106–7; desertions from, 11; *inkosi*, 71, 72; labor market and, 51–53; movement back and forth among, 50; prerogatives of, 51
Children: apprenticeship of, 19–21; care of, 65; labor system abuses, 16; registration as apprentices, 16; rural day labor, 103; social stages, 58–59; social status of, 56; work of, 58–59
Choice: in careers, 61–63; in marriage, 31–32, 38
"Chronological net," 87
Cira, 44
Clarence, Ralph, 21
Clocks, 87
Cloete, Colonel Henry, 13, 36, 46–47, 114, 115, 118, 119
Clothing, 69, 141–42
Coetzee family, 29
Colenso, Frances, 4, 81
Colenso, John William, 19–20, 30, 37
Collective bargaining, 128
Collis, J., 11
Colonists: apprenticeship law and, 19; attitudes toward Africans, 1–4, 78, 141–43;

belief in African inferiority, 3; inappropriate allocation of work by, 68–69; labor interests, 100; servant's perspective of, 69–71; women's dislike of laundering, 111–12; Zulu language and, 82. *See also* Boers (*voortrekkers*)
Commercial agriculture: "Kafir time" and, 83–86; labor interests, 100; relocation policy and, 116–17; *togt* system and, 104–6
Commercial laundries, 136, 137–38
Communication: about time computation, 82; labor market and, 74; translation problems, 82–83
Competitiveness: *lobolo* and, 35; of refugees, 27; of women, 28
Construction work, 109–10
Cooke, M. Joscelin, 94
Cooking, power and, 44. *See also* Food
Cope, T., 126
Corporal punishment, 18
Cosmology, concept of time and, 84
Courts, labor disputes and, 98–99
Cowives, status of, 44, 56. *See also* Women
Crown lands, 47–49
Cultural values: hospitality and, 128; occupations and, 56–60; working-class ethic and, 119
kaCungele, Velana, 57
Curfews, 92, 132
Currency, 95–97

Day (*ilanga*): work during, 83–85; Zulu concept of, 83
Day labor (*togt*). *See Togt* (day labor) system
Deserters, 11–13, 38; charges made against servants, 98–99; confiscation of property, 13; fines for harboring, 17; punishment of, 11
kaDhlovu, Mkando, 65
Dhoby, 137–39
Diamond mines, 74, 132
Dingane, 11, 12, 31, 32, 33, 38, 57, 65, 92
Dingiswayo, 67
Disease. *See* Illness
District magistrate (*landdrost*), 16
Diviners, 57
Dlamini, Paulina, 46
Dohne, Reverend, 15, 58
Drakensberg foothills, 47
Dunne, J. J., 128
Dunn, John, 126
Durban, 10, 50, 62, 87, 89, 90, 92, 102, 106, 141, 143, 145; food hospitality requests, 121–22;